# THE ENCYCLOPEDIA OF AMERICAN RELIGIONS

## FIRST EDITION • SUPPLEMENT

# THE ENCYCLOPEDIA OF AMERICAN RELIGIONS

## FIRST EDITION · SUPPLEMENT

> Includes Cumulative Indexes to
> Both Volumes of the First Edition
> and This Supplement

**J. Gordon Melton**

Gale Research Company
Book Tower
Detroit, Michigan 48226

Amy Marcaccio, *Editorial Coordinator*
Michaeline R. Nowinski, *Production Editor*
Carol Blanchard, *Production Director*
Arthur Chartow, *Art Director*
Mary Beth Trimper, *Senior Production Associate*


Frederick G. Ruffner, *Publisher*
James M. Ethridge, *Executive Vice-President/Editorial*
Dedria Bryfonski, *Editorial Director*
John Schmittroth, *Director, Directories Division*
Robert J. Elster, *Managing Editor, Directories Division*

**Library of Congress Cataloging-in-Publication Data**

Melton, J. Gordon.

Encyclopedia of American religions.

"Includes cumulative indexes to both volumes of the
first edition and this supplement."
1. Sects--United States.    2. Cults--United States.
I. Title.
BL2530.U6M443  Suppl.        291'.0973        85-20537
ISBN 0-8103-2091-6

Printed in the United States of America

# Contents

# Introduction

*The Encyclopedia of American Religions,* published in 1979, provided the first comprehensive study of religious and spiritual groups in the United States since the 1936 edition of *Census of Religious Bodies.* The overwhelming reception of the *Encyclopedia* confirmed the need for such a compilation, and it has become the standard reference work on the subject of American religions.

## Need for Supplement

In the years since the *Encyclopedia* was published, American religion has not remained static, but has continued to change at a rapid pace. Since publication of the first edition in 1979, previously unknown religious bodies have emerged from their obscurity. Some were in the initial stages of formation at the time the major research for the *Encyclopedia* was done and were unknown beyond a small circle of adherents. Others have come into existence since the time the *Encyclopedia* was published. In addition, some of the groups represented in the first edition have gone out of existence or merged with other groups, while others have undergone name changes. This *Supplement* to the first edition of *The Encyclopedia of American Religions* is intended to supply information about groups not reported in the first edition as well as to update information about groups whose status and/or names have changed.

## Contents and Arrangement

This *Supplement* to the first edition of *The Encyclopedia of American Religions* contains a main body of descriptive listings; an appendix of groups that have undergone name and/or status changes; and four cumulative indexes that cover material in both the *Supplement* and the first edition.

The main body of the *Supplement* provides information on 113 churches, religious bodies, and spiritual groups not covered in the first edition of the *Encyclopedia,* although a few groups covered in the first edition have been included where additional information has become known. As in the original edition, descriptive listings are organized into chapters which correspond to religious families. References are made to general historical information as it appears in the first edition. Because many groups listed in the *Supplement* are splinters from older groups, specific cross references to parent bodies in the first edition are indicated within the particular *Supplement* entry where appropriate.

## Compilation Methods

Information contained within the entries has been obtained from questionnaire responses from the religious groups and, in some cases, by follow-up telephone conversations. Published sources have also been consulted for additional background information.

## New Entry Format

Beginning with this *Supplement,* the *Encyclopedia* features a new entry format designed to highlight important items of information within the text. Following the entry number and name of the religious group are descriptive paragraphs that detail the origin and history, beliefs, and organization of the group. Separate headings are provided for mailing address of the headquarters (both national and international where appropriate), membership statistics, name and address of the major periodical(s), and post-secondary educational institutions sponsored and/or supported by the group.

A select list of bibliographical source materials appears at the end of each entry. These source lists replace the cumbersome footnote sections that appeared in the first edition and are representative of the comprehensive files on each group maintained at the Institute for the Study of American Religion. These files, which include recent annual reports where available, have been consulted in the compilation of each entry, although their detailed listing is not possible.

## Appendix Lists Name/Status Change

More than 100 religious groups that have undergone changes in name or status are listed (alphabetically by religious group name) and annotated in the Appendix following the body of descriptive text. Among the types of changes covered are groups whose names have changed since publication of the first edition of the *Encyclopedia,* groups that have gone out of existence, groups that have merged into existing bodies, and groups whose merger has resulted in completely new churches. All entries in the Appendix are indexed in the Religious Group Index. A complete description of the Appendix, including an explanation of the types of information typically supplied in an entry, is given on page 91.

## Cumulative Indexes

In the first edition of the *Encyclopedia,* separately alphabetized general indexes appeared at the end of each volume. For the *Supplement,* these indexes have been merged into a single alphabetical listing, combined with index entries for the *Supplement,* and divided into the following four cumulative indexes:

> RELIGIOUS GROUP INDEX. An alphabetical listing of religious groups and other organizations mentioned in the descriptive text of the first edition and the entries and Appendix of this *Supplement.* Where appropriate, references to main entries appear in boldface type.

> PERSONAL NAME INDEX. An alphabetical listing of persons mentioned in the descriptive text and entries of the first edition of this *Supplement.*

> PUBLICATIONS INDEX. This index lists books, journals, newsletters, and other publications noted in the first edition and this *Supplement.* (This index does not list source material used in the compilation of the *Encyclopedia.*)

> SUBJECT INDEX. Provides subject access to material in the *Encyclopedia* through a selected list of terms.

Because of the change in format between the first edition and this *Supplement,* citations in the indexes refer users to both page numbers (for the first edition) and entry numbers (for the *Supplement*).

## Institute for the Study of American Religion

The Institute for the Study of American Religion, now located in Santa Barbara, California, was founded in 1969 for the purpose of researching and disseminating information on the numerous religious groups in the United States. The *Encyclopedia* and its *Supplement* have been compiled in part from the Institute's collection of more than 25,000 volumes and their thousands of files covering individual religious groups.

Users with particular questions about a religious group, with corrections of errors in the *Encyclopedia,* or information about any group not listed are invited to write to the Institute in care of its director:

> Dr. J. Gordon Melton
> Institute for the Study of American Religion
> Box 90709
> Santa Barbara, California 93190-0709

# Chapter 1

# The Liturgical Family (Western)

For general information about the Western Liturgical Family, please see
pages 1-5 of Volume 1 of the *Encyclopedia of American Religions.*

## The Western Roman Tradition

### The Old Catholic Movement

For general information about the Old Catholic Movement, please see
pages 29-33 of Volume 1 of the *Encyclopedia of American Religions.*

★1★

**American Orthodox Catholic Church—Western Rite Mission, Diocese of New York**

Joseph J. Raffaele, a Roman Catholic layperson, founded St. Gregory's Church, an independent traditionalist Latin-rite parish, in Sayville, New York, on August 28, 1973. Three months later, he was ordained by Bishop Robert R. Zaborowski of the Archdiocese of the American Orthodox Catholic Church in the U.S. and Canada (now called the Mariavite Old Catholic Church). Raffaele developed a congregation among traditionalists who felt spiritually alienated from the post-Vatican II Roman Catholic Church. The parish grew slowly, and Raffaele and his assistants continued to work secular jobs (the standard Old Catholic pattern), devoting evenings and weekends to the church. The parish moved from Sayville to Shirley to Ronkonkoma. During the mid 1970s Bishop Zaborowski insisted upon the acceptance of Mariavite (i.e., Polish) liturgical patterns by the congregations under his jurisdiction. Both St. Gregory's and Fr. Raffaele left the Mariavite Old Catholic Church. Shortly after that action, Archbishop Zaborowski issued an excommunication decree.

Raffaele joined the Mt. Athos Synod under Bishop Charles C. McCarthy (a bishop in the American Orthodox Catholic Church under Archbishop Patrick Healy). On July 18, 1976, McCarthy consecrated Raffaele and raised his associate priest, Gerard J. Kessler, to the rank of monsignor. Six months later, in December 1976, St. Gregory's and Raffaele, due to some personal disagreements with McCarthy, left the Mt. Athos Synod and became an independent jurisdiction, the American Orthodox Catholic Church—Western Rite Mission, Diocese of New York.

The new jurisdiction continues as a traditionalist Latin Rite Catholic church, though Eastern Rite usage is allowed. The jurisdiction accepts the Baltimore Catechism (minus the papal references) as a doctrinal authority and uses the 1917 Code of Canon Law (again minus the papal references). Clerical celibacy is not demanded, but female priesthood is rejected. No collection is taken on Sunday at worship services. Communion is open to all.

In 1978 St. Matthias, in Yonkers, New York, was begun as the first mission parish. In 1979 St. Gregory's moved into a newly purchased building in Medford, New York. That same year, Raffaele consecrated Elrick Gonyo as an independent Uniate bishop in Stuyvesant, New York. In 1979, Raffaele and Gonyo consecrated Kessler as the auxiliary bishop for the jurisdiction.

The Congregation of the Religious of the Society of St. Gregory the Great provides a structure for priests, brothers, and nuns who wish to live an ordered life. There is also a third order lay fraternal organization for women (deaconesses).

**Headquarters:** 318 Express Drive South, Medford, Long Island, New York 11763.

**Membership:** In 1985 the American Orthodox Catholic Church—Western Rite Mission reported one congregation in New York with statewide outreach, serving approximately 200 members, and a Spanish-speaking parish in Miami, Florida. It had two active bishop-priests and five priests.

**Periodical:** *Glad Tidings,* 318 Express Drive South, Medford, Long Island, New York 11763.

**Sources:**

*"Milestones," American Orthodox Catholic Church.* Medford, N.Y.: St. Gregory's Church, 1983.

★2★

**Canonical Old Roman Catholic Church**

The Canonical Old Roman Catholic Church can be dated from the announcement in 1966 by Fr. Anthony J. Girandola, a Roman Catholic priest, that he was married and the father of a child. In spite of the Roman Catholic ban on married priests, he continued to operate as a priest and began to organize an independent parish in St. Petersburg, Florida.

He attained some fame as a spokesperson for the growing number of married priests and later authored an auto-biography, *The Most Defiant Priest.* Eventually, the time spent away from the parish forced him to turn the work over to Fr. John J. Humphreys. Shortly after assuming control, Humphreys separated entirely from Girandola and re-organized the work as Our Lady of Good Hope Old Roman Catholic parish and became a priest in the jurisdiction of Archbishop Richard Marchenna (the Old Roman Catholic Church [see Vol. 1, p. 42]).

In 1974 Marchenna consecrated Robert Clement as bishop for the Eucharistic Catholic Church, an avowed homosexual church in New York. After the consecration, Archbishop Gerard George Shelley, head of the British branch of the jurisdiction, excommunicated Marchenna and reorganized his following as the Old Roman Catholic Church in England and America. Shelley consecrated Humphreys on May 24, 1975, and Humphreys became head of the American branch of the church, which took the name Historical and Canonical Old Roman Catholic Church.

Shelley died on August 24, 1980. Fr. Michael Farrell of San Jose, California, was elected to succeed him and was consecrated by Humphreys on June 13, 1981. However, a month later, on July 28, 1981, he resigned. On April 22, 1984, Humphreys was elected primate.

**Headquarters:** 5501 62nd Avenue, Pinellas Park, Florida 33565.

**Membership:** The Canonical Old Roman Catholic Church has only a few parishes in the United States and several small chapels in England. Bishop Humphreys is assisted by John J. Greed, bishop of Massachusetts.

★ 3 ★
## North American Old Catholic Church, Ultrajectine Tradition

The North American Old Catholic Church, Ultrajectine Tradition was formed in the late 1970s by a group of former Roman Catholics associated with the Queen of the Holy Rosary Mediatrix of Peace Shrine, an independent shrine at Necedah, Wisconsin, created as a result of the visions of the Virgin Mary seen by Mary Ann Van Hoof. Van Hoof had her first apparition of the Virgin on November 12, 1949, one year after a reported apparition in Lipa City, Philippines. Then on April 7, 1950 (Good Friday), a series of apparitions were announced by the Virgin and as promised occurred on May 28 (Pentecost), May 29, May 30, June 4 (Trinity Sunday), June 16 (Feast of the Sacred Heart), and August 15 (Feast of the Assumption). As word of the apparitions spread, crowds gathered. Over 100,000 people attended the events of August 15, 1950.

On June 24, 1950, the chancery office of the Diocese of LaCrosse (Wisconsin) released information that a study of the apparitions had been initiated. In August, Bishop John Treacy announced that preliminary reports had questioned the validity of the apparitions, and he placed a temporary ban on special religious services at Necedah. He lifted the ban for the announced event on August 15. In spite of the

ban, an estimated 30,000 people attended a final apparition on October 7, at which it was claimed that the sun whirled in the sky, just as at the more famous site of Marian apparitions, Fatima, Portugal, in 1917. On October 18, the group which had grown around Van Hoof published an account of the visions and announced that a shrine was to be built and completed by May 28, 1951, the anniversary of the first public apparition.

In spite of the negative appraisal of Bishop Treacy and an editorial in the Vatican's newspaper in 1951 condemning the visions, the activity at Necedah continued and people attended the public events at which Van Hoof claimed to be conversing with the Virgin Mary. Finally, in June, 1955, Treacy issued a public statement declaring the revelations at Necedah false and prohibiting all public and private worship at the shrine. Approximately 650 pilgrims attended the August 15, 1955 (Feast of the Assumption), apparition in defiance of Treacy's ban. In September, details of the exhaustive study of the shrine, by then operating under the corporate name For God and Country, Inc., were released. The report attacked Van Hoof as a former spiritualist who had never been a practicing Roman Catholic.

While the report of the diocese lessened support, worship at the shrine continued and efforts were made to have a second study done. Finally, in 1969, Bishop F.W. Freking, Treacy's successor as bishop of LaCrosse, agreed to reexamine the case. For a while during the study, the shrine was closed to visitors. In 1970 the commission again reported negatively, and in June, 1972, Freking warned the corporation officers to cease activities or face church sanctions. Such sanctions were invoked in May, 1975, when seven people were put under an interdict.

The break with the Roman Catholic Church was formally acknowledged in May, 1979, with the presentation to the faithful of Old Catholic Bishop Edward Michael Stehlik as archbishop and metropolitan of the North American Old Catholic Church, Ultrajectine Tradition. On May 28, 1979, Stehlik dedicated the shrine, twenty-nine years after the first public apparition. The church is at one in doctrine with the Roman Catholic Church, except in its rejection of the authority of the papal office. Stehlik had been consecrated by Bishop Julius Massey of Plainfield, Illinois, pastor of an independent Episcopal Church. Massey had been consecrated by Denver Scott Swain of the American Episcopal Church (now the United Episcopal Church of America [see Supp., entry 14]).

The North American Old Catholic Church, Ultrajectine Tradition faced one crisis after another. During 1980 Stehlik and the priests he brought around him came under heavy attack in the press for falsifying their credentials. Stehlik's assistant, Bishop David Shott, was arrested for violation of parole from an earlier conviction for child molestation. Then in January, 1981, Stehlik quit the church, denounced the apparitions as a hoax, and returned to the Roman Catholic Church. He was succeeded by Francis diBenedetto, whom he had consecrated. However, on May 29, 1983, diBenedetto, in the midst of a service at the shrine, announced his resignation, further labeled the shrine a hoax, and returned to the Roman Catholic Church. In the wake of diBenedetto's leaving, a large number of the adherents also quit and returned to communion with the Roman Catholic Church.

On May 18, 1984, Mary Ann Van Hoof died. Without her visionary leadership, the future of the shrine is in doubt, as is that of the North American Old Catholic Church. Over the years the shrine itself has developed into a complex of structures. In line with a strong anti-abortion polemic, The Seven Sorrows of Our Sorrowful Mother Infants' Home was created to assist unwed mothers and unwanted children. The construction on the St. Francis of Assisi Home for Unfortunate Men continued through 1984.

**Headquarters:** For My God and My Country, Necedah, Wisconsin 54646.

**Membership:** As of 1984 over 300 adults residing near Necedah actively supported the shrine. The much larger number of supporters around the United States is unknown.

**Educational Facilities:** A seminary planned in the late 1970s functioned briefly prior to Bishop diBenedetto's resignation.

**Periodical:** *The Shrine Newsletter,* For My God and My Country, Necedah, Wisconsin 54646.

**Sources:**

Swan, Henry H. *My Work at Necedah.* 4 vols. Necedah, Wis.: For My God and My Country, 1959.

Van Hoof, Mary Ann. *The Passion and Death of Our Lord Jesus Christ.* Necedah, Wis.: For My God and My Country, 1975.

_____. *Revelations and Messages.* 2 vols. Necedah, Wis.: For My God and My Country, 1971, 1978.

★4★
**The Old Roman Catholic Church (English Rite) and the Roman Catholic Church of the Ultrajectine Tradition**

A single church body with two corporate names, the Old Roman Catholic Church (English Rite) and the Roman Catholic Church of the Ultrajectine Tradition is headed by Bishop Robert W. Lane. Lane, a priest in the Old Roman Catholic Church (English Rite) headed by Archbishop R.A. Burns (see Vol. 1, p. 43), was consecrated by H.V. Fris on September 15, 1974. Both Burns and Lane perceived that Fris had failed to follow the correct form for the ceremony, and later that same day, Burns reconsecrated Lane.

Burns died two months later. Lane left Fris's jurisdiction and placed himself under Archbishop R.A. Marchenna of the Old Roman Catholic Church (see Vol. 1, p. 42). Meanwhile, during the last year of his life, Burns had allowed the corporation papers of his jurisdiction to lapse. Lane learned of the situation and assumed control of the corporate title. He was at this time serving as pastor of St. Mary Magdelen Old Catholic Church in Chicago.

According to Lane, in 1978 Marchenna offered him the position of co-adjutant with right to succession. He had, however, developed some disagreements with Marchenna and both refused the position and left the Old Roman Catholic Church. He had previously incorporated his work for Marchenna in Chicago as the Roman Catholic Church of the Ultrajectine Tradition. Upon leaving the Old Roman Catholic Church, Lane formed an independent jurisdiction which continues both former corporations.

The Old Roman Catholic Church (English Rite) and the Roman Catholic Church of the Ultrajectine Tradition are thus two corporations designating one community of faith maintaining a Catholic way of life. It is like the Roman Catholic Church in most of its belief and practice. It retains the seven sacraments and describes itself as "One, Holy, Catholic, Apostolic, and Universal." It differs in that it uses both the Tridentine Latin mass (in both Latin and English translation) and the Ordo Novo. It has also dropped many of the regulations which govern Roman Catholic clergy, most prominently the provision prohibiting the marriage of clergy.

**Headquarters:** 4416 North Malden, Chicago, Illinois 60640.

**Membership:** In 1984 Bishop Lane reported four congregations in the United States, one each in Chicago; New York City; Nashville, Tennessee; and Anchorage, Alaska. In addition, one congregation in Hamburg, Germany, and a mission in Poland were reported.

**Educational Facilities:** Seminary of St. Francis of Assisi, Chicago, Illinois (currently inactive).

★5★
**Our Lady of the Roses, Mary Help of Mothers Shrine**

Our Lady of the Roses, Mary Help of Mothers Shrine emerged from the visionary experiences of Veronica Lueken (b. July 12, 1923), a New York housewife, which began in 1968. Initial visitations from St. Therese of Lisieux (1873-1897) were followed on April 7, 1970, by a visit from the Blessed Virgin Mary. The Virgin announced that beginning April 7, 1970, nine years to the day after the initial apparitions of the Virgin to some children at Garabandal, Spain, she would begin regular visits to Lueken. As announced, she appeared to Lueken outside St. Robert Bellarmine Catholic Church in Bayside, Queens, New York. At the first apparition, the Virgin announced she would return on the eve of the major feast days of the church, especially those dedicated to her. She requested that a shrine and basilica be erected on the grounds occupied by St. Bellarmine's. She revealed herself as "Our Lady of the Roses, Mary Help of Mothers," and designated Lueken as her voicebox to disseminate the future messages.

The messages have focused upon the denouncement of many modern trends, especially changes within the Roman Catholic Church. Prediction of an imminent chastisement of the world on the level of the destruction of Sodom and Gomorrah or the flood in Noah's time have added an urgency to the warnings against doctrinal and moral disintegration. Admonitions have been given against abortion, the occult, immodest dress, and freemasonry. Within the church, the messages have denounced the taking of communion in the hand instead of the mouth, the Catholic Pentecostal Movement, the use of recent Bible translations (which replaced the Douay-Rheims version), and religious textbooks which omit vital teachings of the Church.

As the apparitions continued, Lueken's following grew. The Roman Catholic Diocese of Brooklyn instituted an investigation, and, in an official statement, the chancery office denied any miraculous or sacred qualities to the apparitions and messages. However, the crowds attending the frequent vigils grew beyond the lawn of St. Robert's into neighboring yards. In April 1975 a restraining order against any outside vigils was obtained, and the following month St. Robert's refused the use of the building for vigils. This crisis forced the moving of the site away from the location of the mandated shrine. Since that time, gatherings have been held at Flushing Meadows Park in Queens.

The break with the Roman Catholic Church was followed by continued polemics. The messages have become increasingly critical of the church. In the fall of 1975, the messages endorsed the idea, popular among some traditionalist Catholics, that an imposter had been substituted for Pope Paul VI. Periodic denounciations of the apparitions came from various Catholic bishops, especially those whose members continued to frequent the shrine. Renewed attempts to vindicate the miraculous nature of the apparitions have centered upon successful prophecies of events, such as the New York blackout and the death of Pope John Paul I, and a set of unusual photographs which show what many people believe to be supernatural lights and manifestations.

The Bayside apparitions have been widely publicized, and accounts of the events and reprints of the messages have appeared in numerous independent Marian publications. Support for the apparitions has come from the Center of Our Lady of the Smile in Lewiston, Maine; The Apostles of Our Lady in Lansing, Michigan; Faithful and True, a publishing center in Amherst, Massachusetts; and *Santa Maria,* an independent periodical in Ottawa, Canada. For several years (1973-77), the Order of Saint Michael, a Catholic lay group in Quebec, supported Lueken in its quarterly *Michael,* but broke with her after a disagreement.

Lueken withdrew from her followers and the public during the mid 1970s. She speaks to no one except her closest followers, though she regularly appears at the site of the apparitions. At such times she is surrounded by a cadre of male followers distinguished by the white berets they wear. Women followers wear blue berets.

**Headquarters:** Box 52, Bayside, Long Island, New York 11361.

**Membership:** Not reported. Depending upon the weather, as many as several thousand people attend the vigils in Bayside, the schedules of which are publicized around the United States and Canada. Literature is mailed to many thousands across North America, though the majority remain otherwise members of the Roman Catholic Church.

**Sources:**

de Paul, Vincent. *The Abominations of Desolations:—Anti Christ Is Here Now.* St. Louis, Mo., 1975.

Grant, Robert. "War of the Roses." *Rolling Stone,* no. 311 (21 February 1980): 42-46.

*Our Lady of the Roses, Mary Help of Mothers.* Lansing, Mich.: Apostles of Our Lady, 1980.

★ 6 ★
## Servant Catholic Church

The Servant Catholic Church first convened on the Feast of All Saints in 1978 and finalized its formation and polity in January 1980. Its bishop-primate, Robert E. Burns, SSD, was consecrated on July 13, 1980, by Archbishop Herman Adrian Spruit of the Church of Antioch (see Vol. 2, p. 153). On November 2, 1980, Patricia duMont Ford was consecrated. She and Ivan MacKillop-Fritts, OCC, abbot-general of the church-sponsored religious order, the Order of the Celtic Cross, constitute the present college of bishops.

The core theology of the Servant Catholic Church is rooted in the perception that the essence of the Christian *kerygma* lies in the proclamation of Christian freedom. This belief is technically termed "eleutheric theology." This theology is impressed upon the church's liturgy as contained in *The Sacramentary and Daily Office.* The church recognizes the sacraments of initiation (baptism), reconciliation (penance), restoration (for healing and wholeness), and the Eucharist. Confirmation and marriage are designated as sacramental rites. Though receiving their orders from Liberal Catholic sources, the Servant Catholic Church has rejected Theosophy as "a heresy and cancer within the church" and adopted a more orthodox theological perspective. It reaches out ecumenically to other orthodox sacramental bodies who share its commitment to justice, effective pastoral ministry, and the admission of women to all priestly orders.

**Headquarters:** 50 Coventry Lane, Central Islip, New York 11722.

**Membership:** In 1984 the church reported three congregations, five priests, and seventy-eight members.

**Educational Facilities:** The Whithorn Institute, Ronkonkoma, New York.

**Periodical:** *The Fourth Branch,* 50 Coventry Lane, Central Islip, New York 11722.

**Sources:**

*The Sacramentary and Daily Office of the Servant Catholic Church.* Central Islip, N.Y.: Theotokos Press, 1981.

★ 7 ★
## The Traditional Roman Catholic Church in the Americas

The Traditional Roman Catholic Church in the Americas was formed in 1977 by John Dominic Fesi, a bishop in the Old Roman Catholic Church headed by Archbishop Richard A. Marchenna (see Vol. 1, p. 42). During his brief membership in the Old Roman Catholic Church, Fesi had risen to the post of chancellor. In 1976 he voiced his disapproval of Marchenna's leadership of the church by resigning his post as chancellor and calling a council meeting to reform the church. Two other bishops, Andrew Lawrence Vanore and Roy G. Bauer, attended the meeting and joined Fesi in issuing a declaration of independence from Marchenna. The document accused Marchenna of "unlawful actions" and the "personal usurpation and misuse of authority and jurisdiction." After issuing the declaration, the three bishops each adopted alternative paths. Fesi formed the Traditional Roman Catholic Church in the Americas.

Fesi had begun his ecclesiastical career as a Franciscan friar in the Archdiocese of the Old Catholic Church in America headed by Archbishop Walter X. Brown (see Vol. 1, p. 42). In 1973 Brown created the Vicariate of Illinois and consecrated Msgr. Earl P. Gasquoine as its bishop. Gasquoine appointed Fesi vicar general with the title of reverend monsignor. Fesi, as part of his work, ran Friary Press which printed a quarterly periodical, *The Franciscan,* and pamphlets for the archdiocese.

In 1974 Fesi left Brown's jurisdiction and sought consecration from Damian Hough, head of the Old Roman Catholic Church (see Vol. 1, p. 42). Assisted by Bishops Roman W. Skikiewicz and Joseph G. Sokolowski, Hough consecrated Fesi on June 30, 1974. Fesi took his friars into the Old Roman Catholic Church headed by Marchenna. Though *The Franciscan* was discontinued, Friary Press became the church's major publishing arm.

During his years with Brown and Marchenna, Fesi and the Franciscans assisted at the Church of St. Mary Mystical Rose, an independent Old Catholic parish in Chicago. Bishop Skikiewicz pastored the congregation which had been founded in 1937 in response to a vision of Maria Kroll, a young Polish immigrant. The church was in effect an independent Old Catholic jurisdiction. Eventually, Fesi was appointed associate pastor. Marchenna appointed Fesi head of the Vicariate of Illinois and eventually the Church of St. Mary Mystical Rose became part of the vicariate. Though a strong congregation, after Skikiewicz's death the support dwindled and the building was sold.

The Traditional Roman Catholic Church in the Americas follows the Old Catholic tradition. It keeps the seven sacraments and teaches that baptism is essential for salvation. Veneration of images and pictures of the saints (who are present in a mystical manner in their image) and especially the Blessed Virgin Mary (whose intercession is essential to salvation) is promoted. Abortion is condemned.

The church is organized hierarchically. Under the bishop is an ecclesiastical structure which includes priests, deacons, subdeacons, acolytes, exorcists, lectors, and doorkeepers. Priests are allowed to marry. A synod meets annually.

**Headquarters:** Friary Press, Box 470, Chicago, Illinois 60690.

**Membership:** In 1984 the church reported eleven parishes, twenty-three priests, and 780 members.

**Educational Facilities:** Our Lady of Victory Seminary, Chicago, Illinois.

**Periodical:** *The Larks of Umbria,* Friary Press, Box 470, Chicago, Illinois 60690.

**Sources:**

Fesi, John Dominic. *Apostolic Succession of the Old Roman Catholic Church.* Chicago: Friary Press, [1975?].

———. *Canonical Standing of Religious in Regards to the Sacred Ministry.* Chicago: Friary Press, 1975.
———. *Reasons for Divorce and Annulment in Church Law.* Chicago: Friary Press, 1975.

★8★
**Tridentine Catholic Church**

The Tridentine Catholic Church was formed in 1976 by Fr. Leonard J. Curreri, formerly a priest in the Traditional Christian Catholic Church headed by Archbishop Thomas Fehervary (see Vol. 1, p. 39). In 1974 Fehervary moved to extend his Canadian-based jurisdiction to the United States by ordaining and commissioning Curreri and two other priests. However, the following year, on April 13, 1977, Curreri was consecrated a bishop by Francis J. Ryan of the Ecumenical Catholic Church of Christ. (He was subsequently reconsecrated subconditionally in December, 1976, by Archbishop Andre Barbeau of the Catholic Charismatic Church of Canada.) Then in 1976 Curreri called a synod at which the Tridentine Catholic Church was organized as a separate jurisdiction.

The Tridentine Catholic Church follows the doctrines and practices of the pre-Vatican II Roman Catholic Church. It rejects the Novus Ordo. It also rejects the doctrine of papal infallibility, the ordination of women to the priesthood, and abortion under any circumstances. It leaves the matter of birth control to individual consciences.

**Headquarters:** c/o Archbishop Leonard J. Curreri, Primate, Sacred Heart of Jesus Chapel, 1740 West Seventh Street, Brooklyn, New York 11223.

**Membership:** In 1984 the church reported twelve congregations and/or missions, ten clergy, and 165 members, all in the United States.

**Sources:**

Curreri, Leonard J. *De Sacramentis.* Brooklyn, N.Y., n.d.
———. *More Questions and Answers on the Tridentine Catholic Church.* Brooklyn, N.Y., n.d.
———. *Questions and Answers on the Tridentine Catholic Church.* Brooklyn, N.Y., n.d.
———. *Successio Apostolica.* Brooklyn, N.Y., 1984.

★9★
**The United Hispanic Old Catholic Episcopate in the Americas**

The United Hispanic Old Catholic Episcopate in the Americas can be traced to December 8, 1958, when Fr. Hector Roa y Gonzalez formed the Puerto Rican National Catholic Church as a Spanish-speaking Old Catholic body for the Commonwealth. The original intentions and hope were to affiliate with the Polish National Catholic Church, and the new church adhered strictly to the Utrecht Declaration to the Catholic Church of September 24, 1889, one of the definitive documents of Old Catholicism. Roa opened negotiations with the primate of the Polish National Catholic Church in 1959.

The Polish Church withdrew from the negotiations in 1960, in part due to the presence of the Protestant Episcopal Church (with whom it was then in full communion) on the island. Roa then turned to Eastern Orthodoxy and in 1961 was received into the Patriarchal Exarchate of the Russian Orthodox Church in the Americas. The next year his church was registered as La Santa Iglesia Catolica Apostolica Ortodoxa de Puerto Rico, Inc., i.e., The Holy Catholic and Apostolic Church in Puerto Rico. The church for a time kept its revised tridentine ritual, with a few necessary Orthodox alterations. However, within a short time, the Orthodox liturgy was translated into Spanish and introduced into the Puerto Rican parishes. Gradually, other changes were introduced, and some members began to feel that the church had lost its identity and was being totally absorbed into Russian Orthodoxy, as its Spanish Western Rite Vicariate.

Roa led the fight against the Russification of the vicariate, but, after the replacement of Archbishop John Wendland as head of the exarchate, he found that he had lost his major support within the jurisdiction. In 1968, with his followers, Roa withdrew and reestablished the Puerto Rican National Catholic Church. In 1979, in recognition of the geographical spread of the church, its name was changed to The United Hispanic Old Catholic Episcopate in the Americas. Roa turned to the Catholic Apostolic Church in Brazil, founded by Dom Carlos Duarte Costa, to receive episcopal orders. He was consecrated by Bishop Luis Silva y Viera in 1977.

The United Hispanic Old Catholic Episcopate in the Americas continues to use the revised tridentine liturgy and accepts the seven traditional sacraments. Following the Eastern practice, clergy are allowed to marry prior to ordination, but bishops are chosen from the unmarried clergy. Clerical celibacy is encouraged.

**Headquarters:** c/o Most Rev. Hector Roa y Gonzalez, 10 Stagg Street, Brooklyn, New York 11206.

**Membership:** In 1982 the episcopate claimed 21,000 members scattered throughout the Western Hemisphere.

**Sources:**

*The Profession of Faith of the United Hispanic Old Catholic Church in the Americas.* 1984.

# The Anglican Tradition

For general information about the Anglican Tradition, please see pages 49-50 of Volume 1 of the *Encyclopedia of American Religions.*

★ 10 ★
**Anglican Catholic Church**

While dissent over what many felt was theological and moral drift in the Protestant Episcopal Church led to the formation of several small protesting bodies, large-scale schism occurred only after a series of events beginning in 1974 gave substantive focus to the conservative protest. In 1974 four Episcopal bishops (in defiance of their colleagues and the church) ordained eleven women to the priesthood. The following year, the Anglican Church of Canada approved a provision for the ordination of women. Then in 1976, with only a token censure of the bishops, the Protestant Episcopal Church regularized the ordinations of the eleven women. It also approved the revised Book of Common Prayer which replaced the 1928 edition which most Episcopalians had used for half a century.

The events of the mid-1970s led to the calling of a Congress of Episcopalians to consider alternatives to the Protestant Episcopal Church and to find a way to continue a traditional Anglican church. In the month leading up to the congress, several congregations and priests withdrew from the Episcopal Church and formed the provisional Diocese of the Holy Trinity. They designated James O. Mote as their bishop elect.

Eighteen hundred persons gathered in St. Louis in September 1977 and adopted a lengthy statement, the "Affirmation of St. Louis," which called for allegiance to the Anglican tradition of belief (as contained in the Thirty-nine Articles of Religion) and practice (as exemplified in the 1928 edition of the Book of Common Prayer). It specifically denounced the admission of women to the priesthood, the liberal attitudes to alternative sexual patterns (especially homosexuality), and both the World and National Councils of Churches. It affirmed the rights of congregations in the management of their own financial affairs and expressed a desire to remain in communion with the See of Canterbury.

Throughout 1977 more congregations left the Protestant Episcopal Church, and others were formed by groups of people who had left as individual members. Following the September congress, three more provisional dioceses were established, and bishops elected. The Diocese of Christ the King elected Robert S. Morse; the Diocese of the Southeast elected Peter F. Watterson; and the Diocese of the Midwest elected C. Dale D. Doren. Bishops were sought who would consent to consecrate the new bishops-elect, and finally four agreed. Paul Boynton, retired suffragan of New York, was the first to withdraw from the consecration service, due to illness. Mark Pae of the Anglican Church of Korea, a close personal friend of Dale Doren's, withdrew under the pressure of his fellow bishops, but sent a letter of consent to Doren's consecration. With Pae's letter, on January 28, 1978, Albert Chambers, former bishop of Springfield, Illinois, and Francisco Pagtakhan, of the Philippine Independent Church, consecrated Doren. Doren in turn joined Chambers and Pagtakhan in consecrating Morse, Watterson, and Mote.

Having established itself with proper episcopal leadership, the new church, tentatively called the Anglican Church of North America, turned its attention to the task of ordering its life. A national synod meeting was held in Dallas in 1978. Those present adopted a new name, the Anglican Catholic Church, and approved a constitution which was sent to the several dioceses, by then seven in number, for ratification. In May 1979, the bishops announced that five of the seven dioceses had ratified the actions of the Dallas synod, and thus the Anglican Catholic Church had been officially constituted.

The early 1980s have been a period of extreme flux for the Anglican Catholic Church. It emerged as the single largest body out of the St. Louis meeting, claiming more than half of the congregations and members, but along the way lost two of its original dioceses and three of its original bishops. The Dioceses of Christ the King and the Southeast and their bishops (Morse and Watterson) refused to ratify the constitution and instead continued as the Anglican Church of North America (see Supp., entry 12). The Diocese of the Southeast soon broke with the Diocese of Christ the King and became an independent jurisdiction. Then, in 1983, Watterson resigned as bishop and joined the Roman Catholic Church. His action effectively killed the diocese whose member churches were absorbed by the other Anglican bodies, primarily the Anglican Catholic Church.

While dealing with the loss of the Dioceses of Christ the King and the Southeast, the church continued to grow as new and independent congregations joined; additions more than made up for losses. Bishop Doren resigned in 1980, but only two congregations followed him. In 1981 several priests and parishes left to form the Holy Catholic Church, Anglican Rite Jurisdiction of the Americas (see Supp., entry 13). The largest schism occurred in 1983 when the Diocese of the Southwest under Bishop Robert C. Harvey withdrew and took twenty-one congregations in Arkansas, Texas, Oklahoma, New Mexico, and Arizona.

The Anglican Catholic Church describes itself as the continuation of the traditional Anglicanism as expressed in the Nicene and Apostles' Creeds. It holds to the liturgy of the Book of Common Prayer, 1928 edition. It rejects women in the priesthood and holds to traditional standards of moral conduct, specifically condemning ''easy'' divorce and remarriage, abortion on demand, and homosexual activity.

**Headquarters:** No central headquarters. For information contact the senior bishop: Rt. Rev. James O. Mote, Diocese of the Holy Trinity, c/o St. Mary's Church, 2290 South Clayton, Denver, Colorado 80210; or The Fellowship of Concerned Churchmen, Route 1, Box 35A, Eureka Springs, Arkansas 72632.

**Membership:** In 1983 the Anglican Catholic Church had 135 congregations and an estimated 3,000 to 5,000 members.

**Educational Facilities:** Holyrood Seminary, Liberty, New York.

**Periodical:** *The Trinitarian,* 3141 South Josephine, Denver, Colorado 80210. Unofficial: *Anglican News Exchange,* Fellowship of Concerned Churchmen, Route 1, Box 35A, Eureka Springs, Arkansas 72632.

**Sources:**

*A Directory of Churches of the Continuing Anglican Tradition.* Eureka Springs, Ark.: Fellowship of Concerned Churchmen, 1983-84.

Laukhuff, Perry. *The Anglican Catholic Church.* Eureka Springs, Ark.: Fellowship of Concerned Churchmen, 1977.

*Opening Addresses of the Church Congress at St. Louis, Missouri, 14-16 September 1977.* Amherst, Va.: Fellowship of Concerned Churchmen, 1977.

★11★
## The Anglican Church of North America

The Anglican Church of North America traces its origin to the Independent Anglican Church founded in Canada in the 1930s by William H. Daw. Later he led his jurisdiction into the Liberal Catholic Church led by Bishop E.M. Matthews (see Vol. 2, p. 152) and in 1955 was consecrated by Matthews. In 1964 Daw and Bishop James Pickford Roberts left Matthews to found the Liberal Catholic Church International. Daw assumed the role of primate, but withdrew in 1974 in favor of Joseph Edward Neth. He resumed the primacy in 1979, when Neth was forced to resign after consecrating a priest of another jurisdiction without church approval.

In 1981 Daw participated in the formation of the Independent Catholic Church International, which brought together a number of independent Old Catholic, Anglican, and Liberal Catholic jurisdictions in both North America and Europe. Meanwhile, the Liberal Catholic Church International and Daw reasserted its Anglican roots in the wake of the formation of the Anglican Catholic Church in Canada and the consecration and untimely death of its first bishop, Carmino J. deCatanzaro. The Liberal Catholic Church International repudiated Theosophy and changed its name to the North American Episcopal Church. In 1983 P.W. Goodrich, primate of the ecumenical Independent Catholic Church International, resigned to become primate of the North American Episcopal Church. Goodrich had originally been consecrated by Daw as bishop for the small Independent Catholic Church of Canada.

Goodrich's leadership of the North American Episcopal Church was shortlived, however, and within a year he was forced out and Archbishop Daw again resumed the primacy. Two bishops, Rt. Rev. Robert T. Shepherd and Rt. Rev. M. B. D. Crawford, have been consecrated to administer the work of the church in America and Canada respectively. The first American parish was established in Atlanta, Georgia, in 1983. In June, 1984, the church's name was changed to the Anglican Church of North America.

The Anglican Church of North America, as other continuing Anglican bodies, accepts the 1977 Affirmation of St. Louis and follows the practices of the Protestant Episcopal Church and the Anglican Church of Canada prior to the changes of the 1970s. It uses the 1928 edition of the Book of Common Prayer. It differs from other continuing Anglican bodies in that it believes that a single jurisdiction should be established for all of North America rather than several jurisdictions divided along national and regional lines. It also stresses the collegiality of all levels of the clergy and the laity.

**Headquarters:** For the United States: Chapel of St. Augustine of Canterbury, 1906 Forest Green Drive, NE, Atlanta, Georgia 30329. For Canada: St. Matthias Cathedral, Roxborough & Ivon Streets, Hamilton, Ontario, Canada L8H 5S5.

**Membership:** In 1984 the church reported ten congregations, eight priests, and 250 members in the United States and Canada.

**Educational Facilities:** St. Matthias' Cathedral Seminary, Hamilton, Ontario, a correspondence school.

**Sources:**

Bain, Alan M. *Bishops Irregular.* London, 1984.

### ★ 12 ★
### Anglican Church of North America, Diocese of Christ the King

The Anglican Church of North America, Diocese of Christ the King shares the history of that larger conservative movement which participated in the 1977 congress at St. Louis and approved the "Affirmation" adopted by the delegates. The diocese was one of the four original provisional dioceses formed and its bishop-elect, Robert S. Morse, was consecrated along with the other new Anglican bishops on January 28, 1978, in Denver by Bishops Albert Chambers, Francisco Pagtakhan, and C. Dale D. Doren (see Supp., entry 10). However, Bishop Morse and other members of his diocese were among those most opposed to the new constitution adopted by the synod at Dallas in 1978 by the group which took the name Anglican Catholic Church. Neither the Diocese of Christ the King nor the Diocese of the Southeast ratified the constitution, preferring to work without such a document. Rather, they called a synod meeting for Hot Springs, Arkansas, on October 16-18, 1979, two days immediately prior to the opening of the Anglican Catholic Church synod at Indianapolis. Those gathered at Hot Springs decided to continue to use the name Anglican Church of North America and adopted canons (church laws) but no constitution.

The new jurisdiction immediately faced intense administrative pressures. In response to the Anglican Church of North America claiming many congregations in California and the South, the Anglican Catholic Church established a new structure, the patrimony, to facilitate the movement into the church of already existing congregations and to assist the formation of new ones in areas not covered by existing diocesan structures. Both Bishop Morse and Bishop Watterson viewed the patrimony as an attempt to steal the congregations under their jurisdiction.

The pressure from the Anglican Catholic Church did not keep the two dioceses in the Anglican Church of North America from facing crucial issues around which internal controversy swelled. Bishop Watterson argued for a strict division of the Anglican Church of North America into geographical dioceses with the understanding that neither bishop would attempt to establish congregations or missions in the other's diocese. The Diocese of Christ the King rejected Watterson's suggestions and the Diocese of the Southeast became a separate jurisdiction. The Diocese of Christ the King proceeded to initiate work in the South.

Once separated, the Diocese of the Southeast experienced continued internal problems. In 1980 nine congregations withdrew with the blessing of Bishop Francisco Pagtakhan (who was becoming increasingly dissatisfied with the Anglican Catholic Church) and formed the Associated Parishes, Traditional Anglo-Catholic. Pagtakhan named Fr.

J. B. Medaris as archdeacon. This new jurisdiction dissolved very quickly and merged back into the Anglican Catholic Church. Finally, in 1984, Bishop Watterson resigned his office and joined the Roman Catholic Church. His jurisdiction dissolved and the remaining congregations realigned themselves with the other Anglican bodies.

The dissolution of the Diocese of the Southeast left the Diocese of Christ the King the only diocese in the church.

The Diocese of Christ the King is at one in faith and practice with the other Anglican bodies, holding to the faith of the undivided primitive church to which Episcopalians have always belonged, as spelled out in the Affirmation of 1977. It rejects both the National Council of Churches and the World Council of Churches. It differs from the Anglican Catholic Church only in matters of administration.

**Headquarters:** c/o Rt. Rev. Robert S. Morse, St. Mary's Church, 6013 Lawton, Oakland, California 94618.

**Membership:** In 1983 the Anglican Church of North America had thirty-five parishes with an estimated 3,000 to 5,000 members.

**Educational Facilities:** Saint Joseph of Arimathea Anglican Theological College, Berkeley, California.

**Sources:**

*A Directory of Churches in the Continuing Anglican Tradition 1983-84.* Eureka Springs, Ark.: Fellowship of Concerned Churchmen, 1983-84.

### ★ 13 ★
### The Holy Catholic Church, Anglican Rite Jurisdiction of the Americas

In the several years following the 1977 congress which met in St. Louis, the Anglican Movement grew to encompass over 200 congregations. However, as it grew, it splintered into several factions over administrative disagreements and the domination of the Anglican Catholic Church by the Anglo-Catholic (high-church) perspective. Some congregations remained outside of the various diocesan structures altogether. Bishop Francisco Pagtakhan of the Philippine Independent Church, who had participated in the original consecrations of the four Anglican bishops in 1978, became increasingly disturbed at the splintering and lack of unity in the Anglican Movement. In 1981, asserting his role as the ecumenical and missionary officer of the Philippine Independent Church, Pagtakhan decided to create an "umbrella" for those in the Anglican Movement who were searching for a home where they could "belong to a genuinely canonical part of the One, Holy, Catholic and Apostolic Church." Thus in March 1980 in Texas, he led in the incorporation of the Holy Catholic Church, Anglican Rite Jurisdiction of the Americas.

On September 26, 1981 (with the permission of the Supreme Bishop of the Philippine Independent Church, Most Rev. Macario V. Ga), Bishop Pagtakhan, assisted by retired bishops Sergio Mondala and Lupe Rosete, consecrated Robert Q. Kennaugh, G. Ogden Miller, and C. Wayne Craig, all former priests in the Anglican Catholic Church.

Kennaugh became head of the Diocese of St. Luke, centered in Corsicana, Texas, and archbishop for the jurisdiction. Miller was named bishop of the Diocese of St. Matthew with headquarters in Napa, California. Craig became bishop of the Diocese of St. Mark with headquarters in Columbus, Ohio. In 1983 Herman F. Nelson was consecrated as bishop for the Diocese of St. John the Evangelist with headquarters in Venice, Florida. Shortly thereafter, Kennaugh resigned as archbishop and Craig was named to that post.

The Anglican Rite Jurisdiction of the Americas has no differences in doctrine and practice with the larger Anglican Movement and emphasizes its thorough commitment to "the unity of genuine continuing Anglicanism." The jurisdiction has moved to establish intercommunion with other Anglican bodies and to accept otherwise independent congregations under its umbrella.

**Headquarters:** The Anglican Diocese of St. Mark the Evangelist, c/o Rt. Rev. G. Wayne Craig, 2535 Sunbury Drive, Columbus, Ohio 43219.

**Membership:** In 1984 the jurisdiction reported eleven congregations and less than 1,000 members.

**Periodical:** *The Evangelist,* De Koven Foundation of Ohio, 82 Frederick Avenue, Akron, Ohio 44310.

**Sources:**
Dibbert, Roderic B. *The Roots of Traditional Anglicanism.* Akron, Ohio: DeKoven Foundation of Ohio, 1984.
*The Prologue.* Akron, Ohio: DeKoven Foundation of Ohio, 1984.

## ★ 14 ★
### The United Episcopal Church of America

The United Episcopal Church of America can be traced to the American Episcopal Church founded in the early 1940s by Denver Scott Swain (not to be confused with the presently existing American Episcopal Church formed by K. C. Pillai in 1968). Swain had been ordained to the priesthood in 1942 by Archbishop C. H. Carfora of the North American Old Roman Catholic Church but soon was suspended from the priesthood for going outside of Carfora's jurisdiction seeking someone to consecrate him. Eventually, around 1943, F. V. Kanski of the American Catholic Church raised Swain to the episcopacy. During the 1940s, the American Episcopal Church applied for membership in both the National Association of Evangelicals and the American Council of Christian Churches. It was denied membership when upon investigation it was discovered that Swain had misrepresented the nature and strength of the church.

It was reported that the American Episcopal Church had dissolved in the 1950s. However, in 1945 Swain consecrated William H. Schneider, who in turn consecrated James Edward Burns in 1948. Eventually Burns became primate and the name was changed to the United Episcopal Church. Burns established the church's headquarters at All Saints Church in East Hanover, New Jersey. He was also subsequently consecrated by Hubert A. Rogers (who succeeded Carfora as head of the North American Old Roman Catholic Church) in 1967 and by Walter Propheta of the American Orthodox Catholic Church in 1968.

In 1976 Burns, assisted by Bishop Edward G. Marshall and Archbishop John W. Treleaven (of the Apostolic Catholic Church of North America), consecrated Richard C. Acker to the episcopacy. Several months later Acker succeeded Burns as archbishop in charge of the United Episcopal Church of America. Acker's parish, St. James Church located in Hopkins, South Carolina, became the new national cathedral of the jurisdiction.

The United Episcopal Church of America describes itself as a conservative independent church which uses the King James Bible, the 1928 edition of the book of Common Prayer, and the 1940 Hymnal of the Protestant Episcopal Church. It combines traditional liturgical form with the widest possible measure of intellectual freedom.

**Headquarters:** 6417 North Trenholm Road, Columbia, South Carolina 29206.

**Membership:** Not reported. The church has several congregations and an estimated membership of several hundred.

**Sources:**

*Apostolic Succession in the United Episcopal Church.* Boston, Mass., 1977.
*The Divine Liturgy, Matins and Vespers, and the Divine Offices of the American Episcopal Church.* McNabb, Ill.: Order of St. James Press, 1947.
Piepkorn, Arthur Carl. "The American Episcopal Church (Lutheran)." *American Lutheran* 30 (November 1947): 10-13.

## ★ 15 ★
### The United Episcopal Church of North America

In 1980 C. Dale David Doren, senior bishop of the Anglican Catholic Church and head of its mid-Atlantic diocese, resigned. He asserted that the Anglican Catholic Church (see Supp., entry 10) was becoming exclusively "high-church" or "Anglo-Catholic" in its stance. With only two congregations, he formed the United Episcopal Church of North America. It adheres to the traditional beliefs and practices of the Protestant Episcopal Church as exemplified in the 1928 Book of Common Prayer and the thirty-nine Articles of Religion.

The UEC tends to the "low-church" end of the Anglican spectrum. Each parish is independent and holds title to properties and control over temporal affairs. The jurisdiction adopted the 1958 Protestant Episcopal Church Constitution and Canons, with specific changes in relation to church properties, as its own. The presiding bishop was given the title of archbishop, but the church invested little power in the office. In 1984 Archbishop Doren consecrated Albion W. Knight as a missionary bishop to assist him in leadership of the jurisdiction's affairs.

**Headquarters:** c/o Most Rev. C. Dale D. Doren, 2293 Country Club Drive, Upper St. Clair, Pennsylvania 15241.

**Membership:** Not reported. Parishes of the church are found in Pennsylvania, Ohio, New York, Maryland, New Hampshire, and Florida. Membership is estimated (in 1984) to be less than 1,000.

**Periodical:** *Glad Tidings,* Box 4538, Pensacola, Florida 32507.

# Chapter 2

# The Liturgical Family (Eastern)

## The Eastern Orthodox Tradition

For general information about the Eastern Orthodox Tradition, please see pages 57-59 of Volume 1 of the *Encyclopedia of American Religions.*

★16★

**The Apostolic Catholic Church of the Americas (a.k.a. American Orthodox Catholic Church)**

The Apostolic Catholic Church of the Americas dates to a 1976 merger of two jurisdictions headed by Bishops Robert S. Zeiger and Gordon I. DaCosta. Zeiger had been consecrated in 1961 by Archbishop Peter A. Zurawetzky of the Church of Christ Catholic Church of the Americas and Europe (now the Old Orthodox Catholic Patriarchate of America [see Vol. 1, p. 37]) as an Orthodox bishop for Westerners. However, in 1962 Zeiger left Zurawetzky's jurisdiction and formed the American Orthodox Catholic Church (see Vol. 1, p. 38), headquartered in Denver, Colorado. The church was conceived as American in its autonomy, Orthodox in its faith and practice, and Catholic in its universality.

Gordon I. DaCosta was a priest and bishop of the Free Protestant Episcopal Church. He left that jurisdiction in 1971 and formed the Anglican Church of the Americas, in Indiana. The Anglican Church of the Americas was designed to continue the work of, and update the structure of, the Free Protestant Episcopal Church (then in the process of losing any American presence), and to avoid any conflict over the similarity of name with the Protestant Episcopal Church. Over the first few years of its existence, the Anglican Church moved toward Orthodoxy in both faith and liturgy and in 1976 merged into the American Orthodox Catholic Church headed by Bishop Zeiger. At the time of the merger, the American Orthodox Catholic Church took on a second name, the Apostolic Catholic Church of the Americas. This second name became its most frequently used designation, though both names are officially correct.

Soon after the merger, Zeiger resigned both his office and membership in the church and joined the Roman Catholic Church as a layman in a Uniate Ruthenian congregation. DaCosta was elected as his successor. (As of 1984 Zeiger remains connected to the church as its registered agent. The church is registered in Colorado while DaCosta resides in Indiana.)

The Apostolic Catholic Church of the Americas describes itself as Western Orthodox. It is Orthodox in that it accepts as authority the Sacred Scriptures, the Apostolic Tradition, the doctrinal decrees of the Seven Ecumenical Councils, and the writings of the church fathers. It rejects mandatory clerical celibacy and the ordination of women. It is Catholic, but not Roman; Evangelical but not Protestant; and Orthodox, but not Eastern.

The church is headed by its three bishops: Gordon I. DaCosta; Herbert Robinson of Bellingham, Washington; and C.F. Quinn, who heads a large congregation in Dallas, Texas. Church property is owned locally by the boards of individual congregations. Thus, church government is a complex mixture of episcopal and congregational polity.

**Headquarters:** c/o Archbishop Gordon I. DaCosta, Box 1000, Gas City, Indiana; Diocese of Texas, c/o Rt. Rev. C.F. Quinn, 4201 Fairmount Street, Dallas, Texas 75219.

**Membership:** In 1984 the church reported nine parishes, missions, and chaplaincies and had an estimated membership of less than 500.

**Periodical:** *The Door,* 4201 Fairmount Street, Dallas, Texas 75219.

★17★

**The Autocephalous Syro-Chaldean Church of North America**

The Autocephalous Syro-Chaldean Church of North America traces its origins to Hugh George de Willmott Newman, popularly known by his ecclesiastical name Mar Georgius. Mar Georgius was the first of the independent bishops to have himself consecrated numerous times in order to embody the several episcopal lineages both East and West, which he in turn passed on to the many individuals he consecrated. Among the people to whom he passed these various lines of apostolic succession was Charles D. Boltwood, a bishop in the British-based Free Protestant Episcopal Church. In 1959, three years after his reconsecration by Newman, Boltwood became primate of the church. Among his first actions, Boltwood consecrated John M. Stanley (May 3, 1959) as bishop of the state of Washington.

During the 1960s, Stanley withdrew from the Free Protestant Episcopal Church and formed the Syro-Chaldean Archdiocese of North America. In so doing he claimed the lineage of the Church of the East received by Newman from W.S.M. Knight who had received the lineage from Ulric Vernon Herford (Mar Jacobus). Stanley, as archbishop of the new jurisdiction, took the ecclesiastical name Mar Yokhannan.

The series of events which led to the formation of the Autocephalous Syro-Chaldean Church of North America began at the meeting of the Holy Synod of Syro-Chaldean Archdiocese, December 13-14, 1974. The synod designated Archpriest Bertram S. Schlossberg as bishop-elect with the task of organizing a Diocese of New York. By that action Schlossberg came under the direct authority of Archbishop James A. Gaines who had authority from the archdiocese for the eastern half of the United States. Together, on April 16, 1976, they incorporated their new work as the Autocephalous Syro-Chaldean Archdiocese of the Eastern United States of America. On October 31, 1976, Gaines consecrated Schlossberg as bishop of the Northeast and in December erected the Diocese of the Northeast, over which Schlossberg was assigned.

The actions of Gaines and Schlossberg were followed by a split with Mar Yokhannan, who attempted to dissolve both the Autocephalous Eastern Archdiocese and the Diocese of the Northeast. Eventually, on April 2, 1977, Mar Yokhannan released Schlossberg and Gaines from "all canonical obedience" and then withdrew from the Syro-Chaldean Archdiocese and joined the Church of the East. Gaines (Mar Jacobus) and Schlossberg (Mar Uzziah) then reorganized all of the work formerly under Mar Yokhannan and in October 1977 incorporated the Autocephalous Syro-Chaldean Church of North America, with Mar Jacobus as metropolitan and Mar Uzziah as bishop of the Northeastern Diocese.

The Syro-Chaldean Church follows the Orthodox theology of the Church of the East. It affirms the Bible as the Word of God and both the Apostles' and Nicene Creeds. It keeps seven sacraments—baptism, confirmation, holy communion, reconciliation, annointing for healing, holy matrimony, and holy orders. It uses the Liturgy of Mar Addai and Mar Mari as its official liturgy, but allows parishes great freedom in choosing other forms of worship.

**Headquarters:** c/o Metropolitan Archbishop Bertram S. Schlossberg, Church of the Risen Savior, 9 Ellington Avenue, Rockville, Connecticut 06066.

**Membership:** In 1984 the church reported 400 members in four parish churches and two missions. It sponsors one missionary in Papua, New Guinea. There are eighteen clergy.

**Educational Facilities:** Christ the King Seminary and School of Discipleship, Rockville, Connecticut.

★ 18 ★
## Byzantine Catholic Church

The Byzantine Catholic Church was formed in 1984 by a merger of the Byzantine Old Catholic Church and the Holy Orthodox Catholic Church, Eastern and Apostolic. The Holy Orthodox Catholic Church, Eastern and Apostolic was a small jurisdiction headed by Bishop Richard B. Morrill. The Byzantine Old Catholic Church was a jurisdiction from out of the Old Catholic tradition whose history is intimately tied to the career of its leader, Bishop Mark I. Miller.

As a child, Miller was adopted and, taking the name of his new parents, was raised as Oliver W. Skelton. He joined the American Orthodox Catholic Church. Upon ordination as a priest, he assumed the religious name Leo Christopher (Skelton), as he became known throughout the Old Catholic movement after his consecration as a bishop by Christopher J. Stanley in 1965. In 1966 Skelton left Stanley and the American Orthodox Catholic Church and became a cardinal in the Orthodox Old Catholic Church headed by Claude Hamel (see Vol. 1, p. 45). Headquartered in Enid, Oklahoma, Skelton functioned under the Old Roman Catholic Church (Orthodox Orders), a corporation he had formed in 1964. Upon leaving Hamel, whom he accused of exercising capricious and authoritarian leadership, Skelton changed the name of his organization to the Orthodox Old Roman Catholic Church II (see Vol. 1, p. 41) and assumed the ecclesiastical name Mark I. He established headquarters in Hollywood, California.

In the mid-1970s, Skelton reorganized the Orthodox Old Roman Catholic Church II and changed its name to the North American Orthodox Catholic Church. During this period he was moving, both theologically and liturgically, away from Old Catholicism and toward Eastern Orthodoxy. In April 1975 he had his secular name changed legally to that of his natural parents and became Mark I. Miller.

Two further reorganizations of his jurisdiction in 1981 and 1983 transformed the North American Orthodox Catholic Church into the Byzantine Old Catholic Church. The major reorganization in 1981 resulted from clergy engaged in what were termed "un-Orthodox actions." Miller promulgated a number of additions to the Disciplinary Canons, most notably new regulations prohibiting the ordination of females and the assumption of the bishopric by married clergy. The name was changed to The World Independent Orthodox Catholic Church (and Her Dependencies). Finally in 1983 the World Independent Orthodox Catholic Church assumed the name which it took into the 1984 merger, the Holy Orthodox Catholic Church, Eastern and Apostolic.

After the new church was formed, His Beatitude Metropolitan Richard (B. Morrill) became the president of the Sacred Synod of Bishops and administrator of the church. His Beatitude Mark (I. Miller) became vice-president of the Sacred Synod of Bishops and ecclesiastical administrator and chief justice of the Spiritual Court of Bishops.

The Byzantine Catholic Church is Orthodox in faith and practice. It uses the several Eastern liturgies (most prominently St. John Chrysostom's, St. Basil's).

**Headquarters:** Box 3682, Los Angeles, California 90078.

**Membership:** In 1984 the Byzantine Catholic Church reported 1,600 members in ten congregations served by twenty priests. Affiliated parishes are also found in England, France, Italy, Nigeria, Brazil, and Chile.

**Educational Facilities:** The International Theological Seminary, Van Nuys, California (see Supp., entry 34).

★ 19 ★
## Catholic Apostolic Church in America

Though officially reconstituted in 1983, the Catholic Apostolic Church in America continues an unbroken existence from 1950 when Stephen Meyer Corradi-Scarella established an American outpost of the Catholic Apostolic Church in Brazil. The Catholic Apostolic Church in Brazil was formed in 1946 by Dom Carlos Duarte Costa, a former Roman Catholic bishop who had been excommunicated by Pope Pius XII because of his criticism of the church during World War II. Corradi-Scarella was consecrated by Costa in 1951 and established the church as an exarchate with headquarters in New Mexico. During the 1960s, following the death of Costa, Corradi-Scarella lost touch with the Brazilian group and began to associate with the various Old Catholics in the United States. By 1970 he called his jurisdiction the Diocese of the Old Catholic Church in America.

The church grew slowly until the 1970s. In 1973 Corradi-Scarella was joined by Francis Jerome Joachim, a priest ordained by Archbishop Bartholomew Cunningham of the Holy Orthodox Church, Diocese of New Mexico. Joachim brought an Eastern Orthodox perspective with him, in contrast to Corradi-Scarella's Catholic tradition, but soon became his chief associate. Corradi-Scarella arranged for Joachim's consecration by Archbishop David M. Johnson of the American Orthodox Church, Diocese of California, on September 28, 1974. Two months later, on December 1, 1974, Corradi-Scarella, then almost seventy years old, resigned in favor of Joachim.

Under Joachim the small jurisdiction grew, at one point having almost 100 clergy, but lost significant strength due to the defections of many to other independent jurisdictions. In 1980 Joachim renamed his jurisdiction the Western Orthodox Church in America (formerly the National Catholic Apostolic Church in America).

The early 1980s marked the period of the rise to prominence of C. David Luther, head of the Servants of the Good Shepherd, a community headquartered in Altoona, Pennsylvania. The community had been formed with the assistance and blessing of Corradi-Scarella in 1977. Joachim participated that same year in Luther's consecration as bishop of Altoona. Luther's success in the recruitment and training of priests for the church partially accounted for his elevation to archbishop in 1981.

At the time of Luther's elevation, the Western Orthodox Church was divided into two jurisdictions. The Archdiocese of Altoona was assigned all of the territory east of the Mississippi River, plus the state of Missouri. The Archdiocese of Albuquerque assumed hegemony in the western states. In 1983 Joachim and Luther permanently divided their work into independent jurisdictions. The Archdiocese of Altoona retained the name Western Orthodox Church in America and the Archdiocese of Albuquerque assumed the former name, Catholic Apostolic Church in America.

The Catholic Apostolic Church is Eastern Orthodox in theology, but both Eastern (St. John Chrysostom) and Western (Tridentine and Novo Ordo) liturgies are used. When the Western liturgies are used, the filioque clause is deleted from the creed.

All of the clergy, including the bishops, work at secular jobs and may marry. Within the church are several orders, including the Society of Priests of Saint Justin Martyr, the Benedictine Fathers, the Order of Saint Dominic, and the Orthodox Franciscan Missioners, each with specialized ministries.

In 1983, at the request of Dom Luis Fernando Castillo-Mendez, primate of the Apostolic Catholic Church in Brazil, the Apostolic Catholic Church in America resumed its position as an exarchate of the Brazilian body.

**Headquarters:** 808 Post Street, Suite 1021, San Francisco, California 94102.

**Membership:** In 1984 the church reported approximately 5,000 members in fifteen parishes and six missions served by thirty-two clergy. Bishops are located in Savannah, Georgia; New York City; Ft. Lauderdale, Florida; and San Francisco. Bishop Forest E. Barber is ordinary for the Dominican Republic.

**Educational Facilities:** Chrysostom University, St. Louis, Missouri; Saint John Chrysostom Theological Seminary, San Francisco, California.

**Periodicals:** *Chrysostomos; Western Orthodox Voice,* 808 Post Street, Suite 1021, San Francisco, California 94109.

# Chapter 3

# The Lutheran Family

For general information about the Lutheran Family, please see
pages 89-96 of Volume 1 of the *Encyclopedia of American Religions.*

★ 20 ★

**The Latvian Evangelical Lutheran Church in America**

The takeover of several European countries by Marxist-Communist governments after World War II placed minority Lutheran churches in a precarious position. Nationals who had fled Communist rule, and refugees who had left during the war and felt unable to return, established a church-in-exile with headquarters in Germany. Latvian Lutherans in the United States organized in 1957 as the Federation of Latvian Evangelical Lutheran Churches in America. The churches reorganized in 1976 to become the Latvian Evangelical Lutheran Church in America. It is the North American affiliate of the Lutheran Church of Latvia in Exile.

The Latvian Lutheran Church follows Lutheran doctrine and affirms the three ancient creeds (Apostles, Nicean and Athanasian) as well as the unaltered Augsburg Confession,

Luther's Small and Large Catechisms and the other parts of the Book of Concord.

The synod, presided over by the church's president, meets every three years.

**Headquarters:** 3438 Rosedale Avenue, Montreal, Quebec H4B 2G6, Canada.

**Membership:** In 1983 the church reported sixty congregations served by fifty-two clergymen and 12,526 members in America and an additional twelve congregations, ten clergy and 2,600 members in Canada.

**Periodical:** *Cela Biedrs,* 425 Elm Street, Glenview, Illinois 60025.

**Sources:**

*Lutheran Churches of the World.* Minneapolis: Augsburg Publishing House, 1957.

# Chapter 4

# The Reformed-Presbyterian Family

For general information about the Reformed-Presbyterian Family, please see pages 109-19 of Volume 1 of the *Encyclopedia of American Religions.*

## Presbyterian Churches

★21★
### The Presbyterian Church (U.S.A.)

The Presbyterian Church (U.S.A.) was formed in 1983 by the union of the United Presbyterian Church in the United States of America and the Presbyterian Church in the United States, the two largest Presbyterian bodies in the United States. It continues the beliefs and practices of the two churches, which originally had split over the same issues that divided the United States at the time of the Civil War.

(As this volume goes to press, the changes brought about by the merger proceed and church structures, offices, and judicatory boundaries are still in flux. Readers are referred to the items on the two parent bodies in Volume 1 of the *Encyclopedia of American Religions* (pp. 124, 135). A more complete statement on the new church will be provided in the next edition of the *Encyclopedia.)*

**Headquarters:** 341 Ponce de Leon Avenue NE, Atlanta, Georgia 30365; 475 Riverside Drive, New York, New York 10115.

**Membership:** In 1983 the church reported 3,131,228 members, 18,969 ministers, and 11,662 congregations. Partnership efforts in Christian mission exists with churches in sixty-three nations.

**Educational Institutions:** Theological seminaries: Austin Presbyterian Theological Seminary, Austin, Texas; Columbia Theological Seminary, Decatur, Georgia; University of Dubuque Theological Seminary, Dubuque, Iowa; Johnson C. Smith Theological Seminary, Atlanta, Georgia; Louisville Presbyterian Theological Seminary, Louisville, Kentucky; McCormick Theological Seminary, Chicago, Illinois; Pittsburgh Theological Seminary, Pittsburgh, Pennsylvania; Presbyterian School of Christian Education, Richmond, Virginia; Princeton Theological Seminary, Princeton, New Jersey; San Francisco Theological Seminary, San Anselmo, California; Union Theological Seminary in Virginia, Richmond, Virginia. Educational Institutions: Agnes Scott College, Decatur, Georgia; Alma College, Alma, Michigan; Arkansas College, Batesville, Arkansas; Austin College, Sherman, Texas; Barber-Scotia College, Concord, North Carolina; Beaver College, Glenside, Pennsylvania; Belhaven College, Jackson, Mississippi; Blackburn College, Carlinville, Illinois; Bloomfield College, Bloomfield, New Jersey; Buena Vista College, Storm Lake, Iowa; Carroll College, Wau-

kesha, Wisconsin; Centre College of Kentucky, Danville, Kentucky; Coe College, Cedar Rapids, Iowa; Davidson College, Davidson, North Carolina; Davis & Elkins College, Elkins, West Virginia; University of Dubuque, Dubuque, Iowa; Eckerd College, St. Petersburg, Florida; College of Ganado, Ganado, Arizona; Grove City College, Grove City, Pennsylvania; Hampden-Sydney College, Hampden-Sydney, Virginia; Hanover College, Hanover, Indiana; Hastings College, Hastings, Nebraska; Hawaii Loa College, Kaneohe, Oahu, Hawaii; Huron College, Huron, South Dakota; College of Idaho, Caldwell, Idaho; Illinois College, Jacksonville, Illinois; Jamestown College, Jamestown, North Dakota; Johnson C. Smith University, Charlotte, North Carolina; King College, Bristol, Tennessee; Knoxville College, Knoxville, Tennessee; Lafayette College, Easton, Pennsylvania; Lake Forest College, Lake Forest, Illinois; Lees Junior College, Jackson, Kentucky; Lees-McCrae College, Banner Elk, North Carolina; Lewis & Clark College, Portland, Oregon; Lindenwood College, St. Charles, Missouri; Macalester College, St. Paul, Minnesota; Mary Baldwin College, Staunton, Virginia; Mary Holmes College, West Point, Mississippi; Maryville College, Maryville, Tennessee; Missouri Valley College, Marshall, Missouri; Monmouth College, Monmouth, Illinois; Montreat-Anderson College, Montreat, North Carolina; Muskingum College, New Concord, Ohio; Occidental College, Los Angeles, California; College of the Ozarks, Clarksville, Arkansas; Peace College, Raleigh, North Carolina; Pikeville College, Pikeville, Kentucky; Presbyterian College, Clinton, South Carolina; Queens College, Charlotte, North Carolina; Rocky Mountain College, Billings, Montana; St. Andrew's Presbyterian College, Laurinburg, North Carolina; School of the Ozarks, Pt. Lookout, Missouri; Schreiner College, Kerrville, Texas; Sheldon Jackson College, Sitka, Alaska; Southwestern at Memphis, Memphis, Tennessee; Sterling College, Sterling, Kansas; Stillman College, Tuscaloosa, Alabama; Tarkio College, Tarkio, Missouri; Trinity University, San Antonio, Texas; Tusculum College, Greeneville, Tennessee; University of Tulsa, Tulsa, Oklahoma; Warren Wilson College, Swannanoa, North Carolina; Waynesburg College, Waynesburg, Pennsylvania; Westminster College, Fulton, Missouri; Westminster College, New Wilmington, Pennsylvania; Westminster College, Salt Lake City, Utah; Whitworth College, Spokane, Washington; Wilson College, Chambersburg, Pennsylvania; College of Wooster, Wooster, Ohio.

**Periodical:** *Presbyterian Survey,* 341 Ponce de Leon Avenue NE, Atlanta, Georgia 30365.

# Chapter 5

# The Liberal Family

For general information about the Liberal Family, please see
pages 145-53 of Volume 1 of the *Encyclopedia of American Religions.*

★22★
## The Church of Eternal Life and Liberty

The Church of Eternal Life and Liberty is a libertarian church founded on June 2, 1974, by Rev.'s Patrick A. Heller, Anna Bowling, and James Hudler. It has no creed but espouses a noncoercive libertarian philosophy. Confirming its strong belief in individual freedom, the church has offered support for tax protesters, draft resistance, and alternative schooling for children in the home. The church also has a strong interest in cryogenics, the practice of freezing the body at death in hopes of its being brought back to life at a future point in time when science has conquered physical death and disease.

The church cooperates with other libertarian churches, particularly the Church of Nature, with whom it holds regular joint meetings. Since the early 1980s, the church has engaged in a constant battle with the Internal Revenue Service, who has questioned its legitimacy as a church body and has moved to deny it tax-exempt status.

**Headquarters:** Box 622, Southfield, Michigan 48037.

**Membership:** In 1984 the church reported approximately 100 members in three congregations, two in Michigan and one in California.

**Periodical:** *Live and Let Live,* Box 622, Southfield, Michigan 48037.

**Sources:**

Heller, Patrick A. *As My Spirit Beckons.* Pontiac, Mich.: The Church of Eternal Life and Liberty, 1974.
_____. *Because I Am.* Oak Park, Mich.: The Church of Eternal Life and Liberty, 1981.

★23★
## The Church of Nature

The Church of Nature was founded in 1979 in Dryden, Michigan, by Rev. Christopher L. Brockman. It is described as a libertarian humanist church which espouses a naturalistic philosophy. The church places a high value upon individual freedom and believes that "living up to one's best nature as a human being is the standard of goodness."

Freedom is essential to goodness. The church has established two sacraments: marriage and affirmation. The latter consists of providing a ceremonial context in which an individual (or group of individuals) can offer an affirmative statement of some truth or concern to members of the church.

The church is part of a growing movement within the larger Libertarian Movement to provide a religious context for libertarian thinking, and the Church of Nature cooperates closely with other libertarian churches such as the Church of Eternal Life and Liberty and the United Libertarian Fellowship.

**Headquarters:** Box 407, Dryden, Michigan 48428.

**Membership:** The Church of Nature reported approximately 100 members in a single congregation in 1984.

**Periodical:** *Exegesis,* Box 407, Dryden, Michigan 48428.

★24★
## Freedom from Religion Foundation

During the mid-1970s complaints began to arise within the membership of American Atheists, Inc.; members accused its founder, Madalyn Murray O'Hair, of undemocratic management of the organization and overt efforts to stifle dissent. Some members withdrew in protest while others were dropped from the membership. In 1978 a group of former members, under the leadership of Anne Nicol Gaynor, organized the Freedom from Religion Foundation. Gaynor was elected president, and within the year over 200 people had joined.

Like its parent organization, the foundation is atheistic in its belief and practice, but includes in its membership people who hold a broad range of freethought, i.e., nontheistic perspectives—humanism, agnosticism, secularism, and atheism. There is no statement of belief, but members generally assert that there is no evidence for the existence of a deity and attack the credibility of the Bible and the adequacy of its moral teachings. The foundation also takes a strong stance in favor of feminist concerns; Gaynor's daughter is editor of a feminist newspaper, *The Feminist Connection.*

Equally important to its goal of educating the public on matters relating to nontheistic belief, the foundation advocates a rigid separation of church and state. It has sought removal of religious objects from public property and has backed lawsuits in which it saw the state unduly supporting a religion. In 1983 it filed a suit challenging President Ronald Reagan's declaration of that year as "The Year of the Bible."

The foundation is headed by an executive council. Gaynor has remained its president and edits its periodical. Membership is open to nontheists, and chapters which meet regularly have been formed around the United States. A national meeting is held annually, usually in the fall.

**Headquarters:** Box 750, Madison, Wisconsin 53701.

**Membership:** In 1984 the foundation reported over 1,800 members throughout the United States and Canada.

**Periodicals:** *Freethought Today,* Box 750, Madison, Wisconsin 53701; *Newsletter* of the New Jersey Chapter, Box 40, Asbury, New Jersey 08802.

**Sources:**

Gaynor, Annie Laurie. *Woe to Women—the Bible Tells Me So.* Madison, Wis.: Freedom from Religion Foundation, 1981.

Green, Ruth. *Born Again Skeptic's Guide to the Bible.* Madison, Wis.: Freedom from Religion Foundation, 1979.

Stein, Gordon. *An Anthology of Atheism and Rationalism.* Buffalo, N.Y.: Prometheus Books, 1980.

## ★ 25 ★
### The Society of Evangelical Agnostics

The Society of Evangelical Agnostics was founded in 1975 by William Henry Young. Young had called himself an agnostic for several years and had harbored a hope that an agnostic organization would emerge. After developing the idea of the society, he placed ads in a number of liberal religious journals such as *The Humanist* and mass circulation periodicals such as *Nation* and the *Saturday Review.* He also began to champion the cause of Agnosticism, frequently speaking to audiences on the subject and writing letters to periodicals whenever he thought Agnosticism had been misrepresented.

The society defines Agnosticism by reference to a tradition of outstanding freethinkers who called themselves by that label, most notably Thomas Henry Huxley (who coined the term), Bertrand Russell, and Robert G. Ingersoll. Its principles consist of three statements: One should approach all questions and issues with an open mind; One should avoid advocating conclusions without adequate or satisfactory evidence; One should accept not having final answers as a fundamental reality in one's life. Agnosticism is distinguished quite strongly from atheism. The latter flatly denies the existence of God while the former affirms God is both unknown and an unknowable factor. Atheism, like Christianity, violates the second principle of Agnosticism by advocating conclusions without adequate evidence.

The society is headed by a board of directors and its administrator, William Henry Young. Young is also the librarian of the Cedar Springs Library, in Auberry, California, which has developed a special collection of freethought literature. The library is the official archive of the society and distributes numerous inexpensive items related to the society's concerns. The society has reprinted many classic statements of Agnosticism as well as original material written by its members. Membership is open to all who consider themselves Agnostics and who contribute a modest annual membership fee. Members are also encouraged to form chapters and hold meetings in their local neighborhoods.

**Headquarters:** 42421 Auberry Road, Auberry, California 93602.

**Membership:** In 1984 the society reported 860 members in the United States (plus an additional 20 foreign members) and six chapters.

**Periodical:** *SEA Journal,* 42421 Auberry Road, Auberry, California 93602.

**Sources:**

*Huxley on Agnosticism.* Auberry, Calif.: Cedar Springs Library, n.d.

Young, William Henry. "The Agnostic as Prophet." *Faith and Thought* 1, no. 2 (Summer 1983): 27-31.

## ★ 26 ★
### The United Libertarian Fellowship

The United Libertarian Fellowship was incorporated in 1975 in Los Altos, California, by William C. White, Kathleen J. White, and C. Douglas Hoiles. The fellowship is a religious order which espouses libertarian ideals of individual freedom and responsibility within a religious context, and it offers a broad framework within which libertarians can develop religiously following their own initiative and perspectives.

The fellowship has a simple statement of beliefs. God is acknowledged as the fundamental force in the universe. Human beings possess the capacity to think and act. That capacity places a duty upon people to search for truth and to act in accord with that truth. Individuals, being capable of influencing their own destiny, must also accept responsibility for their actions and the consequences which flow from them. The guidance of personal conduct begins in refraining from the initiation of the use of force or fraud on another person and the general assumption that others are free and should be allowed that freedom to develop their own religious nature.

The fellowship describes worship as "focusing the mind in search for truth." Five sacraments are observed as outward manifestations and public observances of the sacred realm in human life. Affirmation, parallel to confirmation in other churches, is a declaration of adulthood and acceptance of adult responsibility. Marriage is contracting to share lives. Consecration is the dedication of a person or property to sacred purposes. The final two sacraments attempt to integrate religious ideals into everyday life by infusing otherwise mundane activity with sacred worth. Transformation is the act of changing physical materials into a new form with more utility and/or value than the original materials possessed. Exchange is the voluntary giving and receiving of objects or labor.

The direction of the fellowship is in the hands of a board, officers, and its ministers. A three-person board of elders manages the fellowship. Membership on the board is for life, and individual members retain the right to name a successor. The board appoints the officers: a president who directs the religious work, a secretary-treasurer who keeps the records, and bishops who manage the temporal affairs. The board also appoints and ordains ministers who have sacramental functions and can, if they choose, establish churches. In keeping with libertarian principles, neither bishops nor ministers are assigned tasks; rather, they are encouraged to work in accordance with libertarian beliefs and spread its fellowship as their individual creativity dictates.

**Headquarters:** c/o Will Buckley, President, 1220 Larnel Place, Los Altos, California 94022.

**Membership:** Not reported. However, in 1982 the church reported that membership had spread throughout the United States and missions had been established in various parts of the world. Membership is estimated to be several hundred.

**Sources:**

*The United Libertarian Fellowship, A Religious Order.* Los Altos, Calif.: United Libertarian Fellowship, 1982.

# Chapter 6

# The Pietist-Methodist Family

For general information about the Pietist-Methodist Family, please see pages 159-60 of Volume 1 of the *Encyclopedia of American Religions.*

## Methodism

For general information about Methodism, please see pages 168-77 of Volume 1 of the *Encyclopedia of American Religions.*

### Non-Episcopal Methodism

For general information about Non-Episcopal Methodism, please see page 180 of Volume 1 of the *Encyclopedia of American Religions.*

### Miscellaneous Schismatic Churches

For general information about Miscellaneous Schismatic Churches, please see page 184 of Volume 1 of the *Encyclopedia of American Religions.*

★27★
### Association of Independent Methodists

The Association of Independent Methodists (AIM) was organized in 1965 in Jackson, Mississippi, by former members of the Methodist Church (now the United Methodist Church). The organization rejected the Methodist Church's episcopal polity, the doctrinal liberalism felt to exist in the ecumenical movement, and the social activism as represented in the church's support of the civil rights movement. Two churches, both in Mississippi, participated in the founding of the association.

Doctrinally, the association accepts the Articles of Religion of Methodism (see Volume 1, pp. 170-75). However, the statement on sanctification was deleted and new articles on the separation of church and state and the separation of the races were added. This latter article affirms "racial pride" as "a rational, normal, positive principle, as essentially constructive and moral." The association has only white members.

The association has experienced steady growth through its first decade. At the first annual meeting of the association, the original congregations had grown to five churches and 582 members. By 1974 they reported twenty-five churches, over 2,000 members, and twelve ministers. The association endorses the World Gospel Mission of Marion, Indiana, as the recommended mission agency for the association. The association supports one AIM family at a mission station in Honduras.

**Headquarters:** Box 4274, Jackson, Mississippi 39216.

**Membership:** In 1984 the association reported 3,000 members in twenty-seven congregations being served by twenty-six ministers.

**Educational Facilities:** Wesley Biblical Seminary, Jackson, Mississippi.

**Periodical:** *The Independent Methodist Bulletin,* Box 4274, Jackson, Mississippi 39216.

**Sources:**

Howard, Ivan C. *What Independent Methodists Believe.* Jackson, Miss.: Association of Independent Methodists, n.d.

# Chapter 7

# The Holiness Family

For general information about the Holiness Family, please see
pages 199-205 of Volume 1 of the *Encyclopedia of American Religions.*

## The Glenn Griffith Movement

For general information about the Glenn Griffith Movement, please see
page 236 of Volume 1 of the *Encyclopedia of American Religions.*

★28★
### Church of the Bible Covenant

In 1966 four Indiana-based ministers of the Church of the
Nazarene (Marvin Powers, Amos Hann, Donald Hicks, and
Granville Rogers) formed a steering committee that led to
the establishment of the Church of the Bible Covenant the
following year at the John T. Hatfield Campground near
Cleveland, Indiana. The four invited their former district
superintendent, Remiss Rehfeldt, to join them.

On August 10, 1967, the new church elected Rehfeldt and
Marvin Powers as general presiding officers. Those who
gathered for that meeting then spread across the country
under the leadership of twelve regional presiding officers
to develop local congregations.

**Headquarters:** Route 8, Box 214, 450 North Fortville Pike,
Greenfield, Indiana 46140.

**Membership:** In 1984 the church reported ninety churches
in the United States and seventy-five churches and preaching
points overseas. Total membership was 2,000 but approximately 4,000 attended church school each Sunday.

**Educational Facilities:** The church maintains three Bible-
training institutions overseas. Covenant Foundation College,
a four-year degree-granting institution, is located at Greenfield, Indiana.

**Periodical:** *The Covenanter,* New Castle, Indiana 47362.

**Sources:**

*Articles of the Church of the Bible Covenant.* Knightsville, Ind.,
1970.

# Chapter 8

# The Pentecostal Family

For general information about the Pentecostal Family, please see
pages 243-52 of Volume 1 of the *Encyclopedia of American Religions*.

## The Apostolic, Oneness, or "Jesus Only" Movement

For general information about the Apostolic, Oneness, or
"Jesus Only" Movement, please see pages 287-88 of Volume 1
of the *Encyclopedia of American Religions*.

### ★29★
### The Apostolic Church of Christ

The Apostolic Church of Christ was founded in 1969 by
Bishop Johnnie Draft and Elder Wallace Snow, both
ministers in the Church of God (Apostolic). Draft, for many
years an overseer in the church and pastor of St. Peter's
Church, the denomination's headquarters congregation, expressed no criticism of the Church of God (Apostolic);
rather, he states that the Spirit of the Lord brought him to
start his own organization. The church differs from its
parent body in its development of a centralized church polity. Authority is vested in the executive board, which owns
all the church property. Doctrine follows that of the Church
of God (Apostolic).

**Headquarters:** 2044 Stadium Drive, Winston-Salem, North
Carolina 27107.

**Membership:** In 1980 the Apostolic Church of Christ had
six churches, 300 members, fifteen ministers, and one
bishop.

**Sources:**

Richardson, James C., Jr. *With Water and Spirit*. Washington,
D.C.: Spirit Press, 1980.

### ★30★
### The Apostolic Church of Christ in God

The Apostolic Church of Christ in God was formed by five
elders of the Church of God (Apostolic): J.W. Audrey, J.C.
Richardson, Jerome Jenkins, W.R. Bryant, and J.M.
Williams. At the time of the split, the Church of God
(Apostolic) was formally led by Thomas Cox, but, due to
his health, Eli N. Neal was acting presiding bishop. The
dissenting elders were concerned with the authoritarian manner in which Neal conducted the affairs of the church as
well as with some personal problems that Neal was experi-
encing. Originally, three churches left with the elders, who

established headquarters in Winston-Salem, North Carolina.
J.W. Audrey was elected the new presiding bishop.

The new church prospered and in 1952 Elder Richardson
was elected as a second bishop. In 1956 Audrey resigned and
Richardson became the new presiding bishop. Under his
leadership the Apostolic Church enjoyed its greatest success.
He began *The Apostolic Gazette* (later the *Apostolic Journal*) which served the church for many years. He also instituted a program to assist ministers in getting an education. However, his efforts were frustrated by several schisms
that cut into the church's growth, most prominently the 1971
schism led by former bishop Audrey.

The church retained the doctrine and congregational polity
of the Church of God (Apostolic).

**Headquarters:** c/o Bethlehem Apostolic Church, 1217 East
15th Street, Winston-Salem, North Carolina 27105.

**Membership:** In 1980 the church had 2,150 members in
thirteen congregations being served by five bishops and
twenty-five ministers.

**Sources:**

Richardson, James C., Jr. *With Water and Spirit*. Washington,
D.C.: Spirit Press, 1980.

### ★31★
### Mount Hebron Apostolic Temple of Our Lord Jesus of the Apostolic Faith

The Mount Hebron Apostolic Temple of Our Lord Jesus
of the Apostolic Faith was founded in 1963 by George H.
Wiley III, pastor of the Yonkers, New York, congregation
of the Apostolic Church of Christ in God. As his work pro-
gressed, Wiley came to feel that he should be accorded the
office of bishop. He had particular accomplishments in the
area of youth work, and his wife, Sister Lucille Wiley, served
as president of the Department of Youth Work. However,
the board of the Apostolic Church denied his request to
become a bishop. He left with his supporters and became
bishop of a new Apostolic denomination.

Wiley has placed great emphasis upon youth work and upon
radio work, establishing an outreach in New York, one in
North Carolina, and another in South Carolina. The temple continues the doctrine and polity of the Apostolic Church
of Christ in God and has a cordial relationship with its
parent organization.

**Headquarters:** Mount Hebron Apostolic Temple, 27 Vineyard Avenue, Yonkers, New York 10703.

**Membership:** In 1980 the temple reported 3,000 members in nine congregations being served by fifteen ministers. There are two bishops.

**Sources:**

Richardson, James C., Jr. *With Water and Spirit.* Washington, D.C.: Spirit Press, 1980.

★ 32 ★
## Shiloh Apostolic Temple

The Shiloh Apostolic Temple was founded in 1953 by Elder Robert O. Doub, Jr., of the Apostolic Church of Christ in God. In 1948 Doub had moved to Philadelphia to organize a new congregation for the Apostolic Church of Christ in God. He not only succeeded in building a stable congregation, Shiloh Apostolic Temple, but assisted other congregations throughout the state to organize. In light of his accomplishments, Doub felt that he should be made a bishop and so petitioned the church. He believed that the state overseer was taking all the credit Doub himself deserved. Doub's petition was denied. He left with but a single congregation in 1953 and incorporated separately in 1954.

The energetic work that characterized Doub's years in the Apostolic Church of Christ in God led Shiloh Apostolic Temple to outgrow its parent body. Doub began a periodical and purchased a camp, Shiloh Promised Land Camp, in Montrose, Pennsylvania. He also took over foreign work in England and Trinidad. The doctrine, not at issue in the schism, remains that of the parent Church of God (Apostolic) from which the Apostolic Church of Christ in God had come.

**Headquarters:** Shiloh Apostolic Temple, 1516 West Master, Philadelphia, Pennsylvania 19121.

**Membership:** In 1980 the church had 4,500 members of which 500 were in the congregation in Philadelphia. The church reported twenty-three congregations of which eight were in England and two in Trinidad.

**Periodical:** *Shiloh Gospel Wave,* 1516 West Master, Philadelphia, Pennsylvania 19121.

**Sources:**

Richardson, James C., Jr. *With Water and Spirit.* Washington, D.C.: Spirit Press, 1980.

★ 33 ★
## The United Way of the Cross Churches of Christ of the Apostolic Faith

The United Way of the Cross Churches of Christ of the Apostolic Faith was founded by Bishop Joseph H. Adams of the Way of the Cross Church of Christ and Elder Harrison J. Twyman of the Bible Way Church of Our Lord Jesus Christ Worldwide. The new church was formed when the two founders, both pastors of congregations in North Carolina, discovered that God had given each a similar vis-ion to form a new church. Also, Adams, as bishop of North Carolina for the Way of the Cross Church of Christ, had developed some concerns with the administrative procedures of the church. The church had grown, in part, from the addition of pastors and their congregations who had previously left other Apostolic bodies.

**Headquarters:** Not reported.

**Membership:** In 1980 the United Way of the Cross Churches had 1,100 members in fourteen churches. There were thirty ministers and four bishops.

**Sources:**

Richardson, James C., Jr. *With Water and Spirit.* Washington, D.C.: Spirit Press, 1980.

# Miscellaneous Pentecostal Bodies

★ 34 ★
## International Evangelism Crusades

The International Evangelism Crusades was founded in 1959 by Dr. Frank E. Stranges, its president, and Rev.'s Natale Stranges, Bernice Stranges, and Warren MacKall. Dr. Stranges has become well-known as president of the National Investigations Committee on Unidentified Flying Objects and for his claims that he has contacted space people. The International Evangelism Crusades was formed as a ministerial fellowship to hold credentials for independent Pentecostal ministers. As a denomination, it is loosely organized as an association of ministers and congregations and unhampered by a dictating central headquarters.

The doctrine of the organization is similar to the Assemblies of God (see Vol. 1, p. 271). A Canon of Ethics is stressed, the breaking of which constitutes grounds for expulsion from the fellowship.

**Headquarters:** 14617 Victory Boulevard, Suite 4, Van Nuys, California 91411.

**Membership:** In 1984 the International Evangelism Crusades reported forty congregations and 125 ministers in the United States and a worldwide membership of 350,000. Associated foreign congregations can be found in fifty-seven countries.

**Educational Facilities:** The International Evangelism Crusades formed the International Theological Seminary in Van Nuys, California (see Supp., entry 18). Three seminaries serve the congregations in Asia: Heavenly People Theological Seminary, Hong Kong; International Christian Seminary of South Korea; and International Theological Seminary of Indonesia.

**Periodical:** *IEC Newsletter,* 14617 Victory Boulevard, Suite 4, Van Nuys, California 91411.

**Sources:**

Stranges, Frank E. *Flying Saucerama.* Venice, Calif., 1966.
————. *Like Father—Like Son.* Palo Alto, Calif., 1961.
————. *My Friend from Beyond Earth.* Van Nuys, Calif., 1974.
————. *The Stranger at the Pentagon.* Van Nuys, Calif., 1974.

# Chapter 9

# The European Free-Church Family

For general information about the European Free-Church Family, please see
pages 319-27 of Volume 1 of the *Encyclopedia of American Religions.*

## The Brethren

For general information about the Brethren, please see pages 341-42
of Volume 1 of the *Encyclopedia of American Religions.*

★35★
### Bible Brethren

The Bible Brethren was formed in 1948 by a small group
who withdrew from the Lower Cumberland (Cumberland
County, Pennsylvania) congregation of the Church of the
Brethren. Clair H. Alspaugh (1903-1969), a farmer and
painter who had been called to the ministry in the congregation in 1942, led the group that assumed a traditional
Brethren posture. Alspaugh protested the Church of the
Brethren's association with the Federal (now National)
Council of Church of Christ in America and the failure of
the Brethren to endorse doctrinal preaching as inspired by
the Holy Spirit.

The original group constructed a church building following simple nineteenth-century Brethren patterns (with a long
preachers' desk and straight-back pews) at Carlisle Springs,
Pennsylvania. A second congregation was formed at Campbelltown, Pennsylvania. It was strengthened by the addition
of a group under Paul Beidler which had withdrawn from
the Dunkard Brethren, but was lost when Beidler led the
entire congregation away in 1974 to form Christ's Ambassadors. A third congregation of Bible Brethren formed
in 1954 as Locust Grove Chapel, near Abbotstown, York
County, Pennsylvania.

**Headquarters:** No central headquarters.

**Membership:** In 1979 there were approximately 100 members
of the Bible Brethren in two congregations.

**Sources:**

Durnbaugh, Donald F., ed. *The Brethren Encyclopedia.* Oak
Brook, Ill.: The Brethren Encyclopedia, Inc., 1983.

Gleim, Elmer Q. *Change and Challenge: A History of the
Church of the Brethren in the Southern District of Penn-
sylvania.* Harrisburg, Pa.: Southern District Conference
History Committee, 1973.

★36★
### Christ's Ambassadors

Christ's Ambassadors traces its origin to a dispute in 1968
within the Dunkard Brethren congregation at Lititz, Pennsylvania. Leaders in the congregation protested an
unauthorized prayer meeting conducted by some of the
members under the leadership of Paul Beidler. Beidler led
the members in withdrawing and forming an independent
congregation. The small group affiliated with the Bible
Brethren congregation at Campbelltown, Pennsylvania, in
1970. However, four years later Beidler led the entire congregation to withdraw from the Bible Brethren and form
Christ's Ambassadors. The group follows traditional
Dunkard Brethren practice and beliefs, but places great emphasis upon the freedom of expression in worship.

**Headquarters:** No central headquarters.

**Membership:** In 1980 Christ's Ambassadors had approximately fifty members meeting in two congregations, one
at Cocalico and one at Myerstown, Pennsylvania.

**Sources:**

Durnbaugh, Donald F., ed. *The Brethren Encyclopedia.* Oak
Brook, Ill.: The Brethren Encyclopedia, Inc., 1983.

★37★
### Christ's Assembly

Krefeld, Germany, in the lower Rhine Valley, was one place
that dissenting Pietists found relative safety and toleration
during the eighteenth century, and several groups, including
the one which would later become the Church of the
Brethren upon its arrival in America, had members among
the Krefeld residents. In 1737 two Danes, Soren and Simon
Bolle, visited Krefeld and joined the Brethren. They soon
returned to Copenhagen and began to preach and gather
a following. While they had been baptized by the Brethren,
they had been influenced as well by other Pietist groups,
most notably the Community of True Inspiration (which
later migrated to America and formed the colonies at
Amana, Iowa). The movement under the Bolles, Christ's
Assembly, spread through Sweden, Norway, and Germany.

During the 1950s Johannes Thalitzer, pastor of Christ's Assembly in Copenhagen, learned of the continued existence of the Brethren in America through his encounter with some remnants of the recently disbanded Danish Mission of the Church of the Brethren. He initiated contact with several Brethren groups, especially the Old German Baptist Brethren, who sponsored a visit by Thalitzer to the United States in 1959. In subsequent visits he became acquainted with all of the larger Brethren factions, but felt each was deficient in belief and/or practice. In 1967 he organized a branch of Christ's Assembly at a love feast with nine Brethren (from several Brethren groups) at Eaton, Ohio.

Christ's Assembly largely follows Brethren practice, but like the Community of True Inspiration places great emphasis upon the revealed guidance of an apostolic leadership. In more recent years it has been further influenced by the Pentecostal (Charismatic) Movement which has swept through most major denominations.

As Christ's Assembly grew it included members from four states and all the major Brethren branches. A second congregation was formed in the 1970s in Berne, Indiana.

**Headquarters:** No central headquarters.

**Membership:** Christ's Assembly has two congregations and an estimated 100 members.

**Sources:**

Benedict, F.W. and William F. Rushby. "Christ's Assembly: A Unique Brethren Movement." *Brethren Life and Thought* 18 (1973): 33-42.

Durnbaugh, Donald F., ed. *The Brethren Encyclopedia.* Oak Brook, Ill.: The Brethren Encyclopedia, Inc., 1983.

★ 38 ★
**Conservative German Baptist Brethren**

The Conservative German Baptist Brethren is a small Brethren body which dates to the 1931 withdrawal of a group under the leadership of Clayton F. Weaver and Ervin J. Keeny from the Dunkard Brethren Church in Pennsylvania. In 1946 Loring I. Moss, a prominent exponent of the conservative element of the Brethren Movement and one of the organizers of the Dunkard Brethren Church, withdrew and formed the Primitive Dunkard Brethren. Noting the similar concern to keep stricter Brethren standards, Moss led his new group into the Conservative German Baptist Brethren, though he later withdrew and joined the Old Brethren.

**Headquarters:** No central headquarters.

**Membership:** In 1980 the Conservative German Baptist Brethren had two congregations, one at New Madison, Ohio, with ten members and one at Shrewsbury, Pennsylvania, with twenty-five members.

**Sources:**

Durnbaugh, Donald F., ed. *The Brethren Encyclopedia.* Oak Brook, Ill.: The Brethren Encyclopedia, Inc., 1983.

★ 39 ★
**Dunkard Brethren Church**

The Dunkard Brethren Church grew out of a conservative movement within the Church of the Brethren which protested what it saw as a worldly drift and a lowering of standards in the church. The movement formed around *The Bible Monitor,* a periodical begun in 1922 by B.E. Kesler, a former German Baptist Brethren minister who had joined the Church of the Brethren in the first decade of the twentieth century. He was one of seven people chosen to write the report on dress standards adopted by the church in 1911. However, in the ensuing decade he saw the dress standards being increasingly ignored. Men began to wear ties and women were adopting fashionable clothes and modern hair styles. Kesler also protested the acceptance of lodge and secret society membership, divorce and remarriage, and a salaried educated ministry (which was pushing aside the traditional lay eldership).

The emergence of the Bible Monitor Movement led to much tension within the Church of the Brethren. In 1923 Kesler was refused a seat at the annual conference. That same year he met with supporters at Denton, Maryland, to further organize efforts to reform the church. Subsequent meetings were held in different locations over the next few years. However, by 1926 it became evident that the church would not accept the movement's perspective, and at a meeting at Plevna, Indiana, the Dunkard Brethren Church was organized.

The Dunkard Brethren Church follows traditional Brethren beliefs and practices, and until recently has rebaptized members who join from less strict branches of the church. The Dunkard Brethren adopted and enforces the dress standards accepted by the Church of the Brethren in 1911. Modesty and simplicity (though not uniformity) of dress is required. No gold or other jewelry is worn. Women keep their hair long and simply styled. They generally wear a white cap. Men cut their hair short. Divorce and remarriage are not allowed. Life insurance is discouraged. No musical instruments are used in worship.

The church has three orders of ministry. Elders marry, bury, and administer the sacraments; ministers preach and assist the elders in their sacramental role; deacons attend to temporal matters. All are laymen elected by their local congregations. The standing committee, composed of all the elders of the church, has general oversight of the church. Together with the ministers and elders elected by the local churches as delegates, they form the general conference, the highest legislative body in the church. Its decisions are final on all matters brought before it. The church is organized into four districts which meet annually.

The Dunkard Brethren Church also supports the Torreon Navaho Mission in New Mexico.

**Headquarters:** No official headquarters. For information contact: Dale E. Jamison, Chairman, Board of Trustees, Quinter, Kansas 67752.

**Membership:** In 1980 the Dunkard Brethren reported 1,035 members in twenty-six congregations.

**Periodical:** *The Bible Monitor,* c/o Editor, 1138 East 12th Street, Beaumont, California 92223.

**Sources:**

*Dunkard Brethren Church Manual.* Dunkard Brethren Church, 1971.

*Dunkard Brethren Church Polity.* 1980.

Durnbaugh, Donald F., ed. *The Brethren Encyclopedia.* Oak Brook, Ill.: The Brethren Encyclopedia, Inc., 1983.

*Minutes of the General Conference of the Dunkard Brethren Church from 1927 to 1975.* Wauseon, Ohio: Glanz Lithographing Co., 1976.

★40★
## Independent Brethren Church

The Independent Brethren Church was formed in 1972. On February 12 of that year, the Upper Marsh Creek congregation at Gettysburg, Pennsylvania of the Church of the Brethren withdrew and became an independent body. Later that year, members from the Antietam congregation left and established the independent Blue Rock congregation near Wayneboro, Pennsylvania. These two congregations united as the Independent Brethren Church. They are conservative in their following of Brethren belief and practice. They have kept the plain dress and oppose any affiliation with the National Council of Churches.

**Headquarters:** No central headquarters.

**Membership:** In 1980 the Independent Brethren Church had approximately eighty-five members in two congregations.

**Sources:**

Durnbaugh, Donald F., ed. *The Brethren Encyclopedia,* Oak Brook, Ill.: The Brethren Encyclopedia, Inc., 1983.

★41★
## Old Brethren Church

The Old Brethren Church, generally termed simply the Old Brethren, is a name taken by two congregations which split from the Old German Baptist Brethren in 1913 (Deer Creek congregation in Carroll County, Indiana) and in 1915 (Salida congregation in Stanislaus County, California). Though widely separated geographically, the two congregations banded together and in 1915 published *The Old Brethren's Reasons,* a twenty-four page pamphlet outlining their position. The Old Brethren dissented from the Old German Baptist Brethren's refusal to make annual meeting decisions uniformly applicable and from their allowing divergences of practice and discipline among the different congregations. Also, the Old Brethren called for greater strictness in plain dress and called for houses and carriages shorn of any frills which would gratify the lust of the eye.

In particular, the Old Brethren denounced the automobile and the telephone. Use of either caused a believer to be hooked into the world and inevitably led to church members being yoked together with unbelievers. In practice, over the years, the Old Brethren have been forced to change and have

come to closely resemble the group from which they originally withdrew. Even prior to World War II, they began to make accommodation to the automobile.

Members of the Old Brethren meet annually at Pentecost, but keep legislation to a minimum. They allow the congregations to retain as much authority as possible.

Beginning with two congregations, the Old Brethren Church has experienced growth, in spite of a schism in 1930 that led to the formation of the Old Brethren German Baptist Church. A third meeting house was built in the 1970s.

**Headquarters:** No central headquarters.

**Membership:** In 1980 the Old Brethren had approximately 130 members and three congregations (Salida, California; Deer Creek, Indiana; Gettysburg, Ohio). Individual members could be found in Tennessee, Mississippi, and Brazil (where a group of Old German Baptist Brethren had settled in 1969).

**Periodical:** *The Pilgrim,* 19201 Cherokee Road, Tuolumne, California 95379.

**Sources:**

Benedict, F.W. "Old Orders and Schism." *Brethren Life and Thought* 18 (1973): 25-32.

Durnbaugh, Donald F., ed. *The Brethren Encyclopedia.* Oak Brook, Ill.: The Brethren Encyclopedia, Inc., 1983.

*The Old Brethren's Reasons.* 1915.

★42★
## Old Brethren German Baptist Church

The Old Brethren German Baptist Church originated among the most conservative members of the Old Brethren Church and the Old Order German Baptist Brethren Church. Around 1930 members of the Old Brethren Deer Creek congregation near Camden, Indiana, began to fellowship with the Old Order Brethren in the Covington, Ohio, area. However, by 1935 the traditionalist Old Brethren found themselves unable to continue their affiliations with the Ohio Brethren. They continued as an independent congregation until they made contact with a few Old Order Brethren near Bradford, Ohio, who met in the home of Solomon Lavy. In 1939 the two groups merged and adopted the name Old Brethren German Baptist Church. They were joined in 1953 by a group of Old Order Brethren from Arcanum, Ohio.

The Old Brethren is the most conservative of all Brethren groups. They use neither automobiles, tractors, electricity, or telephones. Their only accommodation to modern mechanization is that they do permit occasional use of stationary gasoline engines and will hire nonmembers for specific tasks requiring machinery. Members follow a strict personal code of nonconformity to the world. Homes and buggies are plainly furnished and simply painted. No gold or jewelry is worn. Farmers do not raise or habitually use tobacco. Members do not vote or purchase life insurance.

**Headquarters:** No central headquarters.

**Membership:** Among the smallest of Brethren groups, in 1980 the Old Brethren had forty-five members in three congregations (Camden and Goshen, Indiana, and Arcanum, Ohio).

**Sources:**

Benedict, F.W. "Old Orders and Schism." *Brethren Life and Thought* 19 (1973): 25-32.

★43★
### Old Order German Baptist Church

As the Old German Baptist Brethren continued to deal with questions of accommodating to a fast-moving society in the early twentieth century, a group of members withdrew in 1921 because of the departure of the Old German Baptist Brethren from the established order and old paths. The petitioners, as they were informally called, could be found throughout the brethren, but were concentrated in the congregations at Covington and Arcanum, Ohio.

Staunchly set against most modern conveniences, the Old Order German Baptists have over the years been forced to accommodate. Automobiles are forbidden, but tractors are now allowed for farm work. Members do not use electricity or telephones. Increasingly, younger members have been forced to leave the farm and seek employment in nonfarm occupations.

**Headquarters:** No central headquarters.

**Membership:** In 1980 the church had less than 100 members and three congregations, all in Ohio (Gettysburg, Covington, and Arcanum).

**Sources:**

Benedict, F.W. "Old Orders and Schism." *Brethren Life and Thought* 18 (1973): 25-32.

Durnbaugh, Donald F., ed. *The Brethren Encyclopedia*. Oak Brook, Ill.: The Brethren Encyclopedia, Inc., 1983.

# Chapter 10

# The Baptist Family

For general information about the Baptist Family, please see pages 357-69
of Volume 1 of the *Encyclopedia of American Religions.*

## General Baptists

For general information about the General Baptists, please see
pages 395-96 of Volume 1 of the *Encyclopedia of American Religions.*

★44★
### Colorado Reform Baptist Church

The Colorado Reform Baptist Church was formed in 1981
by a small group of Baptist congregations that agreed to
share a mutual commitment to a loose and free association
in order to further common aims, including cooperation in
mission and educational work. The church finds its basis
in the Reformist tradition of Roger Williams and Anne Hut-
chinson. Not to be confused with Reformed theology, the
Reformist tradition is Arminian and stresses the mission of
Christ to correct and address the social condition of humanity. Tenets of civil rights and religious liberty are strongly
affirmed.

The church is Trinitarian in its theology. It departs from
many Baptists by its observance of seven ordinances: baptism, the gifts of the Holy Spirit, marriage, repentance, healing, communion (the Lord's Table), and spiritual vocations
(ordination). The church has a congregational polity. A conference, representing all the congregations, meets annually. It selects a board of directors and a bishop to lead the
church and oversees the boards and agencies. A very active
social action ministry to address the problems of racism,
sexism, hunger, poverty, political prisoners, and other issues
is supported. Ecumenical activities are carried out through
the Association of Baptist Fellowships.

**Headquarters:** c/o Bishop William Conklin, Box 12514,
4344 Bryant Street, Denver, Colorado 80211.

**Membership:** In 1984 the church reported forty-three
member congregations with ninety-six ordained ministers.
Each of the approximately 2,200 members is considered a
lay minister. Missions are currently supported in Costa Rica,
Mexico, Colombia, Gran Cayman, and West Germany.

**Educational Facilities:** Colorado Reform Theological
Seminary/Reform Baptist Theological Seminary, Denver,
Colorado.

**Periodical:** *Baptist Voice; Roger Williams Review,* Box
12514, Denver, Colorado 80211.

# Chapter 11

# Independent Fundamentalist Family

For general information about the Independent Fundamentalist Family, please see pages 411-17 of Volume 1 of the *Encyclopedia of American Religions.*

## Fundamentalism

For general information about Fundamentalism, please see pages 424-27 of Volume 1 of the *Encyclopedia of American Religions.*

★45★
**Becarah Church**

The Becarah Church began as an independent congregation formed by former members of the Norhill Methodist Episcopal Church, South, of Houston. C.Y. Colgan, a layman in the Northill congregation, disagreed with the modernist tendencies of a new pastor and withdrew to found the Becarah Church, named for the congregation Colgan had attended previously in Philadelphia. Over the next several years, the congregation became associated with Dallas Theological Seminary and turned to it for assistance in locating a new pastor in 1936 when Colgan returned to Philadelphia. J. Ellwood Evans became the first of several pastors to serve the church between 1936 and 1950, at which time Robert B. Thieme (b. April 1, 1918) became pastor.

Robert Thieme had just finished college with a major in Greek literature and entered Dallas Theological Seminary when World War II broke out. He went into the Army Air Force and rose to the rank of lieutenant colonel. After the war he returned to Dallas and graduated *summa cum laude* in 1949. He entered the doctoral program but never finished. He accepted the call to Becarah Church in May 1950, took charge of the congregation, and immediately reorganized it. On the Sunday of his first worship service, he asked for and received the resignation of the entire board of deacons. Under Thieme's strong leadership Becarah Church has continued to grow as an independent congregation; but also, through its publication and dissemination of Thieme's books and tapes, the church has become the fountainhead of a national movement built around Thieme's teachings.

Thieme, a graduate of Dallas Theological Seminary, carried the school's fundamental dispensational theology to a congregation which already had accepted that theological perspective. The eighteen article statement of beliefs of the church agrees with the twenty-one articles of the doctrinal statement of the school. However, since 1969 Thieme has become the target of theological controversy due to statements in several of his books and lectures. This controversy has alienated Thieme, the Becarah Church, and Thieme's supporters around the United States from many within the Fundamentalist Movement, some of whom have denounced his teachings as heresy.

The prime point of controversy and disagreement concerns Thieme's position on the nature and effects of Christ's death. Based upon his very sophisticated study of the Greek texts, Thieme argues that Christ's physical death was for himself alone, a result of his bearing our sins on the Cross. His spiritual death, i.e., his separation from God, was substitutionary and hence efficacious for humanity's salvation. This position leads Thieme to further assert that the blood of Christ is to be understood in a symbolic manner and was not literally shed for humanity's salvation.

Besides the main point of theological controversy concerning Christ's death, Thieme's teaching material has become noteworthy for its use of a distinctive jargon not found elsewhere in fundamentalist writings. He has also taken strong positions in favor of a "just" war and the legitimate participation of the Christian in the military. He has denounced anti-Semitism as incompatible with Christian faith. Through his doctrine of "right pastor," he has developed the concept of the role of the pastoral minister. As reflected in the constitution of Becarah Church, Thieme teaches that the leadership of the local congregation is vested in the pastor "whose absolute authority is derived from Scripture (Hebrews 13: 7, 13)."

The Becarah Church has made a concerted effort to publish and distribute Thieme's many books and tracts, as well as tapes of his sermons and lectures. Thieme regularly tours the United States, speaking at Bible conferences sponsored by Becarah Church. As a result of the response to his teachings, congregations and less formal groups of people who accept Thieme's teachings have arisen across the United States. Each congregation is, like Becarah Church, an independent congregation.

Distribution of Thieme's material is carried out by Becarah Tapes and Publications, Houston, Texas, which issues several hundred thousand copies per year. Several tape franchises have been authorized, such as Bible Doctrine Tape

Supply in Tucson, Arizona. Foreign distributors can be found in England, Australia, Canada, South Africa, and New Zealand. The church supports missionaries through Operations Grace World Missions, a subsidiary.

**Headquarters:** 5139 West Alabama, Houston, Texas 77056.

**Membership:** Not reported. There are an estimated several thousand members of Becarah Church within the greater Houston area and several dozen congregations which have accepted Thieme's basic doctrinal emphases.

**Educational Facilities:** Becarah Church supports the independent Tulsa Seminary of Biblical Languages in Tulsa, Oklahoma.

**Sources:**

King, George William. "Robert Bunger Thieme, Jr.'s Theory and Practice of Preaching." Ph.D. diss., University of Illinois, Urbana, 1974.

Thieme, R.B. *Anti-Semitism.* Houston, Tex.: Becarah Tapes and Publications, 1979.

_____. *Blood of Christ.* Houston, Tex.: Becarah Tapes and Publications, 1979.

_____. *Freedom through Military Victory.* Houston, Tex.: Becarah Tapes and Publications, 1973.

_____. *The Integrity of God.* Houston, Tex.: Becarah Tapes and Publications, 1979.

Wall, Joe Layton. *Bob Thieme's Teachings on Christian Living.* Houston, Tex.: Church Multiplication, Inc., 1978.

Walter, Robert G. *The False Teachings of R.B. Thieme, Jr.* Collinwood, N.J.: The Bible for Today, 1972.

**★ 46 ★**
### The Independent Bible Church Movement

During the early twentieth century as the Fundamentalist-Modernist controversy reached its peak, many independent fundamentalist Bible churches were founded as congregations withdrew from the older denominational bodies and isolated groups formed new congregations. While many of these congregations affiliated with one of the fundamentalist associations, others have remained independent and have affiliated informally over the years with other congregations, publishing houses, missionary enterprises, and schools as deemed expedient. Among the most popular schools have been the Moody Bible Institute (Chicago, Illinois) and Dallas Theological Seminary (Dallas, Texas).

During the 1970s the number of independent Bible churches has increased and leadership from the more prominent fundamentalist colleges and seminaries has added impetus to the movement to plant independent fundamentalist congregations throughout the United States. Among those taking the lead in this new impulse, Church Multiplication, Inc., was formed in 1977 by people associated with Dallas Theological Seminary. It grew directly out of the New Church Development Committee of the Spring Branch Community Church in Houston, Texas. Its purpose has been to enhance church growth and assist in the formation of new independent Bible Churches. Operating in the Southwest, it has a primary focus in Texas, Arkansas, Louisiana, Oklahoma, and New Mexico.

Independent Bible churches are fundamentalist in theology and believe in the infallibility of the Bible and the deity of Christ (exemplified in his virgin birth, his substitutionary atonement, literal resurrection from the dead, and his pre-millennial second advent). They basically accept the dispensational approach to Scripture as outlined in the Scofield Reference Bible. Most distinctively, such churches are congregationally unaffiliated to any denomination or congregational association.

**Headquarters:** No official headquarters. For information contact Church Multiplication, Inc., Box 79203, Houston, Texas 77279.

**Membership:** Unknown. The directory published by Church Multiplication, Inc., in 1983 lists 248 congregations in the states of Texas, Oklahoma, Arkansas, Louisiana, and New Mexico.

**Educational Facilities:** Independent Bible Churches support and draw pastors from a number of colleges and seminaries such as Dallas Theological Seminary, Dallas, Texas; Moody Bible Institute, Chicago, Illinois; Wheaton College, Wheaton, Illinois; Philadelphia College of the Bible, Philadelphia, Pennsylvania; and the Bible Institute of Los Angeles.

**Periodical:** Unofficial: *CMI Newsletter,* Box 79203, Houston, Texas 77279.

**Sources:**

*Bible Church Directory.* Houston, Tex.: Church X Multiplication, Inc., [1983?].

*Biblical Principles of Church Government.* Houston, Tex.: Church X Multiplication, Inc., 1983.

Leafe, G. Harry, Ken Sarles, and Joe L. Wall. *Bible Church History and Distinctives.* Houston, Tex.: Church Multiplication, Inc., 1983.

# Alternate Bible Student Perspectives

For general information about Alternate Bible Student Perspectives, please see page 446 of Volume 1 of the *Encyclopedia of American Religions.*

## British Israelism

For general information about British Israelism, please see pages 446-49 of Volume 1 of the *Encyclopedia of American Religions.*

**★ 47 ★**
### The Church of Israel

Though born within the context of Mormonism, the Church of Israel has largely dropped the elements of Latter Day Saint belief and moved into an acceptance of the Identity message of British Israelism. The church was formed in 1972 by Daniel Gayman and approximately thirty-five members of a small congregation called the Church of Christ at Halley's Bluff (a.k.a. the Church of Christ at Zion's Retreat), located in rural Vernon County, Missouri (see Supp., entry 58). This Church of Christ was a splinter of the Church of Christ (Temple Lot) which claims to be the original Church of Christ founded by Mormon prophet Joseph Smith, Jr. During the 1960s, Daniel Gayman, the son of one of the church's founders, became a pastor and was appointed to edit the church's periodical, *Zion's Restorer.* Gayman began almost immediately to come into open conflict with the church leaders because he promoted some extreme racist views on white supremacy. He also used the church's youth camp as a seminary for white supremists and as a training ground in the use of weapons and military defense. Both anti-black and anti-Semitic articles appeared regularly in *Zion's Reporter.*

Tension within the church culminated in 1972 when Gayman called a church meeting in which two bishops were deposed and new officers elected. The name of the church's periodical was changed to *Zion's Watchman* and the priesthood totally dissolved. The bishops dismissed at this meeting, together with their supporters, filed suit. Eventually the court ruled in their favor, and Gayman's faction was forced to return most of the property (all but 20 of the 441 acres) and was denied use of the name Church of Christ. In 1974 Gayman's group reincorporated as the Church of Our Christian Heritage. It adopted its present name in 1981.

The Church of Israel has almost completely left its Mormon roots and no longer uses the Book of Mormon or other Mormon writings. It does use both the Apocrypha and the Old Testament pseudophygraphal literature, but does not ascribe to either the authority of the Bible. The teachings of Joseph Smith have been replaced with the Kingdom Identity Message and its white Anglo-Saxon supremacy perspectives, which identifies Anglo-Saxons as the literal descendents of the Israel of the Old Testament. Gayman also sees the British people as the principle bearers of the first-century Christian Church's apostolic succession which was brought to England by Joseph of Arimathea soon after Jesus's resurrection.

Gayman has also developed a variation of the two-seed-in-the-spirit theory first popularized by Daniel Parker, a nineteenth-century Baptist minister. Basing his interpretation on Genesis 3:15, Parker argued that Abel and Cain represented two seeds carried by the human race, the former of God and Adam, the latter of Satan. Every person was born of one of the two seeds and was thus predestined from the beginning to be part of God's family or Satan's dominion. Gayman developed Parker's idea along racial lines. He teaches that white Anglo-Saxons have descended from Seth (the substitute for the murdered Abel). Blacks and Jews descend from Cain, a product of Satan's impregnating Eve.

Following the court's decision and the resultant loss of land and buildings, Gayman recovered quickly. In 1977-78 a chapel was constructed at Nevada, Missouri, and both Christian Heritage Academy, an elementary school, and a ministerial training school were opened. Gayman actively promoted the church around the country as a popular speaker at Kingdom Identity gatherings. A Home Bible Study Program had enrolled 125 by 1982.

In 1981, at the time the present name was adopted, a total reorganization took place. The church was divided into twelve dioceses, each designated by one of the twelve tribes of Israel. (Note: There is no diocese for Joseph; rather, there are two tribes for Joseph's sons, Manasseh and Ephraim.

There is also no tribe for Levi. The Levites, seen as scattered throughout the nations, represent a continuing priesthood.) Each diocese is headed by a bishop. Gayman assumed the bishopric over the tribe of Manasseh, i.e. the United States. Ephraim is equated with the British Commonwealth, and the other dioceses represent the various northern and western European nations. Only the diocese of Manasseh has been activated.

**Headquarters:** Box 62-83, Schell City, Missouri 64783.

**Membership:** Not reported. The Church of Israel has two congregations, one at Schell City and one at York, Pennsylvania. It has several hundred members.

**Educational Facilities:** Kingdom Identity Bible Institute, Schell City, Missouri 64783.

**Periodical:** *The Watchman,* Box 62-83, Schell City, Missouri.

**Sources:**

Gayman, Dan. *The Holy Bible, the Book of Adam's Race.* Nevada, Mo.: The Church of Our Christian Heritage, 1978.

———. *The Two Seeds of Genesis 3:15.* Nevada, Mo., n.d.

———. *White Christian Roots.* Nevada, Mo.: The Church of Our Christian Heritage, 1978.

Jenista, Dwain A. "The Church of Christ at Halley's Bluff," 1977. The Institute for the Study of American Religion collection.

Schwartz, Alan M., et al. Special issue: "The 'Identity Churches': A Theology of Hate." *ADL Facts* 28, no. 1 (Spring 1983).

★48★
### The Covenant, the Sword, the Arm of the Lord

The Covenant, the Sword, the Arm of the Lord (C.S.A.) was founded in the mid-1970s by Jim Ellison, an Identity minister in San Antonio, Texas. He had had a vision of the coming collapse of the American society and decided to flee the city and establish a survivalist community in the Ozark Mountains. He moved to Elijah, Missouri, and then in 1976 purchased a 224-acre tract of land in Arkansas, adjacent to the Missouri border, near Pontiac, Missouri. The commune, called Zarephath-Horeb, is viewed as a purging place, the name having been adopted after its Biblical counterpart.

The C.S.A. teaches the Kingdom Identity Message, i.e., it identifies the white Anglo-Saxon race as the literal descendents of Ancient Israel and hence the heir to the covenants and promises God made to Israel. The Anglo-Saxons have been called to be the light of the world, and black people were created for perpetual servitude. The C.S.A. also believes that the Bible teaches that the two-edged sword of God's Spirit is coming soon in judgment to the earth, and God's Arm will be manifest to administer that judgment. The C.S.A. will be that Arm of God. In preparation for the difficult times ahead, the community is storing food and stockpiling weapons and ammunition.

The C.S.A., in line with Ellison's vision, expects the imminent collapse of America, the sign of judgment, and an ensuing war. In that war, Armageddon, whites will be set against Jews, blacks, homosexuals, witches, Satanists, and foreign enemies. At that point, the settlement in Arkansas will become a Christian haven.

The community is largely self-supporting. A farm produces much of the food. Education and medical services are provided internally, and most families live without electricity or plumbing.

Since its founding, the C.S.A. has been a matter of concern for law-enforcement officials. Following a revelation in 1978, the group began to acquire sophisticated weaponry adequate for modern warfare. In 1981 it opened a survival school and gave training to the public in the use of firearms and survivalism. In 1984 a warrant was issued for Ellison's arrest when he failed to appear before a grand jury investigating the murder of an Arkansas state trooper. A gun found in the possession of the accused was registered to Ellison. In spite of a splintering in the winter of 1981-82 over the continuance of paramilitary training and the leaving of those most in favor, the tension which has grown out of the C.S.A.'s potential for violence remains an unresolved concern.

**Headquarters:** Route 1, Box 128, Pontiac, Missouri 65729.

**Membership:** Less than 100 people live at the Zarephath-Horeb settlement, but several hundred nonresident supporters can be found around the South and Midwest.

**Periodical:** *C.S.A. Journal,* Route 1, Box 128, Pontiac, Missouri 65729.

**Sources:**

Schwartz, Alan M., et al. Special issue: "The 'Identity Churches': A Theology of Hate." *ADL Facts* 28, no. 1 (Spring 1983).

**★ 49 ★**
**New Christian Crusade Church**

The New Christian Crusade Church was formed in 1971 by James K. Warner. In the 1960s Warner had been a member of the American Nazi Party headed by George Lincoln Rockwell. He broke with Rockwell and later associated himself with the National States Rights Party led by J.E. Stoner and with the Knights of the Ku Klux Klan. The New Christian Crusade Church teaches the Kingdom Identity Message, i.e. British Israelism, which identifies the present day Anglo-Saxon people as the literal racial descendents of Ancient Israel. The church believes that the present-day Jews come from the Khazars, a warrior people of Turkish-Mongol origins who inhabited the Volga River valleys near the Black Sea in the tenth century. The church is both anti-Semitic and antiblack.

Associated with the church is the Christian Defense League, an open membership organization founded by Warner for individuals who support the church's racial policies. Warner also established the Sons of Liberty, a publishing and literature-distribution company. The Knights of the Ku Klux Klan use the church's post office box as their mailing address.

**Headquarters:** Box 426, Metairie, Louisiana 70004.

**Membership:** Not reported. The New Christian Crusade Church consists of a single independent congregation, but it is the literature and information dissemination center for other independent British Israel churches in North America. Through its affiliated Christian Defense league, the church is in direct contact with people who share its beliefs throughout North America.

**Periodicals:** *The CDL Report; Christian Vanguard,* Box 426, Metairie, Louisiana 70004. *The Crusader,* from the Knights of the Ku Klux Klan, also is distributed from the church's headquarters.

**Sources:**

Polk, Keen. *"Everything After Its Kind."* Metairie, La.: Sons of Liberty, n.d.
Schwartz, Alan M., et al. Special issue: "The 'Identity Churches': A Theology of Hate." *ADL Facts* 28, no. 1 (Spring 1983).

# Chapter 12

# The Adventist Family

For general information about the Adventist Family, please see
pages 453-62 of Volume 1 of the *Encyclopedia of American Religions.*

## The Church of God Movement

For general information about the Church of God Movement, please see
page 469 of Volume 1 of the *Encyclopedia of American Religions.*

★50★
**The Church of God Evangelistic Association**

The Church of God Evangelistic Association is an association of Church of God congregations formed in 1980. Many of the founders were former members of the Worldwide Church of God. Initially four congregations supported the association leadership of David J. Smith, the editor of *Newswatch Magazine.* Smith, later joined by associate editor John W. Trescott, has produced numerous booklets, a Bible correspondence course, and many cassette tapes for distribution. Evangelistic efforts have been assisted by a radio show heard on stations in Arkansas, Missouri, and Tennessee.

The Church of God Evangelistic Association follows the non-Trinitarian beliefs of other Adventist Church of God groups. The association teaches that God's church is a spiritual organization and not limited to any one earthly organization. Christian believers should be organized to effectively serve God and carry out their commission of evangelism, baptising those who repent, and of teaching, but such organizations should not impede the individual's spiritual growth or subvert personal conscience. The association is sabbatarian and observes the annual Passover feast as a time to partake of the memorial Lord's Supper.

**Headquarters:** 11824 Beaverton, Bridgeton, Missouri 63044; Box 1073, St. Ann, Missouri 63074.

**Membership:** Not reported. In 1982 the association listed thirty-three congregations supporting the association, though some of these were also members of other Church of God congregational associations. The periodical circulated 1250 copies.

**Periodical:** *Newswatch Magazine,* 11824 Beaverton, Bridgeton, Missouri 63044.

**Sources:**

Trescott, John W. *The Gospel of the Kingdom of God.* St. Ann, Mo.: Church of God Evangelistic Association, 1983.

———. *Was Jesus an Imposter?* St. Ann, Mo.: Church of God Evangelistic Association, n.d.

★51★
**Fountain of Life Fellowship**

The Fountain of Life Fellowship was organized in 1970 by James L. Porter, a former member of the Worldwide Church of God. Five years previously he had published a study of the feast days of the Old Testament and the seventh day sabbath. The study began with his discovery of what he felt to be the proper method of entering the Kingdom of God, calling directly upon the name of Jesus in prayer. Porter also began to teach the necessity of the baptism of the Holy Spirit with the accompanying sign of speaking in tongues. He places an emphasis upon the centrality of all nine gifts of the Spirit (I Corinthians 12) and the fruits of the Spirit (Galatians 5: 22-23).

The fellowship was organized as a fellowship of believers. Initially Porter began a radio program but soon dropped it in favor of printing and circulating a periodical. The fellowship is headed by a board. No membership role is kept, but supporters gather annually for the Feast of Tabernacles. Believers meet locally in fellowship groups. Teachings follow Church of God emphases. Worship is weekly on the sabbath, and the Old Testament festivals are celebrated annually. Porter travels around the United States to meet with believers.

**Headquarters:** Valley Center, Kansas 67147.

**Membership:** Not reported. Several hundred people receive regular mailings from the fellowship.

**Periodical:** *Fountain of Life Fellowship,* Valley Center, Kansas 67147.

**Sources:**

*Directory of Sabbath-Observing Groups.* Fairview, Okla.: Bible Sabbath Association, 1980.

Porter, James L. *The Sabbaths of God.* New York: Exposition Press, 1965.

Porter, Virginia. *Genesis for Children.* Valley Center, Kans.: Fountain of Life Fellowship, 1984.

# The Sacred Name Movement

For general information about the Sacred Name Movement, please see pages 476-77 of Volume 1 of the *Encyclopedia of American Religions.*

## ★ 52 ★
### Assemblies of The Called Out Ones of "Yah"

The Assemblies of The Called Out Ones of "Yah" began in 1974 when Sam Surratt, a believer who had previously been convinced that "Yah" was the correct name of the Creator and "Yeshuah" that of His son, the Messiah, felt compelled to create a unity of the truly Called Out Ones of Yah. Surratt felt that the true church would be guided by Yah through Yeshuah and the Holy Spirit, rather than by one leader, and that leaders would be chosen by casting lots. Following a Biblical pattern, the Called Out Ones are led by twelve apostles, the seven, and the seventy. The seven, which constitute the officers for the assemblies, are elected for two-year terms and, together with the seventy (directors at large), comprise the board of directors for the assemblies.

The assemblies follow the main ideas of the Sacred Name Movement and are very clear in their rejection of both the Trinitarian position and the "Oneness" or "Jesus Only" position of some Pentecostals. The assemblies are Pentecostal and teach the importance of the baptism of the Holy Spirit and the reception of the gifts of the Spirit (I Corinthians 12). Members of the assemblies refrain from military duty but will accept alternative humanitarian government service. Members tithe ten percent of their increase (net income) annually. A second tithe is given at the annual feast days (Deuteronomy 14: 22-26), and every third year there is a poor fund tithe. Baptism is by immersion. Weekly worship is on the Sabbath.

In the early 1970s Surratt began to send literature to Sacred Name and Sabbatarian believers across the United States and into foreign fields. He built a mailing list of many thousands that has produced some new members who have begun local assemblies. Branch chapters were designated wherever two or more of the Called Out Ones gathered.

**Headquarters:** 231 Cedar Street, Jackson, Tennessee 38301.

**Membership:** Not reported. According to the assemblies, The Called Out Ones of "Yah" consists of that great multitude which no one can number from all nations which Yah is calling of all Babylonish religions to serve with Yeshuah in the coming Kingdom. It numbers more than 144,000.

**Periodical:** *Called Out Ones Bible Thought Provocative Messenger,* 231 Cedar Street, Jackson, Tennessee 38301.

**Sources:**

Surratt, Sam. *"Judge" or "Be Judged," That's the Question.* Jackson, Tenn.: Assemblies of The Called Out Ones of ''Y a h,'' [1977?].
———. *The Point of No Return.* Jackson, Tenn.: Assemblies of The Called Out Ones of "Yah," [1977?].

———. *Virgin Lamps.* Jackson, Tenn.: Assemblies of The Called Out Ones of "Yah," 1977.

## ★ 53 ★
### The Assembly of Yahvah (Alabama)

Among those who accepted the spelling of the name of God as "Yahvah" (as opposed to Yahweh), the spelling espoused by Elder L.D. Snow, is the Assembly of Yahvah, a small group in Alabama. This group also believes in the Pentecostal Baptism of the Holy Spirit and the operation of the nine gifts of the Spirit (I Corinthians 12) in the life of believers today. Like most Sacred Name bodies, it believes in keeping the Saturday Sabbath and in baptism by immersion. Members are admonished to keep a holy life, with particular emphasis upon decent dress and the avoidance of the habitual use of intoxicating substances.

**Headquarters:** Box 89, Winfield, Alabama 35594.

**Membership:** Not reported. The assembly has two congregations affiliated with it, one at Winfield and one at Jackson Gap, Alabama. There are less than 200 members.

**Periodical:** *The Elijah Messenger,* Box 89, Winfield, Alabama 35594.

**Sources:**

*Directory of Sabbath-Observing Groups.* Fairview, Okla.: Bible Sabbath Association, 1980.

## ★ 54 ★
### Assembly of YHWHOSANA

The Assembly of YHWHOSANA is a small Sacred Name group in Colorado. It differs from other Sacred Name groups in its designation of YHWH (as opposed to Yah, Yahweh, or Yahvah) as the true revealed name of the Almighty and YHWHOSHUA (YHWH + HOSHUA) for the name of the Messiah (as opposed to Yahshua or Yahoshua). The Assembly of YHWHOSANA is not affiliated with any other Sacred Name body.

The Assembly is Pentecostal in that it accepts the baptism of the Holy Spirit, evidenced by speaking in new tongues and shown by a marked improvement in life as manifested by the fruits of the Spirit (Galatians 5:22-23). It is also separatist; members refrain from participation in any other religious group as all other religious groups exist in disobedience to the law of YHWH. The Roman Catholic Church is especially criticized as it is identified with the Great Whore (Revelation 17-18). The United States government is identified with the Beast of Revelation 13.

Within the assembly, sex gender roles are sharply defined. Only men may become ministers. Holidays are forbidden, though Passover is celebrated. Natural foods are eaten when possible, and, among other artificial foods, soda pop is expressly forbidden. Members are expected to show their separation by paying no income tax or social security and by not voting, using doctors, or attending Bible schools. Baptism is by immersion.

**Headquarters:** c/o David K. Johnson, 50006 Olson Road, Boone, Colorado 81025.

**Membership:** The assembly has two congregations, one in Boone and one in Pueblo, Colorado.

## ★55★
### The House of Yahweh (Abilene, Texas)

Among the people with whom Jacob Hawkins, founder of the House of Yahweh in Odessa, Texas, communicated his discovery of the true organization of the Called Out Ones of "Yah" was his brother Bill. Israyl Bill Hawkins joined his brother Jacob in building the sanctuary of the House of Yahweh in Odessa. However, in 1980, Israyl Bill Hawkins began to hold Sabbath services in his mobile home in Abilene, Texas. He had become convinced of the necessity of establishing the House of Yahweh according to Micah 4: 1-2. He taught that the formation of the House of Yahweh in Odessa by his brother was but the initial stirring by Yahweh that led to the establishment of Yahweh's true house, the House of Yahweh in Abilene. Israyl Bill Hawkins asserted that the chartering of his house in Abilene by the state of Texas and its recognition as a church by the Internal Revenue Service fulfilled Micah's prophecy. Through the IRS, the United States, a powerful nation, recognized the House of Yahweh and fulfilled the prophecy that the house would be established on the tops of the mountains (i.e., nations. Micah 4:1-2). Also, the house was established in Abilene, a place of gathering at a point due west of Jerusalem, to prepare the world for the second coming of Yahshua, just as the Biblical Abilene (Luke 3:1) had been the starting point of John the Baptist's preparation of Yahshua's first coming.

The House of Yahweh in Abilene is organized similarly to the House of Yahweh in Odessa, with which it shares a common set of beliefs.

**Headquarters:** Box 2442, Abilene, Texas 79604.

**Membership:** Not reported. The bimonthly periodical is mailed to several hundred believers around the United States.

**Periodical:** *The Prophetic Word,* Box 2442, Abilene, Texas 79604.

**Sources:**

*Yahweh's Passover and Yahshua's Memorial.* Abilene, Tex.: House of Yahweh, n.d.

## ★56★
### The House of Yahweh (Odessa, Texas)

The House of Yahweh was founded in 1973 in Nazareth, Israel, by Jacob Hawkins, an American who had gone to Israel in 1967 to work on a kibbutz in the Negev. Hawkins learned of the discovery in 1973 of an ancient sanctuary dating to the first century that had "House of Yahweh" engraved over its entrance in Hebrew. In his own study of Scripture, he had determined that the name of the people called out by Yahweh was the "House of Yahweh." Thus he was led to found Yahweh's House anew. He began to correspond with people about his discovery and his subse-

quent actions. In 1973 he returned to the United States and built a sanctuary of The House of Yahweh in Odessa, Texas.

Members of the House of Yahweh direct their worship toward Yahweh the Father, whose title is Elohim, and His son Yahshua, whose title is Messiah. Yahshua's shed blood cleanses believers from sin if they keep the Ten Commandments, Yahweh's law. Members tithe one-tenth of their income to the support of the ministry. They are Sabbatarians.

The House of Yahweh observes the Old Testament feast days as mentioned in Leviticus 23. Further, it teaches that all believers must come together for the feasts of Passover, Pentecost, and Tabernacles, and members travel from around the United States and the world for these events. In like measure, holidays such as Christmas, Easter, Halloween, and Sunday as a day of worship are condemned as pagan and un-Biblical. Yahshua was born in the spring (around Passover), not in December.

The House of Yahweh is organized on a Biblical pattern with twelve apostles and seventy elders.

**Headquarters:** c/o Jacob Hawkins, Box 4938, Odessa, Texas 79760.

**Membership:** Not reported. In 1980 the House of Yahweh reported congregations in the United States, Israel, India, South Africa, West Africa, Burma, Australia, and Belgium.

**Periodical:** *The Prophetic Watchman,* c/o Jacob Hawkins, Box 4938, Odessa, Texas 79760.

**Sources:**

*Directory of Sabbath-Observing Groups.* Fairfield, Okla.: Bible Sabbath Association, 1980.

## ★57★
### New Life Fellowship

The New Life Fellowship was formed by nine ministers, representing four Sacred Name congregations, who gathered at Van Buren, Arkansas, and drew up the doctrinal statement "A Declaration of Those Things Most Commonly Believed among Us." This group differs from other Sacred Name organizations in its adoption of a Pentecostal perspective that places strong emphasis upon the gifts of the Spirit as outlined in I Corinthians 12 and initially evidenced by speaking in tongues. They also believe in the organization of the church under the five-fold ministry as outlined in Ephesians 4:11; apostles, prophets, evangelists, pastors, and teachers lead the church fellowship as a whole. Locally, elders and deacons lead individual congregations.

At the time of the fellowship's formation, a 260-acre tract of land near Natural Dam, Arkansas, was purchased for the purpose of establishing an intentional community. The New Life Community is attached to the congregation at Van Buren.

The New Life Fellowship accepts the Sacred Name emphases and acknowledges Yahweh as the Father Creator and Yahshua as His son and humanity's Savior. Weekly worship is on the seventh-day Sabbath (Saturday), and the Old Testament feasts are kept. The annual feast of Tabernacles is a time for members of the fellowship to gather from around the United States.

**Headquarters:** Box 75, Natural Dam, Arkansas 72948.

**Membership:** The fellowship began with four congregations in Van Buren, Arkansas; Henryetta, Oklahoma; Murrysville, Pennsylvania; and Jim Falls, Wisconsin. In 1983 a congregation in Eaton Rapids, Michigan, was added. Missionary work is supported in Haiti and Europe.

**Periodicals:** *New Life; Fellowship,* Box 75, Natural Dam, Arkansas 72948.

**Sources:**

*Directory of Sabbath-Observing Groups.* Fairview, Okla.: Bible Sabbath Association, 1980.

# Chapter 13

# The Latter Day Saints Family

For general information about the Latter Day Saints Family, please see
pages 1-8 of Volume 2 of the *Encyclopedia of American Religions.*

## Missouri Mormons

★58★
### The Church of Christ at Halley's Bluff

The Church of Christ at Halley's Bluff, also known as the
Church of Christ at Zion's Retreat, was founded in 1932
by former members of the Church of Christ (Temple Lot)
(see Vol. 2, p. 12) who left in a dispute over baptism. The
original congregation was located in Denver, Colorado, but
by the end of the decade five other congregations had
joined the small denomination. In 1941 the church moved
its headquarters to Zion's Retreat, a 441-acre tract of land
in northeast Vernon County, about seventy miles south of
Independence, Missouri, the site of Zion according to Mormon prophet Joseph Smith, Jr.

In 1942 the congregation in Cranston, Rhode Island,
moved to Zion's Retreat. They were soon joined by the remaining members in Denver, and the group in Independence
came in 1946. The remaining congregation, located in
Delevan, Wisconsin, separated from the group in Missouri
in 1966 and continues to exist today as an independent
congregation.

The peace within the church in Missouri was disturbed in
the 1960s after Daniel Gayman, one of its pastors, became
editor of the church's periodical. He began to advocate
strong racist and antiblack sentiments. Then in 1972 Gayman called a meeting of the church, deposed several bishops,
and had himself elected to lead the church. The deposed
bishops, General Hall and Duane Gayman, and their supporters filed suit and the court returned the property and
the use of the church's several names to them. Meanwhile,
the Hall-Gayman group had reincorporated as the Church
of Christ at Halley's Bluff.

With the loss of its members in Wisconsin and the defection of Daniel Gayman's supporters, the Church of Christ
at Halley's Bluff remains as but a small remnant within the
family of Latter Day Saint Churches.

**Headquarters:** c/o Duane Gayman, Schell City, Missouri
64783.

**Membership:** In 1984 there remained an estimated twenty-
five members in the Church of Christ at Halley's Bluff.

**Sources:**

Jenista, Dwain A. "The Church of Christ at Halley's Bluff,"
1977. The Institute for the Study of American Religion
collection.

## Polygamy-Practicing Groups

For general information about the Polygamy-Practicing Groups, please
see pages 14-16 of Volume 2 of the *Encyclopedia of American
Religions.*

★59★
### Apostolic United Brethren

The Apostolic United Brethren was formed in 1951 when
the majority of the members and leaders of the United Effort Order (see Supp., entry 61), the largest of the polygamy-
practicing groups, rejected the actions of the president of
its ruling Council of Friends, Joseph White Musser
(1872-1954). Musser, who had become a polygamist in the
early twentieth century, had been among the original
members of the Council of Friends established in 1929 by
Lorin C. Woolley. During the several decades of the leadership of the order by John Barlow, Musser had arisen as the
major writer-apologist for polygamy. He ran the Truth
Publishing Company in Salt Lake City, from which he
published a number of books and a periodical, *The Truth.*
In 1951, when Barlow died, Musser became the new council president.

Two years prior to Barlow's death, Musser had suffered a
stroke that left him partially incapacitated. The initial
mistrust of his ability to provide adequate leadership was
heightened when he appointed his personal physician, Rulon
C. Allred, to fill a vacancy on the council. This mistrust
became open revolt when he also added a Mexican,
Margarito Bautista, to the council. Musser met the resistance
by dismissing the entire council, appointing a new council
made up entirely of his supporters, and naming Allred as
his successor. Most of the membership, including the
residents at Short Creek, Arizona, where several of the
dismissed council members lived, rejected Musser, but

several thousand followed him. He reorganized his followers as the Apostolic United Brethren. He also began a new periodical, *The Star of Truth,* which he edited until his death in 1954.

During the period of Rulon Allred's leadership, the Apostolic United Brethren grew several times over. A respected naturopathic physician in the Salt Lake City suburb of Murray and a polygamist since the 1930s, Allred moved quickly to consolidate the Apostolic United Brethren among polygamists, particularly in Mexico. He led in the establishment of a colony in Pinesdale, Montana, where a large meeting hall was dedicated in 1970. His leadership came to an abrupt end on May 10, 1977, when members of a rival polygamist group, Ervil LeBaron's Church of the Lamb of God, assassinated him. He was succeeded by his brother Owen Allred.

The Apostolic United Brethren is among the more liberal of the polygamy-practicing groups in that it allows sexual activity apart from any intent to produce children. It has also moved far beyond the polygamy issue in its criticism of the Church of Jesus Christ of Latter Day Saints. It has condemned the larger Mormon body for its changes in traditional practice and belief, specifically its changing the garment worn during temple services, allowing blacks into the priesthood, and granting leadership concessions to women.

**Headquarters:** 1194 West 16600 South, Bluffsdale, Utah 84065.

**Membership:** Not reported. Of approximately 30,000 polygamists, 5,000 to 7,000 are affiliated with the Apostolic United Brethren.

**Sources:**

Allred, Rulon C. *Treasures of Knowledge.* 2 vols. Hamilton, Mont.: Bitterroot Publishing Co., 1982.

Bradlee, Ben, Jr., and Dale Van Atta. *Prophet of Blood.* New York: G.P. Putnam's Sons, 1981.

*The Most Holy Principle.* 4 vols. Murray, Utah: Gems Publishing Co., 1970-75.

Musser, Joseph W. *Celestial or Plural Marriage.* Salt Lake City: Truth Publishing Co., 1944.

★ 60 ★
### Sons Ahman Israel

Sons Ahman Israel was founded at Saratoga Hot Springs, Utah, at dawn on January 25, 1981, by presiding Patriarch David Israel and four other former members of the Church of Jesus Christ of Latter Day Saints. The group believes in the continued visitation of and revelation by angels, and David Israel regularly receives such revelations in the form of morning and evening oracles. Besides the Bible and the *Book of Mormon,* a wide variety of materials are accepted as scripture, including ancient apocryphal writings (such as the *Gospel of Thomas,* the *Gospel of Philip,* the *Book of Enoch,* the writings found at Nag Hammadi) and modern Mormon revelations (such as the *Oracles of Mohonri* and *The Order of the Sons of Zadok*). Members believe in a secret oral tradition which passed from Moses to the Essenes,

the Gnostics, and eventually to Joseph Smith, Jr. That tradition is preserved in such books as the *Pistis Sophia,* an ancient Gnostic text, and the *Sephir Yetzira,* a prime text from Hassidic Judaism.

A 22-item statement of "S.A.I. Beliefs" affirms belief in a heavenly hierarchy consisting of a Heavenly Father and Mother, their son, Jesus Christ, the Holy Spirit, angels and archangels, and ministers of the flame (just men made perfect). Human beings are the literal offspring of the heavenly Parents and have come into earthly existence to experience the mystery of mortality. Redemption for humans comes only through surrendering their life to Yetshuah the Christ and subsequently developing a relationship to Him in the holy temple ordinances and ritualistic ceremonies. The Sons Ahman Israel also follows the Old Testament feasts and holy days.

The Sons Ahman Israel had absorbed much of its ritual practice from the Christian Kabbalah. A monthly ritual cycle begins with each new moon when baptisms are held. On the second lunar day, charisms (holy annointings) are made and on the third day a eucharistic supper is prepared. The fourth through the fifteenth days are for participation in ceremonial priesthood rituals. The full moon is a time for a monthly feast.

The Sons Ahman Israel is headed by a presiding patriarch and matriarch, under whom function (when the organization is at full strength) a first presidency (of three people), a council of twelve apostles, seven arch seventies, and twelve stake princes. Each stake is headed by twelve high counselmen, a quorum of seventy, and twelve bishops. The church practices polygamy but also believes in the perfect equality of the sexes. Women are accepted into the priesthood on an equal basis with men.

**Headquarters:** Box 186, Washington, Utah 84780.

**Membership:** Unreported. As of 1984 it is estimated to be less than 100.

**Educational Facilities:** School of the Prophets, Mt. Kolob, Utah.

**Periodical:** *Stone Magazine,* Box 186, Washington, Utah 84780.

★ 61 ★
### United Effort Order

The United Effort Order, the largest of the polygamy-practicing groups among the Latter Day Saints, began in 1929 when Lorin C. Woolley organized a Council of Friends dedicated to seeing that no year passed without at least one child being born within a plural marriage. Woolley, who claimed to have been commissioned by President Taylor in 1886, acted only after all of the others present at that time were dead. Woolley had been actively publishing and spreading the story of the authority he and others had from the late-president of the Church of Jesus Christ of Latter Day Saints since 1912 but experienced only modest success until 1929, when Joseph White Musser compiled the various accounts of the 1886 revelation and published them. He also joined J. Leslie Broadbent, John Y. Barlow, Charles Zitting, Legrand Woolley, and Louis Kelsh as a member of the Council of Friends.

Lorin Woolley died in 1934. He was succeeded by Broadbent, who died a few months later, who in turn was succeeded by Barlow, the man most known for his early leadership of the group and of its main colony in rural Arizona, Short Creek (presently known as Colorado City). Short Creek had become a haven for polygamists who had gathered there in the late 1920s to escape the problems created by both law enforcement agents and the increased discipline of the Church of Jesus Christ of Latter Day Saints. Soon after becoming president of the Council of Friends, Barlow contacted some of the more vocal advocates of polygamy at Short Creek and worked out an agreement between them and the council. Eventually he moved to Short Creek with some of his followers, and within a few years the polygamists dominated the settlement. Barlow created the United Trust, incorporated formally in 1942 as the United Effort Plan, but commonly known as the United Effort Order. Meanwhile, Musser, who remained in Salt Lake City, began publication of *The Truth,* the periodical for the group, and the most influential organ promoting polygamy by any group.

Under Barlow's leadership the colony at Short Creek flourished and the United Effort spread throughout Mormon communities in the West, particularly in Idaho, Montana, and Southern California. Many of the polygamists who had fled to Mexico in previous years also accepted Barlow's authority. Having survived a 1935 raid which attempted to destroy the Short Creek community, the only major trouble for the United Effort came in 1944 when an antipolygamy crusade swept through Salt Lake City. Musser and other leaders were arrested and spent several months in jail while the crusade lasted.

Barlow's death in 1951 led to internal crisis and schism within the United Effort. Musser, the new president of the ruling council, was in poor health, and many people rejected his appointments of his physician, Rulon Allred, and a Mexican leader, Margarito Bautista, to fill council vacancies. In response, Musser disbanded the entire council and appointed a new one made up of his supporters. That action split the group, the majority of which supported the leadership at Short Creek. The older members of the council elected a new president, Charles Zitting, while Musser reorganized his following as the Apostolic United Brethren (see Supp., entry 59).

Zitting died within months of his election and was succeeded by Leroy Johnson, a council member added by Barlow. Johnson was almost immediately plunged into a new crisis. On July 26, 1953, the governor of Arizona conducted a massive raid on Short Creek. Most of the men were arrested and the women and children placed in the state's custody. Only after several months, during which time the governor realized the political and financial disaster of his actions, were the colonists allowed to return to their homes where they have lived quietly in recent decades.

The United Effort Order is among the strictest of the several polygamy-practicing groups. It approves of sex only for the intention of producing children and demands abstinence while a female is either pregnant or breast-feeding.

**Headquarters:** c/o Leroy Johnson, Colorado City, Arizona 86021.

**Membership:** Not reported. Of the approximately 30,000 polygamists, it is estimated that 7,000 to 10,000 are affiliated with the United Effort Order. Several hundred reside at the colony at Colorado City, Arizona.

**Sources:**

Anderson, J. Max. *The Polygamy Story: Fiction and Fact.* Salt Lake City: Publishers Press, 1979.

Bradlee, Ben, Jr., and Dale Van Atta. *Prophet of Blood.* New York: G.P. Putnam's Sons, 1981.

Musser, Joseph White. *Celestial or Plural Marriage.* Salt Lake City: Truth Publishing Co., 1944.

Young, Kimball. *Isn't One Wife Enough.* New York: Henry Holt and Company, 1954.

# Chapter 14

# The Communal Family

For general information about the Communal Family, please see
pages 23-31 of Volume 2 of the *Encyclopedia of American Religions*.

## Communes Founded Before 1960

★62★
**The Synanon Church**

The Synanon Church began in 1958 as Synanon Foundation, Inc., a therapeutic group for alcoholics and drug addicts. Charles E. Dederich, a former member of Alcoholics
Anonymous, began the organization informally in his apart-
ment in Ocean Park, California. As the group grew and
began to experience some benefits, it rented a clubhouse and
incorporated. The following year it moved to Santa Monica,
and over the next few years gained a reputation for
reeducating drug addicts. From its base in Santa Monica,
during the 1960s Synanon communities formed along the
West Coast, particularly San Francisco, Marin County, and
Oakland, and outposts opened in the East, Midwest, and
Puerto Rico. Residents totaled 1400 by the end of the
decade. In 1968 Dederich moved to Marin County, where
within a few years three rural Synanon communities
developed near the town of Marshall.

The religious nature of Synanon, coming as it did out of
another religious organization, Alcoholics Anonymous, had
been tacitly recognized from almost the beginning of its existence. However, Dederich also recognized that many of
the people Synanon was attempting to assist had rejected
organized religion; therefore, Synanon was not formally called a religion. Those outside Synanon tended to view it as
another therapeutic community. As community life developed, the religious nature of Synanon life could not be
denied. Discussions of Synanon's role as a religion in the
1960s led to a change of Articles of Incorporation in
January, 1975, which designated the Synanon Foundation
as the organization through which the Synanon religion and
church is manifest. On November 17, 1980, the present
name, The Synanon Church, was formally adopted.

Synanon derives its theological perspective from Eastern
thought (Buddhism and Taoism) and from those Western
mystics who had absorbed a prominent Asian religious com-
ponent in their teachings (most notably, Ralph Waldo Emerson and Aldous Huxley).

As a community, Synanon seeks to manifest the basic principle of oneness, and members seek to manifest that integration (or oneness) in themselves and in their relations with
each other. The Synanon Game, described as the group's
central sacrament, is the principle tool utilized in adherents'
search for unity. Similar to encounter groups, the Synanon
Game is "played" by a small group of people who meet
together as equals in a circle to share in an intense and emo-
tionally expressive context. When successful, the game leads
to mutual confession, repentence, and absolution while providing overall pastoral care.

Synanon residents follow the golden rule, and helping others
is basic in the practical philosophy that all residents attempt
to follow. Residents also believe that the most effective way
to redeem humanity from alienation and achieve unity and
integration is to form religious communities based upon the
beliefs of the Synanon religion and church.

The Synanon Church is organized hierarchically. It is headed
by a six-member executive committee of the board of directors. The board is composed of the ministers of the church.
The ministers oversee the communities, schools, and offices
of the church, besides performing their normal ministerial
functions.

Since its earliest days, Synanon has been a matter of controversy. In December, 1961, Dederich went to jail for the
first time, on a zoning code violation. Synanon has also been
attacked in articles by individuals who disagreed with its
practices and techniques. One such attack, considered particularly defamatory, led to a libel suit against the *San Francisco Examiner*. Synanon received not only a large cash settlement, but an additional $2,000,000 in damages from the
Hearst Corporation, the *Examiner's* publisher, for, among
other things, the burglarizing of the Synanon offices.

Possibly the most controversial event affecting Synanon oc-
cured in 1978 when an attorney representing a person suing
The Synanon Church was bitten by a rattlesnake. In the year
following this incident, Dederich, who along with two
church members had been charged in the case, suffered three
strokes. As the trial date approached, with Dederich's health
failing and unable to pursue the defense of the case, those
charged settled the case by pleading no contest.

During the last several years, over forty people associated with The Synanon Church have been indicted on various charges by grand juries. None of these well-publicized indictments went to trial, as charges were dropped in each case for lack of evidence. (It is the position of The Synanon Church that, had Dederich's health permitted a trial, he and the others charged in the rattlesnake incident would also have been found innocent). As of 1984, The Synanon Church continues a process of adjudication of charges leveled by various government agencies, especially the Internal Revenue Service which has questioned its tax exempt status.

**Headquarters:** 46216 Dry Creek Road, P.O. Box 112, Badger, California 93603.

**Membership:** In 1984 The Synanon Church had three communities, two located at Badger, California, and one at Houston, Texas. Approximately 550 adherents reside in the communities. Other nonresident adherents can be found across the United States and in several countries.

**Educational Facilities:** Synanon College; Charles E. Dederich School of Law, 46216 Dry Creek Road, P.O. Box 112, Badger, California 93603.

**Sources:**

Dederich, Charles E. *The Tao Trip Sermon*. Marshall, Calif.: The Synanon Publishing House, 1978.

Endore, Guy. *Synanon*. Garden City, N.J.: Doubleday, 1968.

Garfield, Howard M. *The Synanon Religion*. Marshall, Calif.: Synanon Foundation, 1978.

Gerstel, David U. *Paradise Incorporated: Synanon*. Novato, Calif.: Presidio Press, 1982.

Michell, Dave, Cathy Mitchell, and Richard Ofshe. *The Light on Synanon*. New York: Seaview Books, 1980.

Olin, William. *Escape from Utopia*. Santa Cruz: Unity Press, 1980.

Yblonsky, Lewis. *The Tunnel Back: Synanon*. New York: Macmillan, 1965.

# Chapter 15

# The Metaphysical Family

For general information about the Metaphysical Family, please see pages 51-59 of Volume 2 of the *Encyclopedia of American Religions.*

# New Thought Groups

## ★63★
## Church of Hakeem

The Church of Hakeem was founded by Clifton Jones, better known to his followers as Hakeem Abdul Rasheed, in Oakland, California, in January 1978. Jones, a Detroit-born black man, attended Purdue University as a psychology major. In the mid-1970s he ran a weight-reduction clinic, which was closed in 1976 when the state Board of Medical Quality Assurance reported that he was using "psychology" rather than diet and exercise to treat clients. He was practicing psychology without a license.

Hakeem turned from weight-reduction to religion and assumed his new name. Like his colleague, Rev. Frederick Eikerenkoetter II (Rev. Ike), founder of the United Church and Science of Living Institute (see Vol. 2, p. 67), Hakeem built upon New Thought perspectives that health, wealth, and happiness came from positive mental attitudes put into positive action. He emphasized positive action as a means to wealth. In contrast to Rev. Ike, however, Hakeem implemented his teachings through a variation of what is known as the Ponsie game, a standard confidence scheme. Members paid into the church with the promise of a 400 percent return within three years. Members would in turn recruit further investors. The early investors receive their promised return. People who joined last receive nothing, not even their original investment. Such schemes are illegal.

In May 1979 Hakeem was indicted and later convicted on six counts of fraud. A group of members signed a class action suit against the church, and the Internal Revenue Service moved against the church for taxes. The cumulative effect of these actions had paralyzed the Church of Hakeem, and its future is doubtful.

**Headquarters:** Oakland, California.

**Membership:** In 1979 congregations of the church had been established in San Diego, Los Angeles, San Francisco, and Sacramento. There were an estimated 5,000 to 10,000 members.

## ★64★
## The Course in Miracles; The Foundation for Inner Peace; Miracle Experiences, Inc.

The Foundation for Inner Peace was founded in 1976 to publish and distribute *A Course in Miracles,* a three-volume textbook in New Thought metaphysics. The material in the *Course* had been received by Dr. Helen Schucman (d. February 9, 1981), a psychologist at the Neurological Institute of Columbia University in New York City. Born a Jew, Dr. Schucman had become an atheist, but in 1965 began to receive the material for the *Course* as dictated by an inner voice. The voice claimed to be Jesus Christ. The dictations occurred over a seven-year period.

In 1975 Dr. Schucman met Judith Skutch, a well-known leader in New York City's psychic community and head of the Foundation for Parasensory Information. During the next year, Skutch read the material and was so impressed that she established the Foundation for Inner Peace. During that year she also met Saul Steinberg, owner of Coleman Graphics, a printshop on Long Island, who offered to print the book. It was published in 1976 without any mention of Dr. Schucman. Though given little fanfare and informally promoted, largely by word of mouth, it quickly found an audience. By 1977 groups studying *A Course in Miracles* sprang up from New York to California. In addition to Coleman Graphics, Steinberg founded a publishing company, Miracle Life, Inc. (now Miracle Experiences, Inc.), and began a newsletter, *Miracle News,* which promotes the *Course* through conferences and workshops and has fostered the emergence of a network of study groups.

The movement which grew around the *Course* soon attracted leaders from among people already accepting of New Thought metaphysics, including some medical and psychological professionals previously aligned with the human potential movement. Several of these professionals, most notably Dr. Gerald G. Jampolsky, founder of The Center for Attitudinal Healing in Tiburon, California, have become national promoters and spokespersons for the *Course.*

As the movement grew, Saul Steinberg emerged as the national conference coordinator and national group coordinator for the *Course.* Regional coordinators and moderators of study groups guide the movement in local communities. Miracle Experiences, Inc., of which Steinberg is the president, coordinates and promotes the national and regional conferences, publishes a newsletter, and distributes the growing body of materials which has appeared in response to the *Course.*

The *Course,* summarized in fifty brief statements in the first chapter of the three-volume work, is a complete presentation of New Thought metaphysics using as a basic metaphor the image of a miracle. A miracle is redefined from its common definition of God's particular and extraordinary action above and beyond the laws of nature; it is a correction introduced into false thinking by an individual. Miracles are examples of correct thinking which atune the individual's perceptions to Truth.

**Headquarters:** Miracle Experiences, Inc., Box 158, Islip Terrace, New York 11752; Foundation for Inner Peace, Box 635, Tiburon, California 94920.

**Membership:** Not reported. By the early 1980s over 200 Miracle Groups were reported in the listing circulated by Miracle Experiences, Inc. Over 100,000 copies of *A Course in Miracles* had been sold.

**Periodicals:** *Miracle News,* Miracle Experiences Inc., Box 158, Islip Terrace, New York 11752; *Miracles,* San Francisco Miracles Foundation, 1040 Masonic Avenue, Apt. #2, San Francisco, California 94117.

**Sources:**

*A Course in Miracles, Manual for Teachers.* New York: Foundation for Inner Peace, 1975.

*A Course in Miracles, Text.* New York: Foundation for Inner Peace, 1975.

*A Course in Miracles, Workbook for Students.* New York: Foundation for Inner Peace, 1975.

Koffend, John. "The Gospel According to Helen." *Psychology Today* 14 (September 1980): 74-78.

Skutch, Robert. "A Course in Miracles, the Untold Story." *New Realities,* Vol. 4, nos. 1 and 2, July-August and September-October, 1984, pp. 17-27; 8-15, 78.

# Chapter 16

# The Psychic and New Age Family (Part One)

For general information about the Psychic and New Age Family (Part One), please see
pages 83-87 of Volume 2 of the *Encyclopedia of American Religions.*

## Teaching Spiritualism

For general information about Teaching Spiritualism, please see
pages 114-15 of Volume 2 of the *Encyclopedia of American Religions.*

★65★
**The Homebringing Mission of Jesus Christ**

The Homebringing Mission of Jesus Christ emerged from the activity of Gabriele Wittek, a German prophetess, who has since 1975 been the instrument for two spirit entities identified as Jesus Christ and as the Cherub of Divine Wisdom, Brother Emmanuel. Wittek was born in the 1930s near Augsburg, West Germany, and raised a Roman Catholic. After World War II, she married and moved to Wurzburg. By this time she had rejected the religion of her childhood. The first anniversary of her mother's death, November 11, 1970, became a crucial turning point in her life. She saw her mother's spirit and was convinced of life after death. She began to attend meetings with a medium through whom the spirit of Christ spoke. The spirit of Christ told her of a great mission to which she had been called.

During the Christmas holidays of 1974, Wittek was contacted by an inner spiritual teacher, Brother Emmanuel, and in January, 1975, by Jesus Christ. Several months later, for the first time, Christ spoke through her in the presence of a group of people. Wittek soon began to speak before a small group in Nuremberg and before the year was out held the first public gathering. The first Christ-cell, as groups that receive and study the teachings are called, was formed in Munich. During these first months of the mission, a process of growth was established. Advertisements were placed in newspapers and magazines, and literature explaining the mission and containing the messages received through Wittek was circulated free of charge.

The work of the mission is to bring the messages revealed by Jesus Christ and His servants through the prophetess, Wittek, to the world. The connection with God that allows the revelation is the "Inner Word," God's language of light that a few purified souls are able to perceive in their mother tongue. The mission, in publishing the material, provides a course of instruction for all who wish to practice contemplation within their inner self, to the end that they may be brought home by Jesus Christ after the temporal body has passed away.

The mission is founded upon four pillars. First, the revelations through Wittek and others provide, in concentrated form, the deeper spiritual knowledge (largely lost in the West) that has been the possession of a few initiated persons. The revelations describe a spiritual path that leads the pilgrim on a path of unfoldment. Second, the mission meetings represent the Inner Spirit-of-Christ Church, not founded upon statutes, dogmas, creeds, rituals, or priests. At these gatherings, all people may be instructed directly by Christ through the Inner Word. Third, the seeker may receive instruction in meditation from the Prayer-, Healing-, Meditation Center. Fourth, upon completing the courses from the Meditation Center, the student may begin the sevenfold path of soul evolution under the direct guidance of Jesus Christ. The mission's primary goal is to make available once again the completely Christian-mystical path to the Godhead to all who sincerely strive for God.

The Homebringing Mission has been quick to translate the revelations into English, and by the early 1980s advertisements began to appear in American periodicals informing the public of its existence. Most materials are distributed free of charge, though donations are accepted for larger booklets and cassette tapes. The mission has had a significant response and experienced a steady growth.

**Headquarters:** c/o Charlotte E. Surprenant, Box 13, Pelham, New Hampshire 03076.

**Membership:** By 1984 communities of the Inner Spirit of Christ Church had been formed in New York, New Haven, Boston, and Denver. An unreported number receive the material in all parts of North America.

**Sources:**

*The Divine Mystical Method of Instruction in the Homebringing Mission of Jesus Christ.* Pelham, N.H.: Homebringing Mission of Jesus Christ, 1982.

*A Former Spiritually Unknowing Person on the Path to God, the Course of Life of the Prophetess in the Homebringing Mission of Jesus Christ.* Pelham, N.H.: Homebringing Mission of Jesus Christ, 1980.

Wittek, Gabriele. *In Harmony with the Absolute Spirit, the Source of All Life.* 1983.

# Theosophy

For general information about Theosophy, please see pages 135-42 of Volume 2 of the *Encyclopedia of American Religions*.

★ 66 ★
**The Temple of the People**

The Temple of the People was founded in 1898 by William H. Dower, a physician, and Mrs. Francis A. LaDue, both members of the Theosophical Society in Syracuse, New York. Known at first simply as The Temple, it arose during the years of tension within the society occasioned by the withdrawal of the American Section from affiliation with the European and Indian branches; the death of William Q. Judge, the American leader; and the rise of Katherine Tingley, Judge's successor. During this period, Dower and LaDue began to receive occult communications from Hilarion, one of the masters who had approached Madame Blavatsky, the founder of the Theosophical Society. The two began to release a monthly periodical, *The Temple Artisan,* which contained the communications. They later compiled them into a book.

In 1903 the small group which had gathered around Dower and LaDue moved to Oceans, California, in San Luis Obispo County, where they created a settlement on a one hundred-acre plot they had purchased. In 1905 they formed the Temple Home Association, a short-lived communal experiment, to which some members with Socialist persuasions ascribed. In 1908 the temple incorporated as the Temple of the People. They began work on a temple building which was completed in the 1920s and became the focus of community life.

The temple found support among Theosophists, and within its first decade had established over twenty supportive groups, called "squares," across the country. After the founders died, the temple declined, but continues today under the leadership of Harold E. Frogostein, the guardian-in-chief. It continues to publish and circulate the communications and the writings of its founders and has a following around the United States.

**Headquarters:** Temple of the People, Halcyon, California 93420.

**Membership:** Not reported.

**Sources:**

Dower, William H. *Occultism for Beginners*. Halcyon, Calif.: Halcyon Book Concern, 1917.
Kagan, Paul. *New World Utopias*. Baltimore, Md.: Penguin Books, 1975.
*Teachings of the Temple*. Halcyon, Calif.: Temple of the People, 1948.
*The Theosophical Movement, 1875-1950*. Los Angeles: Cunningham Press, 1951.

# The Alice Bailey Movement

For general information about the Alice Bailey Movement, please see pages 144-47 of Volume 2 of the *Encyclopedia of American Religions*.

★ 67 ★
**School for Esoteric Studies**

The School for Esoteric Studies was established in 1956 by former staff members of the New York headquarters of the Arcane School (see Vol. 2, p. 147). Each had been a close co-worker of Alice Bailey. The school is located in New York City and offers training for discipleship in the New Age. Its course, given via correspondence to students throughout the world, focuses on study of the Ancient Wisdom teachings, meditation, and service as a way of life. Discipleship is seen not as devotion towards any individual or group, but as intelligent cooperation with the Spiritual Hierarchy (i.e., the masters of Wisdom, or the Christ and His Disciples) towards the working out of the Plan of Light and Love within humanity.

The teaching staff at the school has written its own lesson material, which is used by students reading the various texts by Alice Bailey. The School is led by its president, Jan van der Linden, and a teaching staff of twenty-two members.

**Headquarters:** 40 East Forty-Ninth Street, Suite 1903, New York, New York 10017.

**Membership:** In 1984 the school reported 227 students of whom 176 were in the United States. It is not organized into local groups.

**Sources:**

Gregor, Norman. *Whither Man?* New York, n.d.
*School for Esoteric Studies*. New York, n.d.

★ 68 ★
**Tara Center**

Within the Theosophical tradition, Charles W. Leadbeater and Annie Besant first promoted the expectation of a world savior whose appearance was equated with the Second Advent of Christ and the arrival of Lord Maitreya, the Buddhist bodhisattva who would assist humanity in making its next forward evolutionary step. They identified Krishnamurti Jeddu as that savior and organized the Order of the Star of the East to communicate their hope. In 1948, almost two decades after Krishnamurti had renounced his Messianic role, Alice Bailey, founder of the Arcane School (see Vol. 2, p. 147), published *The Reappearance of the Christ*, in which she argued that the time was ripe for the appearance of a new world teacher (avatar) who would come as both Son of God and head of the Spiritual Hierarchy, the group of exalted beings believed by Theosophists to form the cosmic government of the universe. She also suggested that preparatory work for the appearance would begin in 1975.

In 1975 a Scottish-born student of Bailey's teachings began to proclaim the imminent appearance of the Christ. Benjamin Creme first voiced his expectations in London and then traveled throughout Europe and to North America. He claimed to have originally come into contact with the Spiritual Hierarchy in 1959. He later received instructions to begin his mission of publicity announcing Maitreya's appearance in 1975. In 1977 he began receiving messages from Maitreya which could be relayed to the general public. The substance of the messages was brief: Humanity has arrived at a situation in which it must either change or die. Humans must begin to manifest their divinity in new ways, specifically through the more traditional values of love and justice, but especially in the sharing of the world's resources with the poor and starving.

According to Creme, the Anti-Christ has come and gone. The Anti-Christ, an energy not a person, the destructive force which destroys the old in preparation for the positive forces of the Christ, wreaked its havoc during the period of 1914-1945 and was fully embodied in Adolf Hitler and his closest associates. With Anti-Christ out of the way, Christ/Maitreya is ready to appear.

During the 1970s, according to Creme, Maitreya materialized a human body into which he incarnated. In 1977 he flew from Karachi to London and took up residence in the Indian-Pakistani community of London, where he began to speak regularly to audiences numbered in the hundreds. On April 24-25, 1982, through advertisements taken out in a number of the world's prominent newspapers, Creme announced that Maitreya's "Day of Declaration" would occur within two months. Followers expected it on or before June 21, 1982. When the Declaration failed to occur and Maitreya failed to appear, Creme blamed the apathy of the media (a sign of general human apathy). He also announced that the Day of Declaration was still imminent though no new specific date was set. In the meantime, the followers were urged to continue their main task of announcing that Christ is in the world and soon to appear.

As people accepted Creme's message, an organization began to emerge, and by 1980 Tara Centers had been established in New York and Hollywood to distribute books and tapes, facilitate Creme's tours and speaking engagements, and develop "transmission groups," small groups of followers who work in meditation to transform the energy emanating from the Spiritual Hierarchy. That transformation makes the energy accessible to the planet to carry on the work of the Christ. Groups now exist across North America and Europe.

**Headquarters:** Box 6001, North Hollywood, California 91603.

**Membership:** Not reported.

**Periodicals:** *Emergence; Share International,* Box 971, North Hollywood, California 91603.

**Sources:**

Bailey, Alice. *The Reappearance of the Christ.* New York: Lucis Publishing Company, 1948.
Creme, Benjamin. *The Reappearance of the Christ and the Masters of Wisdom.* London: Tara Press, 1980.
*Update on the Reappearance of the Christ.* North Hollywood, Calif.: Tara Center, 1983.

# Liberal Catholicism

For general information about Liberal Catholicism, please see pages 149-51 of Volume 2 of the *Encyclopedia of American Religions.*

★ 69 ★
## The New Order of Glastonbury

The New Order of Glastonbury began in 1979 when seven independent Old and Liberal Catholic priests decided to establish an ordered community. The previous year, one of their number, Frank Ellsworth Hughes, had been consecrated by Archbishop Herman A. Spruit of the Church of Antioch (see Vol. 2, p. 153). The group incorporated in 1980 and only later decided to add a missionary ministry as a means of serving the lay public. Several of the clergy have established chapels and begun to build a congregation.

The order is very eclectic but generally follows a Liberal Catholic perspective. Their statement of principles espouses a belief in One God, manifest as the Creator; the Cosmic Christ, the Son; and the Holy Spirit, the Comforter. In life and worship, the order combines emphases from Catholic (apostolic succession, seven sacraments); Protestant (freedom of belief and mode of worship); and Metaphysical (the study of comparative religion, occult and psychic reality) traditions. A variety of liturgies is approved from the more orthodox (such as the Tridentine Latin or Byzantine) to the theosophical liturgy of the American Catholic Church written by Paul Wadle.

The order is governed by a board of directors, consisting of six members of the order. Most Rev. Frank Ellsworth Hughes was elected as the first presiding bishop. The order admits both married men and women to all levels of its ministry. Fr. Merle D. Mohring, Sr. served as the first president of the board of directors, while his wife, Most Rev. Martha Theresa (Martha Jo Mohring) served as secretary-treasurer, and more recently was appointed acting presiding bishop.

**Headquarters:** Box 324, Rialto, California 92376.

**Membership:** In 1984 the order reported five congregations, served by thirteen priests, and 100 members.

**Educational Facilities:** Seminary of Our Lady, St. Mary of Glastonbury, Rialto, California.

**Periodical:** *Gateways,* Box 324, Rialto, California 92376.

**Sources:**

*The New Order of Glastonbury, History and Apostolic Succession.* Rialto, Calif.: New Order of Glastonbury, [1980?].

★ 70 ★
## The Paracletian Catholic Church

The Paracletian Catholic Church was founded in 1982 by Leonard R. Barcynski and Vivian Barcynski, two bishops in the Church of Antioch (see Vol. 2, p. 153). The Barcynskis had become well-known during the 1970s for their many books on magick and the occult written under their pseudonyms, Melita Denning and Osborne Phillips. They have been leaders for over a decade in the Aurum Solis, a ritual magick organization which they helped reconstitute in 1971 (see Supp., entry 74).

In 1978 the Barcynskis moved to the United States and soon after met Archbishop Herman Adrian Spruit, who in June 1982 consecrated them and established a Diocese of St. Paul (Minnesota) which the Barcynskis jointly administered. However, in October of that year, they broke with the Church of Antioch (see Vol. 2, p. 153) and established an independent jurisdiction.

The articles of association of the Paracletian Catholic Church indicates that the church's main purposes are "to spread the love and knowledge of Christ, to administer the sacraments of the Catholic and Apostolic tradition in their plenitude, and to perform charitable works." The church attempts to give expression through the forms of the Catholic liturgical tradition to the teachings of Western occultism as transmitted through the Aurum Solis. As defined by the Aurum Solis, the purpose of life in this world is to discover one's True Will and to do it. God is envisioned as the Divine Spark within, which motivates people to search out their true Vocation or Will.

**Headquarters:** 590 Dayton Avenue, #2, St. Paul, Minnesota 55102.

**Membership:** Not reported, but estimated to be less than 100.

**Sources:** The following books were written by the Barcynskis under their pseudonyms.

Denning, Melita, and Osborne Phillips. *Astral Projection.* St. Paul: Llewellyn Publications, 1979.

_____. *The Development of Psychic Powers.* St. Paul: Llewellyn Publications, 1981.

_____. *The Magical Philosophy.* 5 vols. St. Paul: Llewellyn Publications, 1974-81.

# Miscellaneous Theosophical Groups

★71★
## Universal Great Brotherhood

The Universal Great Brotherhood was formed by Serge Raynaud de la Ferriere (b. 1916), a Frenchman who had been involved in the esoteric from his childhood. As a young man, he traveled to Egypt, where, according to his biography, he was initiated as the "Sublime Crowned Cophto and Great Priest Khediviat." At the age of 22, in London, he received a degree of Doctor of Hermetic Science and the next year, in Amsterdam, Doctor of Universal Science. During World War II he became closely identified with the Theosophical Society in France and joined the Theosophical and Astrological Lodge in London. After the war, his occult work expanded and he became active in a Masonic body.

De la Ferriere's early esoteric work prepared him for an encounter with Master Sun W.K., described as the "Superior Power of Tibet," who gave de la Ferriere his mission to

begin the exposition of initiatic principles to the general public. De la Ferriere founded the Universal Great Brotherhood and for the next three years traveled widely, establishing the brotherhood in centers around the world. Very early in his travels, he went to Venezuela where he met Jose Manuel Estrada, who was to become his leading student.

Estrada (b. 1900) had, for nine years, announced the arrival of an avatar (an incarnation of God) and had gathered a group waiting upon the avatar. After their meeting, Estrada accepted de la Ferriere as the awaited one and became his first disciple. De la Ferriere spent eighteen months with Estrada and his group, and on March 21, 1948, reopened the Universal Great Brotherhood in a public manner.

In 1950, de la Ferriere turned over the management of the brotherhood to Estrada and retired to a quiet life of esoteric work and writing. Estrada assumed the title of director general. The work grew steadily in Latin America through the 1950s and 1960s. In 1969 Estrada sent Rev. Gagpa Anita Montero Campion to the United States. She settled in St. Louis and began to teach yoga classes. She shared the teachings of the brotherhood with her pupils and in 1970 organized the first brotherhood center. It soon spread to Ann Arbor, Michigan; Chicago; and New York City.

The brotherhood describes itself as an educational organization rather than a religion. It is an initiatic school designed to assist humanity in its transition to a new age, often spoken of as the transition from the Age of Pisces to the Age of Aquarius. The birthplace of this new age is the Americas, hence the reopening of the brotherhood in the West.

The brotherhood is dedicated to the attainment of peace by raising the consciousness of humanity both individually and collectively. The brotherhood offers a number of services to pre-initiates. It sponsors health care programs with special emphases on preventive medicine and natural cures. The organization strongly advocates vegetarianism. It also sponsors a variety of classes to promote personal growth, such as hatha yoga, martial arts, astrology, and meditation. In this regard it also promotes the Cosmic Ceremony, a Universal form of worship that allows each person to get in touch with his or her own highest concept of the divine.

Participants in brotherhood public programs, designated *followers,* may be invited to become initiates. Once initiated they become members of the Esoteric College and receive the title *Gegnian,* or Little Novice. Afterward they pass upward through several degrees: first degree, *Getuls,* or Novice; second degree, Reverend *Gag-pa,* or Affiliated; third degree, Right Reverend *Gelong,* or Adept; and the fourth degree, Respectable *Guru,* or Instructor. Currently held by only the international leaders, still higher degrees are, in principle, open to all. The fifth degree, Honorable *Sat Chellah,* or Disciple, is held by Domingo Dias Porta; and the sixth degree, Venerable *Sat Arhat,* or Missionary, is held by Estrada. Only one person can hold the seventh degree as *Sat Guru,* the Master, presently de la Ferriere. Administratively, the brotherhood is headed by the superior council, which operates under the Sat Guru and makes all the decisions concerning the activities of the brotherhood internationally. Under it are national and regional councils.

**Headquarters:** Administrative Council of U.S.A., Box 9154, St. Louis, Missouri 63117.

**Membership:** The brotherhood has opened centers in seventeen countries. In the United States, centers can be found in St. Louis (4); Chicago; Ann Arbor; Brooklyn; Oklahoma City; Shaker Heights, Ohio; Los Angeles; and Jamaica Plain, Massachusetts.

**Sources:**

*Biography, the Sublime Maestre, Sat Guru, Dr. Serge Raynaud de la Ferriere.* St. Louis: Educational Publications of the I.E.S., 1976.

Montero-Campion, Anita. *My Guru from South America: Sat Arhat Dr. Jose Manuel Estrada.* St. Louis, 1976.

★72★
### Universal White Brotherhood

The Universal White Brotherhood, named for the spiritual hierarchy of advanced esoteric adepts, was brought to France in 1937 by Omram Michael Aivanhov (b. 1900), a Bulgarian esoteric teacher. According to Aivanhov, the true brotherhood is a line of masters who periodically appear to give humanity its lofty impulses. In secret for several thousand years, it was reestablished in its outer form in the nineteenth century in Bulgaria through Peter Deunov (d. 1944). As Deunov's student, Aivanhov brought the brotherhood to France and, upon Deunov's death, succeeded him as its master.

The brotherhood is seen not as a new religious sect, but as a new form of the eternal religion of Christ, thus continu-ing the Church of St. John, the embodiment of the tradition of true Christian spirituality. By the Church of St. John, the brotherhood refers to the small number of spiritual elites, working in secret, alongside of the larger Church of St. Peter, i.e., official and public religion. The meaning of life is to discover the elder brothers (the spiritual elites) of the brotherhood and to participate in their work of helping humanity become one family. The brotherhood exists to give to the perfected beings an opportunity to act through humanity to bring about the Kingdom of God on earth.

The Universal White Brotherhood was brought to America after the appearance of the English translations of Aivanhov's work in the early 1980s. Aivanhov made his first visit to America in 1983.

**Headquarters:** International: Editions Prosveta, BP 12, Frejus 83601 France; United States: Prosveta U.S.A., Box 49614, Los Angeles, California 90049.

**Membership:** In 1983 the brotherhood had approximately 4,000 members in France, Belgium, and Switzerland; 2,000 in French Canada; and several hundred in the United States.

**Sources:**

Aivanhov, Omram Michael. *Life.* Frejus, France: Editions Prosveta, 1978.

———. *Sexual Force or the Winged Dragon.* Frejus, France: Editions Prosveta, 1982.

———. *The Universal White Brotherhood Is Not a Sect.* Frejus, France: Editions Prosveta, 1982.

Popenoe, Cris and Oliver Popenoe. *Seeds of Tomorrow.* San Francisco: Harper & Row, 1984.

# Chapter 17

# The Psychic and New Age Family (Part Two)

## Unclassified New Age Groups

★ 73 ★
### The International Community of Christ

The International Community of Christ was founded in 1957 in Peru by Gene Savoy, author and archeologist. Savoy had had a vision that a messenger of God would come into the world as a little child; he was to gather a following and wait for him. The expected child, Jamil, was born in 1959 in New Smyrna, Florida, and lived only three years. During that time, however, the child Jamil traveled to Peru where he taught Savoy and the small group there assembled. In 1972 Savoy returned to the United States and established the International Community of Christ at Reno, Nevada. He initiated publication of the material which Jamil had revealed, primarily two books: *The Decoded New Testament,* a volume which explains the secret system of spiritual regeneration originally taught by Jesus, and *Jamil: the Child Christ,* which tells the story of the brief life on earth of the child messenger.

The teachings of the community are based upon the belief that Jesus had taught a secret system of spiritual initiation and development which was handed down through oral tradition. Never being committed to writing, it was lost when all its bearers were martyred, leaving only, a very poor substitute, the New Testament. This secret oral tradition has been reestablished and supplemented by Jamil.

The community teaches that God is not anthropomorphic, but a totality that includes all dimensions, generated and ungenerated. Christ (not to be confused with the man Jesus, who like Jamil was a messenger) is not a deity, but a universal force which can link humans to the Godhead. The Gospel, the secret teachings, is a system detailing how to get along with nature and bring the energies of nature into the self. Individuals can use the Christ energy to evolve spiritually and to experience the universal consciousness of God and immortality. The details of the system, termed "Cosolargy," are given only to members of the community.

Admission to the community is through initiation and acceptance by the Jamilian University of the Ordained into the Academy and Sacred College. Originally the course of study was advertised in various periodicals such as *Fate Magazine* and *East-West Journal,* but as the community has grown, it has commenced a direct mail solicitation effort. Those who respond are invited to pursue a correspondence course that includes the secret oral teachings on tape, or, in areas where community teachers reside, to take classes with tutorial assistance.

**Headquarters:** Box 4500, Reno, Nevada 89505.

**Membership:** Not reported. Members and teachers can be found across the United States, especially in the larger urban areas.

**Educational Facilities:** Jamilian University of the Ordained, 643 Ralston Street, Reno, Nevada 89503.

**Sources:**

"The Emerging New Christianity and the Secret Church." *East-West Journal* 5, no. 12 (15 December 1975): 18-23.

# Chapter 18

# The Magick Family

For general information about the Magick Family, please see pages 249-53
of Volume 2 of the *Encyclopedia of American Religions.*

## Ritual Magick

For general information about Ritual Magick, please see pages 253-58
of Volume 2 of the *Encyclopedia of American Religions.*

★74★
### The Aurum Solis

Aurum Solis, the Order of the Sacred Word, was founded
in England in 1897 by Charles Kingold and George Stanton
as a school of Western Kabbalistic magick. Like the Golden
Dawn, the Aurum Solis teaches a system of high magick,
i.e., a disciplined approach to self-transformation. Its
system, much of which has been published in the five volume
set *The Magical Philosophy* by Melita Denning and Osborne
Phillips, centers upon the myth of the sacred king (i.e., the
magician), who chooses of his own free will the path of
sacrifice but subsequently rises again and passes into the light
of attainment.

Melita Denning and Osborne Phillips are the pennames of
Vivian and Leonard R. Barcynski, who currently serve as
grand master and administrator general of the order. Both
had encountered the order while living in England and participated in its reconstitution in 1971. They brought the order
to America in 1978 when they moved to St. Paul, Minnesota.
Under their pennames they have authored numerous books
on various occult topics.

Membership in the order is by invitation only, though in-
quiries are invited. The Barcynskis also head the Paracletian Catholic Church, a liturgical church in the Liberal
Catholic tradition, which has an open membership (see
Supp., entry 70). It is based upon the Christian expression
of Aurum Solis teachings. Members of either the order or
church are not necessarily members of the other
organizations.

**Headquarters:** c/o The Administrator General, Box
43383-OSV, St. Paul, Minnesota 55164.

**Membership:** Not reported, but estimated at no more than
a few hundred.

**Sources:**

*The Constitution of the Aurum Solis.* N.p., n.d.

Denning, Melita, and Osborne Phillips. *The Magical Philosophy.*
5 vols. St. Paul: Llewellyn Publications, 1974-81.

_____. *The Magick of Sex.* St. Paul: Llewellyn Publications, 1982.

_____. *The Magic of the Tarot.* St. Paul: Llewellyn Publications,
1983.

_____. *Psychic Self-Defense and Well Being.* St. Paul: Llew-
ellyn Publication, 1980.

## Neo-Paganism

For general information about Neo-Paganism, please see pages 286-87
of Volume 2 of the *Encyclopedia of American Religions.*

★75★
### SM Church

The SM Church emerged in the mid-1970s in Berkeley,
California, among people who defined themselves as being
into SM (i.e., sadism and masochism) and who had, in addition, come to believe in the ancient historical practices of
Goddess worship (which had appeared in the previous
decade throughout the San Francisco Bay area). The church
began as discussions on the SM experience led to questions
of spiritual meaning associated with intense SM fantasy,
beyond simple sexual gratification. Early positive explora-
tions led to the establishment of the "Temple of the Goddess" of the SM Church.

The SM Church is opposed to the male father image which
has dominated Western religion and encourages members
to focus upon the feminine aspects of God, which it seeks
to uncover in ongoing research into periods and cultures
which emphasized Goddess worship. The church differs
from many other Neopagan groups in that it believes in a
powerful female deity, equivalent to the male monotheistic
God.

The church is feminist in orientation and from the beginning excluded male dominant-female submissive patterns
from its organization. It allows both homosexual and
heterosexual patterns of female dominance within the
church's philosophy. Undergirding its approach is a belief
in the great transition of Western culture. The church
believes that society could collapse and, in that event,
females would have to take control. The church is attempting to plan for that possibility.

Ritual life, initially adopted from other Neopagan group patterns, includes a unique emphasis upon the use of controlled pain and mortification experiences as a sacrament of penance. On occasion, such rituals are designed to allow both males and females to experience the extremes of female dominance fantasies, though the church denies that female rule in the envisioned postmodern society would be vindictively harsh. Further, the sacramental atmosphere of the rituals attempts to separate them from any identification with commercialized exploitation of SM practices.

The church has published a set of purposes which includes: the purchase and/or erection of church facilities, the continuance of the seminary which trains women for the priesthood, the development of ordered communities as models of a matriarchial society, and assistance in improving the image of the SM community (through various charity projects). The church has initiated plans to build a monastery as a full-scale model of a female-dominated society.

The church is governed by a board of directors. Associated with it is the Essemian Society, a nonreligious social-educational group whose activities derive from SM Church perspectives.

**Headquarters:** c/o Robin Stewart, Priestess, Box 1407, San Francisco, California 94101.

**Membership:** Not reported. Membership in both the SM Church and the Essemian Society is limited to a single congregation in San Francisco. There are an estimated 100 members.

**Educational Facilities:** The SM Seminary, San Francisco, California.

**Sources:**

Budd, Russell. "Interview: The SM Organizations of San Francisco." *Woman/Slave,* no. 14 (October-December 1982): 30-37.

Green, Gerald, and Caroline Green. *SM, the Last Taboo.* New York: Ballantine Books, 1974.

★ 76 ★
**The Venusian Church**

The Venusian Church was formed in 1975 by Ron Peterson, a Seattle businessman, and chartered the following year by the Universal Life Church. During the 1960s and early 1970s, Peters, a former member of the Seventh-Day Adventist Church, followed a spiritual pilgrimage which centered upon the release of sexual feelings occasioned by the strict sexual code under which he was raised. He found assistance within the human potentials movement and became an advocate of helping others who wished to confront their sexual feelings. Meanwhile, he had also become a professional pornographer.

Peterson gathered around him a group of interested people, including several sex therapists and human potentials counselors, and began to explore the potential of sex and sexual experience in releasing human creativity and opening the realm of the spiritual. A Temple of Venus, which featured both pornographic films and sexually explicit presentations that attempted to communicate the church's attitude about open sexuality to the general public, was opened in Seattle. In 1977 a retreat center, Camp Armac, was opened and became the focus of church activities. A variety of seminars, workshops, social events, and worship services were offered, all in an atmosphere in which clothes were optional and sexual experimentation was condoned and even encouraged.

The leaders of the church resisted any attempts to systematically build a belief system or pattern of worship, and the life of the group slowly emerged out of the spontaneous experiences in the various gatherings of the members. First came the worship of nature in the form of the Goddess and the acknowledgment of Her at communal feast and in the celebration of the solar equinox and solstice. Then in 1979, church members discovered the preexisting Pagan Movement. Having found in Neopaganism a larger movement which already possessed a complete religious system toward which the Venusian Church seemed to be heading, the church began to absorb both thought and practices from their new acquaintances, especially from the Church of All Worlds.

In 1979 Camp Armac closed and for several years the church conducted its programs in the homes of members. In 1981 the church purchased a large tract of land near Redmond, Washington. A former warehouse was converted into a church center, named the Longhouse, and a stonehenge was erected for outdoor rituals.

Because of its strong opinions on the centrality of sex and its varied attempts to communicate its beliefs through programs which featured nudity and even overt sexual acts, the church has been in constant tension with legal authorities. On several occasions, people working at the Temple of Aphrodite were arrested for lewd conduct. The church has also been in a long-term battle to reclaim its tax-exempt status which was revoked by the Internal Revenue Service.

The beliefs of the Venusian Church follow that of Neopaganism. It affirms the centrality of Nature and seeks to discover means to reestablish links with those original, natural patterns currently distorted by society, especially in its repression of creative sexual expression. Sex is considered divine. The church is self-consciously eclectic in belief and antidogmatic. It encourages the influx of any ideas which prove useful to the overall accomplishment of the church's goals.

The church is formally headed by a board of directors, but management of the church center and development of programs is placed in a loosely organized council of active members. Ministers are selected from among the members after demonstrating their leadership abilities and competence in dealing with people.

**Headquarters:** P.O. Box 21263, Seattle, Washington 98111.

**Membership:** In 1984 the church had approximately 150 members in the single center outside Seattle. Most members live in or close to Seattle.

**Periodical:** *Longhouse Calendar,* 23301 Redmond—Fall City Road, Redmond, Washington 98053.

# Chapter 19

# The Eastern and Middle Eastern Family
# (Jews and Muslims)

For general information about the Eastern and Middle Eastern Family (Jews and Muslims), please see pages 307-8 of Volume 2 of the *Encyclopedia of American Religions.*

## Jewish Faith

For general information about the Jewish Faith, please see pages 308-14 of Volume 2 of the *Encyclopedia of American Religions.*

### Black Jews

For general information about Black Jews, please see pages 330-31 of Volume 2 of the *Encyclopedia of American Religions.*

★77★
### Rastafarians

The Rastafarian Movement, a Jamaican black nationalist movement, grew out of a long history of fascination with Africa in general and Ethiopia in particular among the masses in Jamaica. The movement can be traced directly to the efforts of Marcus Garvey, founder of the Universal Negro Improvement Association, who, among other endeavors, promoted a steamship company that would provide transportation for blacks going back to Africa. In 1927 Garvey predicted the crowning of a black king in Africa, as a sign that the redemption of black people from white oppression was near. The 1930 coronation of Haile Selassie as emperor of Ethiopia was seen as a fulfillment of Garvey's words.

Haile Selassie was born Ras Tafari Makonnen out of a lineage claimed to derive from the Queen of Sheba and King Solomon. He proclaimed his title as King of Kings, Lord of Lords, His Imperial Majesty the Conquering Lion of the Tribe of Judah. Elect of God. His name Haile Selassie means "Power of the Holy Trinity." Reading about the coronation, four ministers in Jamaica—Joseph Hibbert, Archibald Dunkley, Robert Hinds, and, most prominently, Leonard Howell—saw the new emperor as not only the fulfillment of the Garveyite expectation, but also the completion of Biblical prophecies such as those in Revelation 5:2-5 and 19:16 which refer to the Lion of the Tribe of Judah and the King of Kings. The four, independently of each other, began to proclaim Haile Selassie the Messiah of the black people. Their first successes came in the slums of West Kingston, where they discovered each other and a movement began.

Howell began to proselytize around the island. He raised money by selling pictures of Haile Selassie and telling the buyers that they were passports back to Africa. He was arrested and sentenced to two years in jail for fraud. Upon his release he moved into the hill country of St. Catherine's parish and founded a commune, the Pinnacle, which, in spite of government attacks and several moves, became the center of the movement for the next two decades. At the Pinnacle, the smoking of ganga (marijuana) and the wearing of long hair curled to resemble a lion's mane (dread locks) became the marks of identification of the group.

As the Rastafarians matured, they adopted the perspectives of Black Judaism and identified the Hebrews of the Old Testament as black people. Their belief system was distinctly racial and they taught that the whites were inferior to the blacks. More extreme leaders saw whites as the enemies of blacks. In the near future, blacks will return to Africa and assume their rightful place in world leadership. Haile Selassie is believed to be the embodiment of God, and, though no longer visible, nevertheless still lives. Some Rastafarians believe Selassie is still secretly alive, though most see him as a disembodied spirit.

Relations with white culture have been intense, lived at the point of "dread," a term to describe the confrontation of a people struggling to regain a denied racial selfhood. Most Rastafarians are pacifists, though much support for the movement developed out of intense antiwhite feelings. Violence has been a part of the movement since the destruction of the Pinnacle, though it has been confined to individuals and loosely organized groups. One group, the Nyabingi Rastas, stand apart from most by their espousal of violence.

Rastafarians came to the United States in large numbers as part of the general migration of Jamaicans in the 1960s and 1970s. They have brought with them an image of violence, and frequent news reports have detailed murders committed by individuals identified as Rastafarians. Rastafarian spokespersons have openly complained that many young Jamaican-Americans have adopted the outward appearance of Rastafarians (dread locks and ganga-smoking) without adopting Rastafarian beliefs and lifestyle.

A major aspect of Rastafarian life is the unique music developed as its expression. Reggae, a form of rock music, became popular far beyond Rastafarian circles, and exponents such as Bob Marley and Peter Tosh became international stars. Reggae has assisted immensely in the legitimization of Rastafarian life and ideals.

In Jamaica the Rastafarian Movement is divided into a number of organizations and factions, many of which have been brought into the Jamaican community in America. Surveys of American Rastafarians have yet to define the organization in the United States though individual Rastafarians may be found in black communities across America, most noticably Brooklyn, New York, Miami, and Chicago.

**Headquarters:** Unknown.

**Membership:** There are an estimated 3,000-5,000 Rastafarians in the United States, though the figures are somewhat distorted by the large number of people who have adopted the outward appearance of Rastafarian life.

**Periodicals:** *Arise,* Creative Publishers, Ltd., 8 Waterloo Avenue, Kingston, Jamaica, West Indies; *Jahugliman,* c/o Carl Gayle, 19C Annette Crescent, Kingston 10, Jamaica, West Indies.

**Sources:**

Barrett, Leonard. *The Rastafarians.* Boston: Beacon Press, 1977.
Owens, Joseph. *Dread.* Kingston, Jamaica: Sangster, 1976.
Williams, K.M. *The Rastafarians.* London: Ward Lock Educational, 1981.

# Islam and Related Groups

For general information about Islam and Related Groups, please see pages 335-37 of Volume 2 of the *Encyclopedia of American Religions.*

## Black Muslims

For general information about the Black Muslims, please see page 339 of Volume 2 of the *Encyclopedia of American Religions.*

### ★ 78 ★
### The Nation of Islam (The Caliph)

As significant changes within the Nation of Islam (see Vol. 2, p. 341) founded by Elijah Muhammad proceeded under his son and successor Wallace Deem Muhammad, the Nation of Islam became a more orthodox Islamic organization. It was renamed the American Muslim Mission and dropped many of the distinctive features of its predecessor. Opposition among those committed to Elijah Muhammad's ideas and programs led to several schisms in the late 1970s. Among the "purist" leaders, Emmanuel Abdullah Muhammad asserted his role as the Caliph of Islam raised up to guide the people in the absence of Allah (in the person of Wallace Fard Muhammad) and his Messenger (Elijah Muhammad). One Islamic tradition insists that a caliph always follows a messenger.

The Nation of Islam under the caliph continues the beliefs and practices abandoned by the American Muslim Mission. A new school, the University of Islam, was begun and the Fruit of Islam, the disciplined order of Islamic men, reinstituted. A new effort aimed at economic self-sufficiency

has been promoted, and businesses have been created to implement the program.

**Headquarters:** Muhammad's Temple of Islam No. 1, 1233 West Baltimore Street, Baltimore, Maryland 21223.

**Membership:** Not reported. As of 1982, the Nation of Islam under the caliph had only two mosques, one in Baltimore and one in Chicago.

**Periodical:** *Muhammad Speaks,* Muhammad's Temple of Islam No. 1, 1233 West Baltimore Street, Baltimore, Maryland 21223.

### ★ 79 ★
### Nation of Islam (Farrakhan)

Of the several factions which broke away from the American Muslim Mission (formerly known as the Nation of Islam and then as the World Community of Islam in the West [see Vol. 2, p. 341]) and assumed the group's original name, the most successful has been the Nation of Islam headed by Abdul Haleem Farrakhan. Farrakhan was born Louis Eugene Wolcott. He was a nightclub singer in the mid-1950s when he joined the Nation of Islam headed by Elijah Muhammad. As was common among Muslims at that time, he dropped his last name, which was seen as a name imposed by slavery and white society, and became known as Minister Louis X. His oratorical and musical skills carried him to a leading position as minister in charge of the Boston Mosque and, after the defection and death of Malcolm X, to the leadership of the large Harlem center and designation as the official spokesperson for Elijah Muhammad.

In 1975 Elijah Muhammad died. Though many thought Louis X, by then known by his present name, might become the new leader of the nation, Wallace, Elijah Muhammad's son, was chosen instead. At Wallace Muhammad's request, Farrakhan moved to Chicago to assume a national post. During the next three years the Nation of Islam moved away from many of its distinctive beliefs and programs and emerged as the American Muslim Mission. It dropped many of its racial policies and began to admit white people into membership. It also began to move away from its black nationalist demands and to accept integration as a proper goal of its programs.

Farrakhan emerged as a leading voice among "purists" who opposed any changes in the major beliefs and programs instituted by Elijah Muhammad. Long-standing disagreements with the new direction of the Black Muslim body led Farrakhan to leave the organization in 1978 and form a new Nation of Islam. He reinstituted the beliefs and program of the pre-1975 Nation of Islam. He reformed the Fruit of Islam, the internal security force, and demanded a return to strict dress standards.

With several thousand followers, Farrakhan began to rebuild the Nation of Islam. He established independent mosques and developed an outreach to the black community on radio. He was only slightly noticed until 1984 when he aligned himself with the presidential campaign of Jesse Jackson, a black minister seeking the nomination of the Democratic Party. The acceptance by Jackson of his support and the subsequent controversial statements by Farrakhan on radio and at press conferences kept Farrakhan's name in the news during the entire period of Jackson's candidacy.

**Headquarters:** Box 20083, Chicago, Illinois 60620.

**Membership:** Not reported. There are an estimated 5,000 to 10,000 members of the Nation of Islam.

**Periodical:** *The Final Call,* Box 20083, Chicago, Illinois 60620.

**Sources:**

Lomax, Louis E. *When the Word Is Given.* Cleveland: World Publishing Company, 1963.

Muhammad, Elijah. *Message to the Blackman.* Chicago: Muhammad Mosque of Islam No. 2, 1965.

Page, Clarence. "Deciphering Farrakhan." *Chicago* 33, no. 8 (August 1984): 130-35.

★ 80 ★
**The Nation of Islam (John Muhammad)**

John Muhammad, brother of Elijah Muhammad, founder of the Nation of Islam, was among those who rejected the changes in the Nation of Islam and the teachings of Elijah Muhammad which led to its change into the American Muslim Mission. In 1978 he left the mission and formed a continuing Nation of Islam designed to perpetuate the programs outlined in Elijah Muhammad's two books, *Message to the Blackman* and *Our Saviour Has Arrived.* According to John Muhammad, who uses the standard title of black Muslim leaders, "Minister," Elijah Muhammad was the last Messenger of Allah and was sent to teach the black man a New Islam.

**Headquarters:** Nation of Islam, Temple No. 1, 19220 Conant Street, Detroit, Michigan 48234.

**Membership:** Not reported. John Muhammad has support around the United States, but the only temple is in Detroit.

**Periodical:** *Minister John Muhammad Speaks,* Nation of Islam, Temple No. 1, 19220 Conant Street, Detroit, Michigan 48234.

**Sources:**

Muhammad, Elijah. *Message to the Blackman.* Chicago: Muhammad Mosque of Islam No. 2, 1965.

———. *Our Saviour has Arrived.* Chicago: Muhammad's Temple of Islam No. 2, 1974.

## Sufism

For general information about Sufism, please see pages 343-45 of Volume 2 of the *Encyclopedia of American Religions.*

★ 81 ★
**The Chishti Order of America**

The Chishti Order of America is one of several Sufi groups in the United States which traces its origin to the Chishti Order, one of the four main branches of Sufism. The Chishti Order was founded by Khwaja Abu Ishaq Chishti, who set-

tled at Chishti in Khurasan, in what is present-day Iran, during the tenth century. The lineage of leaders of the Chishti Order stayed in Persia until the succession of Khwaja Muinuudin Chishti (1142-1236), the most renowned saint in the order's history. He took the order to India and is regarded as the true founder of the modern order.

Khwaja Muinuudin was born in Sistan, Persia, and raised as a Sufi. The constant warfare he witnessed during his early life reinforced the mystic tendencies he inherited through his family. He studied with Hazrat Khwara Usman Harvani, a teaching master of the Chishti Order, for twenty years and was, upon his departure, granted the *khalifat,* or succession, of his teacher. He traveled to Lahore and Delhi before settling in Ajmer, then the seat of an important Hindu state. He became a major force in establishing Islam in India. His tomb in Ajmer is a sacred shrine as well as the location of the international headquarters of the order.

Over the centuries various leaders of the order have founded new branches. The two most important are the Nizami (founded by Nizanu'd-Din Mahbubiilahi) and the Sabiri (founded by Makhdum Ala'u'd-Din Ali Ahmad Sabir). Both orders were started by students of Baba Farid Shakarganj in the thirteenth century. The Chishti Order of America derives its lineage from the Sabri branch of the Chishti Order. The Nizami branch is represented in America by the Sufi Order (see Vol. 2, p. 345).

The Chishti Order of America was founded in 1972 by Hakim G.M. Chishti as the Chishti Sufi Mission, an affiliate of the Chishti Sufi Mission Society of India in Ajmer. Hakim was a student of Mirza Wahiduddin Begg who was the senior teacher at Ajmer during the 1970s. When Begg died in 1979, Hakim was granted his succession, a fact confirmed at a ceremony in Ajmer in 1980. At the same time, the Chishti Sufi Mission was renamed the Chishti Order of America.

Khwaja Muinuudin stressed the essence of Sufism as the apprehension of Divine reality through spiritual means and the suppression of the lower self. He taught the need of absolute devotion to one's spiritual master (Pir) as a necessity for salvation. He also stressed the obligation of humanitarian action in the face of the caste system.

**Headquarters:** Eastern Branch: c/o Hakim G.M. Chishti, 390 Soundview Drive, Rocky Point, New York 11778; Western Branch: Box 3396, College Station, Tucson, Arizona 85722.

**Membership:** Not reported. In 1981 Chishti sheikhs were to be found in New York, Chicago, and Los Angeles.

**Sources:**

Begg, W.D. *The Holy Biography of Hazrat Khwaja Muinuudin Chishti.* Tucson, Ariz.: Chishti Sufi Mission of America, 1977.

★ 82 ★
**Jerrahi Order of America**

The Jerrahi Order of America is the North American affiliate of the Halveti-Jerrahi Sufi Order headquartered in

Turkey. The Halveti (also spelled Khalwati) is regarded as one of the original source schools of Sufism, and members attribute its founding to several thirteenth-century Muslim ascetics. The Halveti experienced many schisms, one of which was founded in the seventeenth century by Hazreti Pir Nureddin Jerrahi (d. 1733). Born in a prominent family of Istanbul, Jerrahi studied law and at the age of nineteen was appointed a judge for the Ottoman Empire's province of Egypt. Just as he was due to sail to his new post, he met Halveti Sheikh Ali 'Ala-ud-Din and gave up his legal career to become a dervish. An accomplished student, he soon received *ijazat*, license to teach, from his teacher.

The Halveti orders have been characterized by both a strict program of training and an emphasis upon individualism (one cause of the continual splintering). It has also invested great reverence in any of its leaders who could demonstrate his power. Jerrahi is considered a *qutb*, a spiritual pole of the universe, and head of the hierarchy of saints. The order spread throughout the Ottoman Empire and beyond, from Yugoslavia to Indonesia.

The most distinctive practice of the Jerrahi Order is *dhikr*, literally, the remembrance of God. Dhikar is the invocation of the unity of God and is performed by the dervishes within a circle headed by their sheikh.

The Jerrahi is currently headed by Sheikh Muzaffer Ozak Al-Jerrahi, who resides in Istanbul. He is the author of a number of books; however, only one, *The Unveiling of Love,* has as yet been translated into English. He established the Jerrahi Order in America within the American-Iranian community in the late 1970s. The Masjid al-Farah, its main center, is located in Manhattan.

**Headquarters:** 864 South Main Street, Spring Valley, New York 10977.

**Membership:** Not reported. Two centers were active in 1982, one in New York City and one in Spring Valley, New York. Periodically Sheikh Muzaffer visits the United States and invites the general public to participate in dhikr performances, which he has held in cities across the United States and Canada.

★ 83 ★
## Khaniqahi-Nimatullahi

The Khaniqahi-Nimatullahi is the Western representative of the Nimatullahi Order of Sufis, an Iranian order founded by Nur ad-din M. Ni'matullah (1330-1431). Ni'matullah was born in Syria, the son of a Sufi master, and studied with several Sufi teachers before meeting his principal teacher, Abdullah al-Yafi-i, in Mecca. After Sheikh Yafi-i's death in 1367, Ni'matullah began a period of traveling, finally settling in Mahan, Persia (Iran), from whence the order spread throughout Persia and India.

The present head of the order is Dr. Javad Nurbakhsh, former head of the Department of Psychiatry of the University of Teheran, Iran. Nurbakhsh brought the order to the West in the 1970s and by 1983 had established centers in London, England, and several United States cities. He also created Khaniqahi-Nimatullahi Publications as the publish-

ing arm of the order, and it immediately began to generate English-language Sufi materials.

Nurbakhsh defines a Sufi as one who travels the path of love and devotion towards the Absolutely Real. Knowledge of the Real is accessible only to the Perfected Ones, the prime model being Ali, the son-in-law of Mohammad, to whom Iranian Shi'ite Muslims trace their authority. Ali traveled the path as a disciple of Mohammad and became not just a spiritual master, but the *qutb,* or spiritual axis, for his time. The head of the Nimatullahi Order continues in the succession of spiritual masters to whom disciples can look for knowledge.

**Headquarters:** 306 West 11th Street, New York, New York 10014.

**Membership:** Not reported. In the United States in 1980, the order had six centers, one each in New York City; Washington, D.C.; Boston; Seattle; San Francisco; and Mission Hills, California. Several hundred people are affiliated with the growing order.

**Sources:**

Nurbakhsh, Javad. *Masters of the Path.* New York: Khaniqahi-Nimatullahi Publications, 1980.
_____. *What the Sufis Say.* New York: Khaniqahi-Nimatullahi Publications, 1980.

★ 84 ★
## The Mevlana Foundation

The Mevlana Foundation was founded in 1976 by Reshad Feild, the first sheikh of the Mevlana school of Sufism to travel to the West. The Mevlana lineage was initiated by Mevlana Jelalu'ddin Rumi (1207-1273), the great thirteenth-century mystic poet. Raised as a Sufi, Rumi was an ecstatic and a visionary. He settled in Qonya, in present-day Turkey, and his tomb became the headquarters of his followers. They formally organized soon after his death.

Sufis share the basic beliefs of Islam but are organized around the leader, the sheikh, of the order who is considered the axis of the conscious universe. Rumi was especially devoted to music, and the Mevlana Order developed a musical emphasis. The order practices the *dhikr*, the remembrance of God, and became noted for its practice of the Turn, a dance in which individual Sufis attempted to establish a universal axis within themselves. For this practice the Mevlana became famous in popular folklore as the "whirling dervishes."

Reshad Feild was raised in London. He studied with a Gurdjieff/Ouspensky group as well as the Druids, and finally became a professional spiritual healer. In the early 1960s he met Pir Vilayat Khan, leader of the Sufi Order, and was initiated as a Sufi sheikh by him. In the fall of 1969, still on a spiritual pilgrimage, Feild encountered a man referred to simply as Hamid. As a result of this encounter, he traveled to Turkey to study. While there he met Sheikh Suleyman Dede, the head of the Mevlana Order.

In 1976 Feild left Turkey and moved to Los Angeles, where he became a Sufi teacher and healer. Shortly after the move, he assisted Dede's visit to America. During this trip, Dede initiated Feild as the first sheikh in the West. Feild founded the Institute for Conscious Life which later became the Mevlana Foundation.

**Headquarters:** Box 305, Boulder, Colorado 80306.

**Membership:** Not reported. Groups affiliated with the foundation can be found in several urban centers in the western United States, Canada, and England.

**Sources:**

Feild, Reshad. *Cooperation in the Three Worlds.* Los Angeles: Institute for Conscious Life, 1974.
_____. *The Invisible Way.* New York: Harper & Row, 1979.
_____. *The Last Barrier.* New York: Harper & Row, 1976.
Subhan, John A. *Sufism, Its Saints and Shrines.* New York: Samuel Weiser, 1970.

# Baha'ism

## ★85★
### Orthodox Baha'i Faith, Mother Baha'i Council of the United States

The Orthodox Baha'i Faith, Mother Baha'i Council of the United States is one of three organizations of former members of the Baha'i Faith who accept the claims of Charles Mason Remey (see The Remey Society, Supp., entry 87) to be the successor of Shoghi Effendi, the Guardian of the Baha'i Faith who died in 1957. After Remey's death in 1974, Joel Marangella was one of two people to assert that Remey had named him the Third Guardian of the Faith. Upon assuming that position, Marangella discovered the organization that Remey had established in America in disarray due to the successful court action initiated by the Baha'i Faith. He moved to reestablish Remey's work through a new organization, the National Bureau of the Orthodox Baha'i Faith in America. In 1972 the headquarters moved from New York City to Albuquerque, New Mexico. Soon after that move a council of nine persons was elected. It assumed the responsibilities of the bureau as the Mother Baha'i Council of the United States. It is composed entirely of individuals residing in the Roswell, New Mexico, area.

The Mother Baha'i Council has continued an aggressive attack upon the organization of the Spiritual Assembly of the Baha'i Faith (the ruling authority for Baha'is), occasionally placing advertisements in Chicago-area newspapers outlining its position. (The United States headquarters of the Baha'i Faith is in Wilmette, Illinois, a Chicago suburb.)

**Headquarters:** 3111 Futura, Roswell, New Mexico 88201.

**Membership:** Not reported. There are an estimated several hundred Orthodox Baha'is connected with the Mother Baha'i Council in the United States. Joel Marangella resides in Germany, and other members can be found throughout Europe.

**Periodical:** *Newsletter,* 3111 Futura, Roswell, New Mexico 88201.

**Sources:**

Bjorling, Joel. *The Baha'i Faith, a Bibliography.* New York: Garland, forthcoming.

## ★86★
### Orthodox Baha'i Faith under the Regency

The Orthodox Baha'i Faith under the Regency is one of three organizations of former members of the Baha'i Faith who accepted the claims of Charles Mason Remey (see The Remey Society, Supp., entry 87) to be the successor of Shoghi Effendi, the Guardian of the Baha'i Faith who died in 1957. Remey claimed to be the Second Guardian. After Remey's death in 1974, Joel B. Marangella was one of two men who claimed to have been appointed by Remey as the Third Guardian. Marangella organized his followers as the Orthodox Baha'i Faith, represented in the United States by the Mother Baha'i Council of the United States.

Among those appointed to a leadership role by Remey, Reginald B. (Rex) King accepted Marangella as the Third Guardian, but later came to the conclusion that both Remey and Marangella had taken actions which were contrary to Baha'i law. He concluded that Remey, rather than being the Second Guardian, was but the regent who assumed control until such time as the Second Guardian appeared and took his rightful place. Upon reaching that conclusion, King withdrew from Marangella and claimed to be the second regent.

King died in 1977. In his will he appointed four members of his family—Eugene K. King, Ruth L. King, Theodore Q. King, and Thomas King—as a council of regents to succeed him. The Orthodox Baha'is follow the teaching of the Baha'i Faith, differing only in their rejection of the authority of the spiritual assembly in favor of the regency.

**Headquarters:** Orthodox Baha'i Faith, National House of Justice of the United States and Canada, Box 1424, Las Vegas, New Mexico 87701.

**Membership:** Not reported. There are an estimated several hundred Orthodox Baha'is in the United States.

**Periodical:** *The Star of the West,* Orthodox Baha'i Faith, National House of Justice of the United States and Canada, Box 1424, Las Vegas, New Mexico 87701.

**Sources:**

Bjorling, Joel. *The Baha'i Faith, a Bibliography.* New York: Garland, forthcoming.

## ★87★
### The Remey Society

The Remey Society is one of three organizations of former members of the Baha'i Faith who accept Charles Mason Remey (1874-1974) as the Second Guardian of the Faith. Remey was a prominent Baha'i for many years. He authored a number of books, designed several Baha'i temples, and served as president of the International Baha'i Council. In 1951 he was one of nine people named by Shoghi Effendi as a hand of the cause.

In 1957 Shoghi Effendi died without having fathered a child, leaving a will, or naming a successor. Remey then joined with the other hands of the cause in proclaiming the formation of a Baha'i World Center made up of nine hands of the cause to assume temporarily the function of the guardian. Remey was one of the nine. However, during the next few years, Remey dissented from the position of the other hands. He argued that the guardianship was a necessary feature of the structure of the faith. He also asserted that, as the president of the International Baha'i Council (a position assigned Remey by Shoghi Effendi), he was the only one in a position to become the Second Guardian. He waited two years for the hands to accept his position. Then, in 1959, he left Haifa, where the Baha'i Faith has its international headquarters, and came to the United States. In 1960 he issued a Proclamation to the Baha'is of the World and circulated it at the annual gathering of the American Baha'is that year. He also issued a pamphlet, *A Last Appeal to the Hands of the Faith,* asking them to abandon plans to elect members of the International Baha'i Council in 1961. The hands continued to reject his claims and expelled him from the faith.

Throughout the 1960s Remey insisted upon his right to be designated the Second Guardian. Finally, in 1968 he appointed the first five Elders of the Baha'i Epoch and announced the organization of his followers under the name The Orthodox Abha World Faith. He retired to Florence, Italy, and lived out the last decade of his life in virtual retirement.

After Remey's death in 1974, two men, Donald Harvey and Joel Marangella, both claimed that he had appointed them as the Third Guardian of the Faith. The Remey Society unites the American followers of Donald Harvey. The society was organized by Francis C. Spataro.

**Headquarters:** 86-11 Commonwealth Boulevard, Bellerose, New York 11426.

**Membership:** Not reported. It is estimated that no more than a thousand people recognize Donald Harvey's claims, of which only a few hundred reside in the United States.

**Periodical:** *The Remey Letter,* 86-11 Commonwealth Boulevard, Bellerose, New York 11426.

**Sources:**

Bjorling, Joel. *The Baha'i Faith, a Bibliography.* New York: Garland, forthcoming.

Remey, Charles Mason. *The Bahai Movement.* Washington, D.C., 1912.

——.*Observations of a Bahai Traveller.* Washington, D.C., 1914.

Spataro, Francis Cajetan. *The Lion of God.* Bellerose, N.Y.: The Remey Society, 1981.

——. *The Rerum.* Bellerose, N.Y., 1980.

## ★ 88 ★
### World Union for Universal Religion and Universal Peace

In the years after the death of Abdul-Baha and the elevation of his grandson, Shoghi Effendi, to the leadership of the Baha'i Faith as the Guardian of the Faith, an American Baha'i, Ruth White, began to question Shoghi Effendi's authority. In her first book, *Abdul Baha and the Promised Age* (1926), she voiced her opposition to his attempts to develop the Baha'i organization by quoting Abdul-Baha to the effect that, "The Baha'i Movement is not an organization. You can never organize the Baha'i Cause." More importantly, she began to voice opposition to Shoghi Effendi's role as guardian, and in her 1929 work, *The Bahai Religion and Its Enemy, the Bahai Organization,* she attacked the authenticity of the Will and Testament of Abdul-Baha, the document upon which Effendi's authority rested.

Though she lectured widely throughout the United States, her only success in recruiting supporters came in Germany where the Bahai World Union was founded by Wilhelm Herrigel and other Baha'is, who were described as friends of Abdul-Baha. The Bahai World Union continued until 1937 when the German government outlawed the Baha'i Faith.

Simultaneously with White's attack upon Effendi, though separate from it, Ahmad Sohrab, a close friend of Abdul-Baha who had accompanied him on his American tour in 1912, and an American Baha'i, Julie (Mrs. Lewis Stuyvesant) Chandler, formed an independent Baha'i network in New York City. They felt that Effendi's increasing efforts to organize the faith were counterproductive. They established the New History Society which offered lectures by Sohrab and other prominent guests (Albert Einstein addressed it on one occasion) and opened the Bahai Bookshop. Members of the New History Society considered themselves participants in the Baha'i movement but separate from the organization headed by Effendi. In response, the Baha'i Faith brought suit against Sohrab, Chandler, and the New History Society seeking to prevent their use of the name "Baha'i." The court ruled against them, however, stating that no group of followers of a religion could monopolize the name of that religion or prevent other groups of followers from practicing their faith.

Like the Bahai World Union, the New History Society found support in Europe and opened offices in Paris in the 1930s. Sohrab became the major spokesperson for the society. He spoke frequently and authored a number of books, including *Broken Silence,* a response to the 1941 court case.

Ruth White and Ahmad Sohrab both died in 1958 and Julie Chandler, in 1961. Since their deaths, their work and thought have been carried on by Hermann Zimmer of Stuttgart, Germany. Zimmer had returned to Germany in 1948 after being released from a POW camp. He picked up the remnants of Herrigel's organization and formed the World Union for Universal Religion and Universal Peace. In 1950 he published *Die Wiederkunft Christi* in which he equated Baha'u'llah with Christ returned in his Second Advent. Though never becoming a large organization, the World Union remains as a rallying point for "Free Baha'is" around the world.

**Headquarters:** No American headquarters located.

**Membership:** No figures available; estimates suggest that only a few hundred "Free Baha'is" reside in the United States.

**Sources:**

*The Baha'i Case Against Mrs. Lewis Stuyvesant Chandler and Mirza Ahmad Sohrab.* Wilmette, Ill.: National Spiritual Assembly of the Baha'is of the United States and Canada, 1941.

Bjorling, Joel. *The Baha'i Faith, a Bibliography.* New York: Garland, forthcoming.

Sohrab, Mirza Ahmad. *Broken Silence.* New York: New History Foundation, 1942.

White, Ruth. *Abdul Baha and the Promised Age.* New York, 1927.

_____. *Bahai Religion and Its Enemy, the Bahai Organization.* Rutland, Vt.: Charles Tuttle, 1929.

Zimmer, Herman. *A Fraudulent Testament Devalues the Bahai Religion into Political Shoghism.* Stuttgart, Germany: World Union for Universal Religion and Universal Peace, 1973.

# Chapter 20

# The Eastern and Middle Eastern Family
# (Hinduism, Sikhism, and Jainism)

## Hinduism

For general information about Hinduism, please see pages 355-60 of Volume 2 of the *Encyclopedia of American Religions.*

### ★89★
### American Meditation Society

The American Meditation Society is the United States affiliate of the International Foundation for Spiritual Unfoldment founded in 1975 in Capetown, South Africa, by Purushottan Narsinhran (b. 1932), whom his followers know by his spiritual name, Gururaj Ananda Yogi. As a child in his native Gujurat, he showed a distinct focus upon spiritual realities. As a child of five he ran away from home to visit the temples in the neighborhood. When found, he explained to his parents that he had visited many temples, but had found to his frustration that "the Gods were lifeless and would not speak to me." His continued search for the Divine culminated when he discovered that what he sought lay within himself. Having found the inner Reality, and having fully and permanently entered the self-realized state, he set himself to the task of becoming a spiritual teacher in the West.

He moved to South Africa and became a successful businessman. In 1975, following a problem with his heart, he retired from business and turned to full-time work as a spiritual teacher. He founded the International Foundation for Spiritual Unfoldment. Within the first year it had spread to nine countries in the British Commonwealth and throughout Europe. In 1977 it was organized in California as the American Meditation Society.

Gururaj Ananda Yogi teaches not a religion, but the basis which underlies all religions. His task is seen as merely to awaken the individual to the same Reality that he discovered, to lead him or her along the path of unfoldment. Meditation is the individual's major tool in turning inward, and it works best if individualized. The society offers basic meditation courses which introduce the variety of ways to meditate. Gururaj assists in the process of individualizing meditation by giving to each person a distinct mantrum, a sound which is intoned during meditation. Individuals send their picture to Gururaj. He meditates upon the picture and hears the sound each person makes with the universe. He presents that distinct sound to each person as a unique personal mantrum.

**Headquarters:** United States: American Meditation Society, Box 244, Bourbonnais, Illinois 60914. International: International Foundation for Spiritual Unfoldment, Box 202, Gatesville, Cape Town 7764, South Africa.

**Membership:** In 1984 the society had approximately 2,000 members in thirty centers. Internationally, the foundation has centers in Canada, Australia, Zimbabwe, Spain, Denmark, Germany, Holland, Ireland, Great Britian, and South Africa.

**Periodical:** American Meditation Society *Newsletter,* Box 244, Bourbonnais, Illinois 60914.

**Sources:**

Partridge, Ted. *Jewels of Silence.* Farmborough, Hamps.: St. Michael's Abbey Press, 1981.

Taylor, Savita. *The Path to Unfoldment.* London: VSM Publications, 1979.

### ★90★
### Dhyanyogi Mahant Madhusudandasji, Disciples of

Indian yoga teacher Dhyanyogi Mahant Madhusudandasji Maharaj left home as a child of thirteen to seek enlightenment. He spent the next forty years as a wandering student, during which time he met and worked with his guru whom he discovered at Mt. Abu in Rajasthan State in Northern India. From his guru he received *shaktipat,* a transmission of power believed to release the latent power of *kindalini,* pictured as residing at the base of the spine. The emergence of that power and the experience of its traveling up the spine to the crown of the head is considered by many Hindu groups to be the means of enlightenment.

In 1962 Dhyanyogi Madhusudandasji ceased his wanderings and began to teach. He established an ashram at Bandhvadi, Gujurat, the first of several in western India. He authored two books, *Message to Disciples* and *Light on Meditation.* During the 1970s followers moved to England and the United States. He made his first visit to his Western disciples in 1976 and began to build a following among American converts.

Dhyanyogi Madhusudandasji's teachings emphasize meditation (dhyan), or raja yoga, and kundalini yoga. He offers shaktipat to *sadhuks* (students). As the kundalini awakens, the student is open to the guru's continuing influence and is able to shed past encumbrances and move on the path of enlightenment.

**Headquarters:** c/o Mr. Manu Michael Hannon, Director, 2026 Redesdale Avenue, Los Angeles, California 90039.

**Membership:** Not reported. Groups of followers can be found in Illinois, New Jersey, and California.

**Sources:**

Dhyanyogi Mahant, Madhusudandasji Maharaj. *Light on Meditation.* 1978.

★91★
### Holm/Church of Divine Influence

Holm, also known as the Church of Divine Influence, was founded during the early 1970s by Lee Lozowick, a former Silva Mind Control instructor. Lozowick gathered a small group of seekers around him and established Holm at Tabor, New Jersey. In 1975 he published his first book, *Beyond Release,* edited from talks he had given, and began to issue a newsletter, *At Holm.* The group's growth fluctuated for several years, and members began to look for a place where a community could be created. Hence, in 1980 the group moved to Prescott Valley, Arizona, and established an ashram.

Lozowick's eclectic spiritual teachings draw heavily upon Hinduism, but also include elements of Gurdjieff, Meher Baba, and Zen Buddhism. The goal of life, according to Lozowick, is "spiritual slavery," a state in which one has been so blessed and transformed that the individual is compelled by inner necessity to fulfill the Will of God. The spiritual life at Holm includes daily *darshan* (sessions with Lozowick), *kirtans* (hymns and chants), and the five life conditions. Members are expected to follow: (1) a daily discipline of exercise (hatha yoga and/or a martial art); (2) a balanced lacto-vegetarian diet free of tobacco, alcohol, and mind-altering drugs; (3) daily study of spiritual literature; (4) celibacy outside of monogamous marriage; and (5) daily meditation. Lozowick also encourages weekly bridge games as a spiritual discipline and to emphasize the spiritual aspect has written a bridge manual entitled, *Zen Gamesmanship.*

Holm recognizes three levels of membership. The core group that manages the affairs of Holm are called the Mandali. The body of full resident members of the community are designated the Order of Ordinary Fools. Other participants, who may attend community activities, participate in Holm study groups in their own community, and offer some minimal financial support, are designated the Order of Divine Fools.

**Headquarters:** c/o Anthony Zuccarello, President, Box 25839, Prescott Valley, Arizona 86312.

**Membership:** In 1984 Holm reported 100 members in the United States and an additional 25 members outside the country. Besides the main ashram in Prescott Valley, study groups have been organized in New York City, Los Angeles, and Boulder, Colorado. There are three ministers.

**Periodical:** *Divine Slave Gita,* Box 25839, Prescott Valley, Arizona 86312.

**Sources:**

Lozowick, Lee. *Acting God.* Prescott Valley, Ariz.: Holm Press, 1980.
_____. *Beyond Release.* Tabor, N.J.: Holm Press, 1975.
_____. *Book of Unenlightenment.* Prescott Valley, Ariz.: Holm Press, 1980.
_____. *The Cheating Buddah.* Tabor, N.J.: Holm Press, 1980.
_____. *In the Fire.* Tabor, N.J.: Holm Press, 1978.
_____. *Laughter of the Stones.* Tabor, N.J.: Holm Press, n.d.

★92★
### Lakshmi

Lakshmi was founded by former English professor Dr. Frederick Lenz. Lenz had become a disciple of Sri Chinmoy (see Vol. 2, p. 375) during the 1960s and studied with him for eleven years. Under the name Atmananda, given to him by his guru, he began to teach yoga in Los Angeles and Southern California. Spontaneously, his students began to report a number of extraordinary experiences during his classes. Lenz was seen, according to reports, to levitate, disappear completely, and/or radiate intense beams of light during group meditations. During the 1970s Atmananda left Sri Chinmoy and formed Lakshmi as an independent organization. At a gathering of approximately 100 of his students in the early 1980s, he announced that Eternity had given him a new name, "Rama."

Rama teaches that humanity is at the end of a cycle. The present period, Kali Yuga, is a dark age. At the end of each cycle or age, Vishnu (the god of the Hindus) is due to take incarnation. While Rama does not see himself to be the same conscious entity as the historic Rama, a previous incarnation of Vishnu, he does claim to be the embodiment of the "particular octave of celestial light which was once incarnated as Rama."

**Headquarters:** Box 2110, Malibu, California 90265.

**Membership:** Not reported. Rama regularly conducts classes in Malibu and Los Angeles. Lakshmi has an estimated several hundred members.

**Periodical:** *Self Discovery,* Box 2110, Malibu, California 90265.

**Sources:**

Rama. *The Last Incarnation.* Malibu, Calif.: Lakshmi Publications, 1983.

★93★
### Ma Yoga Shakti International Mission

The Ma Yoga Shakti International Mission was formed in 1979 by Ma Yogashakti Saraswati, an Indian female guru, who migrated to the United States in 1977. She established ashrams in New York and Florida and alternates her time between them. She also has four ashrams in India (Bombay, Calcutta, Delhi, and Gondia). Ma Yogashakti teaches a balanced approach to all yogas—hatha, raja, bhakti, and karma. Full moon *Purnima* (devotional services) are held monthly. Her teachings are spelled out in a number of books she has written, including: *Chhandogya Upanishad, Prayers and Poems from Mother's Heart, Shree Satya Narayana Vrata Katha, Adhyatma Sandesh,* and *The Invisible Seven Psychic Lotuses.*

**Headquarters:** 114-23 Lefferts Boulevard, South Ozone, New York 11420.

**Membership:** In 1984 the mission had three centers, one in New York and two in Florida (Deerfield Beach and Palm Bay), with an estimated 200 members.

**Periodical:** *Yogashakti Mission Newsletter,* 114-23 Lefferts Boulevard, South Ozone, New York 11420.

**Sources:**

Yogashakti, Ma. *Prayers and Poems from the Mothers Heart.* Melbourne, Fla.: Yogashakti Mission, 1976.

★94★
**Moksha Foundation**

The Moksha Foundation was founded in 1976 as the Self-Enlightenment Meditation Society by Bishwanath Singh, known by his religious name Tantracharya Nityananda. Nityananda began studying yoga at the age of seven. He became a student of Shrii Shrii Anandamurtiji and eventually served as a monk with the Ananda Marga Yoga Society. In 1969 he had a realization that he was a siddha yogi in his previous incarnation and that he had been reincarnated in this life to teach meditation and yoga. He left the Ananda Marga Yoga Society and began independent work, eventually establishing centers in India and England. He also renounced his vows as a monk and married.

In 1973 Nityananda moved to Boulder, Colorado, and established the Self-Enlightenment Meditation Society. The center served as a residence for several of his closest students. He taught meditation, tantric yoga philosophy, and lathi, a martial art, and offered personal instruction and initiation for his followers. From his Colorado headquarters, he regularly journeyed to meet with students in Chicago, Minneapolis, New York, and Los Angeles.

In 1981 Nityananda traveled to Europe on a speaking tour. While on the Continent, he was invited to lecture in Sweden. After leaving the plane in Stockholm, he disappeared. His body was found several months later; he had been murdered.

Mira Sussman, a resident student at the Boulder center, succeeded to leadership of the foundation and has continued the program initiated by Nityananda.

**Headquarters:** 745 31st Street, Boulder, Colorado 80303.

**Membership:** Not reported. At the time of Nityananda's death, he had approximately fifty students in Boulder, with other United States groups in several cities. The centers previously founded in London and in Bihar, India, continued, and he regularly visited them.

**Periodical:** *Tantric Way,* 745 31st Street, Boulder, Colorado 80303.

★95★
**Narayanananda Universal Yoga Trust**

The Narayanananda Universal Yoga Trust was created in 1967 by Swami Narayanananda Maharaj (b. April 12, 1902), a native of the hill country of Coorg in Southern India. At the age of twenty-seven, he began his religious quest. He traveled to the Ramakrishna Math in Belur, Bengal (outside of Calcutta). He joined the monks and took his vows as a *sannyasin* (the renounced life). He studied under Swami Shivananda, the math's president, and in 1932 departed for the Himalayas to complete his spiritual quest. In February, 1933, he experienced *nirviklpa samadhi,* described as the merger of his individual consciousness with the great Ocean of Consciousness occasioned by the awakening of his *kundalini,* the latent energy pictured as lying coiled like a serpent at the base of the spine.

After the experience of samadhi, Narayanananda remained a recluse, refusing to take disciples or form an organization. Then in 1947, moved by the suffering of people at the time of the separation of Pakistan from India, he agreed to take disciples. Over the next twenty years the number of disciples grew and included some Europeans. The growth in the number of followers led Narayanananda to create the trust which at its inception included centers in Denmark, Germany, and Switzerland.

Narayanananda teaches what he terms Universal Religion. He emphasizes meditation, strict morality, and mind control (i.e., the detached life) as the path to union with the Divine. He also emphasizes kundalini yoga.

In 1977 Swami Narayanananda authorized Swami Turiyananda to start an ashram in the United States. He settled in Chicago and opened one center. An ashram/retreat was begun in Winter, Wisconsin. Narayanananda made his first visit to the United States in 1980 and conducted classes at both locations.

**Headquarters:** N U Yoga Ashrama, 1418 North Kedzie, Chicago, Illinois 60651.

**Membership:** In 1980 the trust had approximately fifteen centers in India, Denmark, Sweden, Norway, Germany, and New Zealand. The two centers in the United States serve several hundred members.

**Sources:**

Narayanananda, Swami. *The Mysteries of Man, Mind and Mind Functions.* N.p., n.d.

_____. *A Practical Guide to Samadh.* Rishikish, India: Narayanananda Universal Yoga Trust, 1966.

_____. *The Secrets of Mind-Control.* Rishikish, India: Narayanananda Universal Yoga Trust, 1970.

_____. *The Secrets of Prana, Pranayama, and Yoga-Asana.* Gylling, Denmark: N U Yoga Trust & Ashrama, 1979.

★ 96 ★

## Raj-Yoga Math and Retreat

The Raj-Yoga Math and Retreat is a small monastic community formed in 1974 by Father Satchakrananda Bodhisattvaguru. Satchakrananda began the practice of yoga in 1967. After only two months of practice, he experienced the raising of the *kundalini,* an internal energy pictured in Hindu thought as a snake coiled and resting at the base of the spine which upon awakening rises to the *crown chakra* (psychic center at the top of the head). That event produced an awareness of Satchakrananda's divine heritage. Following that event, he spent a short time in a Trappist monastery, attended Kenyon College, and then became coordinator for the Northwest Free University, where he taught yoga.

In 1973 Satchakrananda was "mystically" initiated as a yogi by the late Swami Sivananda (1887-1963), the founder of the Divine Life Society (see Vol. 2, p. 364), through a trilogy of "female Matas" at a retreat he attended on the Olympic (Washington) Peninsula. The following year, with a small group of men and women, he founded the math (monastery). In 1977 he was ordained a priest by Archbishop Herman Adrian Spruit of the Church of Antioch (see Vol. 2, p. 153), and has attempted to combine both Hindu and Christian traditions at the math. Spiritual disciplines include the regular celebration of the mass, though the major practice offered is the Japa Yoga Sadhana, consisting of the successive practice of *japa* (mantra) yoga, meditation, *kriyas* (cleansings), mudras, *asanas* (hatha yoga postures), and *pranayam* (disciplined breathing). Japa yoga allows practitioners to become aware of their divine nature.

The math is located in the foothills of Mt. Baker overlooking the Nooksuck River near Deming, Washington. It accepts resident students for individual instruction, but offers a variety of classes for nonresidents through the Karma Leela Institute. For those unable to travel to the math for instruction, Satchakrananda has put together a japa yoga workshop packet.

**Headquarters:** Box 547, Deming, Washington 98244.

**Membership:** The resident community at the math fluctuates between two and twenty. Several hundred individuals are associated with the math through their attendance at the Karma Leela Institute.

**Sources:**

*Letters to Satchakrananda.* Deming, Wash.: Raj-Yoga Math and Retreat, 1977.

Satchakrananda, Yogi. *Coming and Going, the Mother's Drama.* Deming, Wash.: Raj-Yoga Math and Retreat, 1975.

★ 97 ★

## Satyananda Ashrams, U.S.A., and International Yoga Fellowship

Swami Satyananda Saraswati (b. 1893), a former disciple of Swami Sivananda (1887-1963) [see the Divine Life Society, Vol. 2, p. 364], pioneered the modern opening of the yoga to all, both sannyasins and householders, regardless of sex, nationality, caste, or creed. After working with Sivananda for twelve years, he wandered India for nine more. In 1964, the year after his guru's death, Satyananda founded the Bihar School of Yoga. He built the Sivananda Ashram on the banks of the Ganges and the Ganga Darshan on a hill overlooking the river valley. Satyananda continued Sivananda's broad approach which integrated the various yogic techniques, but gave particular emphasis to tantra. Also, like Sivananda, he actively spread his teachings, first throughout India, and beginning with a world tour in 1968, to the West. During the 1970s he established ten ashrams and many centers in India and outside of India; followers could be found in Australia, Indonesia, Columbia, Greece, France, Sweden, England, and Ireland. As the movement spread, he organized the International Yoga Fellowship.

Satyananda's teachings came to the United States in two separate manners. First, in 1975 Llewellyn Publications, an occult publisher in St. Paul, Minnesota, released a major work by Swami Anandakapila (a.k.a. John Mumford), a leading disciple of Satyananda's in Australia. The publication of *Sexual Occultism* was followed by a United States tour in 1976 and feature articles in *Gnostica,* a major occult periodical. Concurrently with the publication of Anandakapila's book, a New York publisher released *Yoga, Tantra and Meditation* by Swami Janakananda Saraswati, a teacher for Satyananda in Scandinavia. Second, during the 1970s many students of Satyananda immigrated to the United States from India, and as their numbers increased they formed small yoga groups. In 1980 Swami Niranjananda Saraswati (b. 1960), a leading teacher with Satyananda who had traveled extensively and organized ashrams for the World Yoga Fellowship, arrived in the United States. On October 28, 1980, he organized Satyananda Ashrams U.S.A., the American affiliate of the International Yoga Fellowship. Niranjananda remained in the United States teaching and organizing local centers. In the summer of 1982, Swami Amritananda, a female guru and designated successor to Satyananda, visited the United States. Her visit was followed immediately by Satyananda's first tour of North America.

Satyananda has emerged as the foremost exponent of the so-called left-hand path of tantric yoga. Tantra is built upon the blending and exchange of male and female energies and consciousness. In left-hand tantra, sexual intercourse is used as a means of reaching *ananda* (or bliss).

The World Yoga Fellowship is one of the largest yoga groups worldwide. Its extensive membership in the United States is somewhat hidden, being largely confined to the Indian-American community.

**Headquarters:** 1157 Ramblewood Way, San Mateo, California 94403.

**Membership:** Not reported. Membership is estimated to be in the thousands as ashrams and centers may be found across the United States and Canada.

**Periodical:** *Yoga,* c/o Bihar School of Yoga, Lal Darwaja, Monghyr 811201, Bihar, India.

**Sources:**

Mumford, John [Swami Anandakapila]. *Sexual Occultism.* St. Paul: Llewellyn Publications, 1975.

Saraswati, Swami Janakananda. *Yoga, Tantra and Meditation.* New York: Ballantine Books, 1975.

Saraswati, Swami Satyananda. *Dynamics of Yoga.* Monghyr, India: Bihar School of Yoga, 1966.

_____. *Tantra-Yoga Panorama.* Rajanandgaon, M.P., India: International Yoga Fellowship Movement, 1972.

★ 98 ★
## Truth Consciousness

Truth Consciousness, formed in 1973, is the organization of followers of Swami Amar Jyoti. Swamiji, as he is called by his students, was born in 1928 in what is today Pakistan. A few months prior to his graduation from college, he renounced his seemingly destined life of comfort and success to follow an inner dictum, "Know yourself and you shall know everything." He began a ten-year period of solitude and meditation, broken in 1960 when he began a pilgrimage around India. He founded Jyoti Ashram in Pune, Maharastra State, and received his first students. In 1961 he took his first trip to the United States, but, even though his first American disciples were drawn to him during that visit, he spent the next decade concentrating on his work in India.

Swamiji returned to the United States in 1973 and began his first ashram in the West. Truth Consciousness is the nonprofit corporation which ties together the various centers which have been created by a growing following. Swamiji divides his time between the Indian and American ashrams and centers.

The primary focus of life in the ashrams of Truth Consciousness is the regular *satsangs,* sessions in which students sit with Swamiji and discuss various concerns (or listen to tapes in his absence). Swamiji emphasizes the search toward self-knowledge and meditation as means for inner exploration. Individuals already are, in essence, that which they seek. Thus along with meditation, he emphasizes the need of constant reminders that affirm the union of the self with joy, love, and peace.

**Headquarters:** c/o Sacred Mountain Ashram, Gold Hill, Salina Star Route, Boulder, Colorado 80302.

**Membership:** In the United States, Truth Consciousness consists of three ashrams (Boulder, Colorado; Rockford, Michigan; and Tucson, Arizona). There is no formal membership, but an estimated several hundred individuals are affiliated with the organization. In India, Ananda Niketan Ashrams, the Trust headed by Swami Amar Jyoti, has two ashrams, one in Pune, Maharasrashtra, and the Rishi Ashram in the Himalayas.

**Periodical:** *Truth Consciousness Journal,* Sacred Mountain Ashram, Gold Hill, Salina Star Route, Boulder, Colorado 80302.

**Sources:**

Frey, Kessler. *Satang Notes of Swami Amar Jyoti.* Boulder, Colo.: Truth Consciousness, 1977.

★ 99 ★
## Vedantic Cultural Society

The Vedantic Cultural Society was formed in 1983 by Hansadutta Swami (a.k.a. Hans Kary), a former initiating guru with the International Society for Krishna Consciousness (ISKCON) (see Vol. 2, p. 371). During the late 1970s, Hansadutta had been the subject of strong criticism by the other gurus in ISKCON because of his unorthodox fund raising, administrative, and recruiting activities. Then in the spring of 1980, he was arrested for possession of illegal firearms. While the charges were later dropped, his advocacy of survivalism and his possession of a number of weapons led to his being sent to India for a year. After consideration of the sacred nature of the relationship of initiating guru and his disciples (which constituted most of the Berkeley temple), the governing council reinstated him. However, his return to Berkeley did not ease the tension, and in 1983 ISKCON excommunicated Hansadutta. He left and took most of the Berkeley temple with him, forming the Vedantic Cultural Society.

In most ways, the Vedantic Cultural Society follows the beliefs and practices of ISKCON, since the cause of the split was neither doctrinal nor devotional.

Hansadutta's troubles did not end with the break from ISKCON. In September of 1983, he was arrested and accused of shooting out several store windows in Berkeley. Several weapons and empty shells were found in his car. As this volume goes to press, the future of the center and its leader is very much in doubt.

**Headquarters:** 2334 Stuart Street, Berkeley, California 94705.

**Membership:** The Vedantic Cultural Center has several hundred members, all in the area of Berkeley, California.

★ 100 ★
## Yoga House Ashram

The Yoga House Ashram was formed in the mid-1970s by Dadaji Vimalananda, a former leader of the Ananda Marga Yoga Society. Dadaji was born in 1942 in Badwel, South India, of a Brahmin family. At the age of six he had an intense initiation experience of divine light filling his room and a voice instructing him on the path of enlightenment. He began to pursue the inner life, and at the age of sixteen became an instructor of meditation. In 1962 he met Shrii Anandamurti, founder of the Ananda Marga Yoga Society (see Vol. 2, p. 381), and was impressed with both his spirituality and his program of service to humanity, especially the sick, the elderly, and the poor. In like measure, Anandamurti was impressed with his young disciple and quickly elevated him to be a teacher of yoga. In 1966 Dadaji left India to spread Ananda Marga. He was responsible for starting centers in Thailand, Singapore, Indonesia, Malasia, Hong Kong, and the Philippines. The government and the United Nations honored him for his efforts on behalf of the victims of the 1968 earthquake that struck Manila.

In 1969 Dadaji came to the United States and assisted in the spread of Ananda Marga. However, in the mid-1970s he left Ananda Marga and founded the Yoga House Ashram. Since that time he has spent his time creating his own following in the San Francisco Bay area of California.

Dadaji came to the United States with a strong desire to bridge the gap between East and West. He teaches a traditional yoga but has retained the emphasis upon social action he found in Ananda Marga. He teaches his students to keep their role in society as they strive for God.

**Headquarters:** Box 3391, San Rafael, California 94902.

**Membership:** Not reported. The work of the Yoga House Ashram is confined to northern California where Dadaji Vimalananda teaches yoga at a variety of locations in the larger San Francisco Bay area.

**Sources:**

Vimalananda, Dadaji. *Yogamritam (The Nectar of Yoga).* San Rafael, Calif.: Yoga House Ashram, 1977.

# Sikhism

For general information about Sikhism, please see pages 386-88 of Volume 2 of the *Encyclopedia of American Religions.*

## ★101★
## Nirankari Universal Brotherhood Mission

The Nirankari Universal Brotherhood Mission is one of several Sant Mat groups which traces its lineage to Jaimal Singh, founder of the Radhasoami Satsang, Beas (see Vol. 2, p. 389). It was founded by Boota Singh (1873-1943), a tattoo artist who in 1929 received a succession from Kahn Singh. Boota Singh became known for his opposition to the rigid conventions and rituals of the Sikhs; he opposed all taboos, castes, creeds, and divisions based upon external habits and appearances. He discarded all dictates concerning what one eats, drinks, or wears. Boota Singh was succeeded by Avtar Singh (1899-1969). After the partition of 1947 (which established Pakistan as a separate state), Avtar Singh moved the headquarters of the Nirankari Mission to Delhi and formally established the Sant Nirankari Mandal. He wrote a constitution and gave it its present organizational structure. He authored *Avtar Baani,* which functions as a holy book for the movement. Under Avtar Singh, the mission flourished and a colony was established on the Januma River in Delhi. In 1969 Avtar Singh was succeeded by Gurbachan Singh, who had the year previous traveled to Europe to establish the work there. By 1973 there were

354 branches with work outside of India in England, Hong Kong, Canada, and the United States.

The spread of the Nirankari Mission to the West began in 1955 when Bhag Mal, a member, moved to England. The mission was formally organized in 1962. Soon after his becoming head of the mission, Gurbachan Singh, who had helped develop the work in the West, formed a foreign section to focus upon growth outside of India. In 1971 he made his first trip to North America. Beginning in Vancouver, he moved to San Francisco where he appointed Dr. Iqhaljeet Rai as president of the Nirankari Universal Mission in the United States. He continued his journey across the United States and visited Toronto and Montreal before returning home. In 1972 headquarters were moved to Madison, Wisconsin.

Internationally, the mission is headed by the Seven Stars, seven men picked by the guru to serve for life. The mission in India, having received some persecution, organized the Sant Nirankari Seva Dal, a defense force to protect the group against acts of violence directed against it.

Essential to the life of the mission is *gian,* the giving of the knowledge by the guru to each member. This process, the exact nature of which is held confidential within the group, establishes the relationship of guru to disciple. As the mission has grown, specific disciples have been appointed to represent the guru in the giving of knowledge. Members of the mission agree to live by the five principles: (1) Nothing is ours. All possessions—physical, mental, material—are a divine loan which we must utilize only as trustees and not as masters. (2) No discrimination based upon caste, creed, colour, religion, or worldly status. (3) No criticism of anyone's diet or dress, as this creates conflict and breeds hatred. (4) No renunciation of the world. One should continue performing one's normal vocations and functions of life and be always righteous. (5) No divulgence of the Divine Secret of the gian except with permission of the True Master.

**Headquarters:** Sant Nirankari Mission (USA), 1015 Thacker Street, Des Plaines, Illinois 60016.

**Membership:** The Nirankari claims more than 8,000,000 members worldwide with work established in twenty-six countries. In the United States, in 1983, the mission reported 2,000 members in twenty centers.

**Periodical:** *Sant Nirankari,* Nirankari Colony, Delhi 110009, India.

**Sources:**

Gargi, Balwant. *Nirankari Baba.* Delhi: Thomson Press, 1973.

# Chapter 21

# The Eastern and Middle Eastern Family (Buddhism, Shintoism, and Zoroastrianism)

## Buddhism

For general information about Buddhism, please see pages 393-402 of Volume 2 of the *Encyclopedia of American Religions*.

### Theravada Buddhism

★ 102 ★
**Thai-American Buddhist Association**

The general unrest in Southeast Asia and the rescinding of the Oriental Exclusion Act in 1965 combined to increase immigration from Thailand to the United States in the late 1960s. Significant Thai-American communities emerged on the West Coast and in several urban areas further inland. Assisted by leadership from Thailand, the new immigrant communities began to organize their predominantly Buddhist religious life. In 1970, at the invitation of the American Thais, the Ven. Phrakhru Vajirathammasophon of Wat Vajirathamsathit toured the United States. During his visit, the Thai-American Buddhist Association was formally organized in Los Angeles and plans were initiated to build the Wat Thai of Los Angeles, a temple complex which would serve the largest of the Thai communities in the West. Later that year, three priests arrived to take up permanent residence.

The 1971 visit by the Ven. Phra Dhammakosacharn, a leading Thai Buddhist priest, was followed by the incorporation of the Wat Thai as the Theravada Buddhist Center and the beginning of a fund raising drive. In 1972 the United States government invited the supreme patriarch, Phra Wannarat of Wat Phra Jetuphon, and a group of Thai priests to make an official state visit. During this visit, the presentation of the land-title deed for the future site of the Wat Thai was held in the office of the Consul General in Los Angeles. The cornerstone was laid and construction commenced. It was finished in stages, and in 1980 the statue of Buddha in the main temple was consecrated.

While work on the complex in Los Angeles proceeded, other wats were being organized in other cities from San Francisco and Denver to Houston, Washington, D.C., and New York.

Theravada Buddhism has as a major practice, insight meditation, described as the practice of mindfulness. Mindfulness is the observation point arrived at by the meditator from which he or she can truly understand mental and physical phenomena as they arise. In general, Theravada Buddhists are among the most conservative in their adherence to the oldest Buddhist traditions and they use the Pali-language texts of early Buddhism, as opposed to the Sanskrit texts used by the Mahayana Buddhists.

**Headquarters:** Wat Thai of Los Angeles, 12909 Cantara Street, North Hollywood, California 91605.

**Membership:** There are over a hundred thousand Thais in the United States, and 40,000 in Los Angeles alone. Wats have now been established in Los Angeles; San Francisco; Sunnyvale, California; Denver; Ogden, Utah; Chicago; Houston; Washington, D.C.; St. Louis; Miami; Tampa; and Mt. Vernon, New York.

**Periodical:** *Duangpratip,* Wat Thai of Los Angeles, 12909 Cantara Street, North Hollywood, California 91605.

**Sources:**

Hamilton-Merritt, Jane. *A Meditator's Diary.* New York: Harper & Row, 1976.

Namto, Achan Sobin. *A Short Introduction to Insight Meditation: Its Theory and Practice.* Denver: Wat Buddhawararam of Denver, n.d.

*Wat Thai of Los Angeles.* Bangkok, Thailand: S. Darongkamas, 1982.

## Zen Buddhism

For general information about Zen Buddhism, please see pages 413-16 of Volume 2 of the *Encyclopedia of American Religions*.

★ 103 ★
**Minnesota Zen Meditation Center**

The Minnesota Zen Meditation Center began in the 1960s with a group of people in Minneapolis who began to practice *zazen,* Zen meditation. They developed an association with the San Francisco Zen Center (see Vol. 2, p. 417) and its assistant priest, Dainen Katagiri-roshi, visited them on several occasions. In 1972 the group extended an invitation to Katagiri-roshi to become the leader of a new Zen center they were establishing. He accepted, and the Minnesota Zen Center was formed in January 1973.

Katagiri-roshi was born in Japan in 1928 and became a Zen monk in 1946. He trained at Eiheji Monastery, the original center of the Soto Shu Sect. He came to the United States in 1963 to work with the North American Buddhist Church, the Japanese-American Soto group, and was assigned to their Los Angeles temple. After five months, however, he was sent to San Francisco to assist Shunryu Suzuki-roshi at both the San Francisco temple (Sokoji) and the independent San Francisco Zen Center. While there, he assisted in the opening of the Tassajara Zen Mountain Center.

Since coming to Minneapolis, Katagiri-roshi has attracted students throughout the Midwest among whom affiliated centers have emerged. In 1978 the center purchased 280 acres in southeastern Minnesota and has begun construction of a year-round center for intensive Zen practice.

The center is governed by a board of directors which is elected at the annual meeting of members. There are three categories of membership—associate, general, and voting—but only the latter may vote at the annual meetings. Katagiri-roshi is consulted in an advisory capacity on the center's administrative affairs.

**Headquarters:** 3343 East Calhoun Parkway, Minneapolis, Minnesota 55408.

**Membership:** In 1984 the center reported 100 members in the United States in four centers under the leadership of ten priests. There is also one affiliate center in Japan with 25 members.

**Educational Facilities:** Hokyo-ji (i.e., Catching-the-Moon Zen Monastic Center), near Houston, Minnesota.

**Periodicals:** *MZNC Newsletter; Udumbara*, 3343 East Calhoun Parkway, Minneapolis, Minnesota 55408.

**Sources:**

Suzuki, Shunryu. *Zen Mind, Beginner's Mind.* New York: Weatherhill, 1970.

# Zen Buddhism in Korea

Buddhism in Korea differs markedly from Buddhism in other Oriental societies in that, during the modern era, the various schools of Buddhist thought began to emphasize their commonality over their differences. As a result, the several organizations were able not only to reverse the process of splintering but finally, in 1935, to unite into a single organization, the Chogye sect, from which most contemporary groups derive.

Buddhism entered what is today called Korea in 372 C.E., when it was brought from China to the Kingdom of Koguryo, a state covering the northern portion of the peninsula. From there it spread southward to the kingdoms of Paekche and Silla. It flourished in the united kingdom created by Silla in 668 C.E. during which time Zen was in-

troduced along with the original Mahayana (called "Chiao" in Korea) forms. Nine schools of Zen developed around nine outstanding masters and six schools of Chiao emerged.

Through the next centuries, Buddhism waxed and waned, always remaining in competition with Confucius's thought and popular folk religion. Zen experienced a revival in the twelfth century when Master Pojo (1158-1210) advocated a union of thought which found favor with the varying Zen schools. A century and a half later, in 1356, under Master T'aego (1301-1382), a merger of all the Zen schools into the Chogyejong was accomplished. Master T'aego was one of several priests who had risen to prominence in the land and had been given the title "national teacher" by the king.

The Yi Dynasty (1392-1910) became a time of great suffering for Korean Buddhism, as the ruling powers generally assumed a hostile posture toward it. Buddhism was suppressed and Zen almost died out, though in the face of opposition Buddhism became more united. In 1424 two of the Chiao sects united with the Chogyejong to form the Sonjong while the remaining Chiao sects united into the Kyojong.

Only in the late eighteenth century did government policies toward Buddhism relax. King Chongyo began to lift negative government regulations and in the nineteenth century Buddhism began a revival, further spurred in the 1890s by the arrival of many Japanese Buddhist priests. In 1904, for the first time, the government ended its control of Buddhist temples. The revival of Buddhism, the cooperation with the Japanese priests, and the new freedom, however, came to an abrupt halt in the second decade of the twentieth century after Japan occupied Korea in 1910. The occupation government reclaimed control of the temples. Nationalistic feelings led to a new sense of unity by Korean Buddhists over against the Japanese. The growth of those sentiments led in 1935 to the merger of the Sonjong and Kyojong into the single Chogye sect which dominates Korean Buddhism to this day.

The migration of Korean Buddhism to America and the formation of Korean Buddhist organizations awaited the end of the Korean War and the large-scale migration of Koreans after the lifting of the Oriental Exclusion Act in 1965. The 1970s saw the proliferation of temples and centers across the United States in the 1970s. (Sources: Kyung-Bo Seo, *A Study of Korean Buddhism Approached through the Chodangjip* [Walnut Creek, Calif.: Walnut Creek Zendo, (1960?)])

★104★
**American Zen College**

The American Zen College began in 1970 as Hui-Neng Zen at Easton, Pennsylvania. The temple was founded by Gosung Shin, the Seventy-seventh Patriarch in the Lin-Che lineage, a line of Zen masters which traces its origin to Buddha Sakyamuni. Gosung Shin had been an abbot in three Korean temples, but came to the United States in 1969 at the request of Zen Master Kyung-Bo Seo to permanently establish the World Zen Center which Kyung-Bo Seo had founded at Spruce Run Mt., Virginia. Shin studied at Harvard briefly and in 1970 settled in Philadelphia where a Hui-Neng Zen Center Association developed as students gathered around him. In the spring of 1981, at the invitation of Mr. Paul Beidler, the group moved to Easton, Pennsylvania, and changed its name to the Hui-Neng Zen Temple (see the Kwan-Yin Zen Temple, Inc., Vol. 2, p. 424). Soon outgrowing the facilities at Easton, the temple moved to a tract of land in rural New York, near Woodhull. The name was changed to the Kwan-Yin Zen Temple. There being no houses on the property, Shin and his followers lived in tents while the temple was being constructed. Eventually they developed a self-sufficient community supported by the proceeds of a health food store in Corning, New York.

Once the center at Woodhull became a stable and growing concern, Shin began a program of planned expansion. In 1977 an urban center opened in Washington and the following year a second rural center was established near Germantown, Maryland. The new name, American Zen College, was adopted and the focus of activity shifted from the New York temple, which remains as a retreat center for advanced students.

The American Zen College center in Washington, D.C., serves primarily the large Korean community in the metropolitan area, while most non-Korean students live at the Seneca Lake Zen Center in Maryland. A daily schedule of chanting, recitation of the sutras, and meditation is followed at the centers, and, on Friday evenings at Seneca Lake, Shin leads a seven-hour period of extended meditation.

**Headquarters:** American Zen College, 16815 Germantown Road (Route 118), Germantown, Maryland 20767.

**Membership:** In 1984 the American Zen College reported 2,500 members at its three centers.

**Periodical:** *Buddha World,* American Zen College, 16815 Germantown Road (Route 118), Germantown, Maryland 20767.

**Sources:**

Shin, Gosung. *Zen Teaching of Emptiness.* Washington, D.C.: American Zen College Press, 1982.

★ 105 ★
**Kwan Um Zen School**

The Kwan Um Zen School was founded in 1983 to connect the various temples and centers previously founded by Master Seung Sahn Sunim. Soen Sa Nim, as he is generally referred to by his students, is the Seventy-eighth Patriarch in the Chogye Order. As a young man in Korea, he became deeply involved in radical politics but turned to Buddhism during World War II. He became a student of Zen Master Ko Bang and eventually abbot of two temples. After the war, he became a leader in the effort to revive the Chogye sect which had suffered much damage in the final years of Japanese occupation. In 1965 he traveled to Japan and during his stay founded three temples. In 1972 he came to the United States and began a small temple in Providence, Rhode Island. That temple became the headquarters from

which he traveled around New England and across the United States. Early branch centers were established in New Haven, Cambridge, and New York City, followed by centers in Los Angeles and Berkeley.

Master Seung Sahn came to the United States with a missionary zeal to plant a new Buddhist tradition in the West. He emphasizes that the purposes of Zen are, first, to understand the True Self, i.e. attain Truth, and, then, to assist other people to attain the "Great Love, Great Compassion, Great Bodhisattva Way." Most people have a significant amount of karma which forms an obstacle to enlightenment, hence the necessity of masters and centers. Like the Japanese Rinzai masters, Seung Sahn uses the koan as a major teaching device. Besides the main practice of daily sitting meditation, each center associated with the school sponsored a silent three or seven day meditation retreat called Yong Maeng Jong Jin (to leap like a tiger while sitting), equivalent to the *sesshin* or extended meditation sessions at Japanese Zen centers.

The growth of the center in Providence led to its purchase of a tract of land in rural Rhode Island upon which it developed a residential community and to which it eventually moved its headquarters. Throughout the early 1980s, Soen Sa Nim extended his travels and developed centers in South America and Europe, with special success in Poland.

**Headquarters:** K.B.C. Hong Poep Won, RFD No. 5, 528 Pound Road, Cumberland, Rhode Island 02864.

**Membership:** In 1984 the Kwan Um Zen School reported fifteen centers and temples in the United States, seven in Poland and others in England, Spain, Brazil, and Canada.

**Periodical:** *Primary Point,* K.B.C. Hong Poep Won, RFD No. 5, 528 Pound Road, Cumberland, Rhode Island 02864.

**Sources:**

Sahn, Seung. *Bone of Space.* San Francisco: Four Season's Foundation, 1982.

_____. *Dropping Ashes on the Buddha.* Edited by Stephen Mitchell. New York: Grove Press, 1976.

_____. *Only Don't Know.* San Francisco: Four Season's Foundation, 1982.

★ 106 ★
**Zen Lotus Society**

The Zen Lotus Society was founded in 1975 in Toronto, Ontario, but dates to the arrival in the United States of an independent Korean Zen monk, Samu Sunim (b. 1941). Samu Sunim was an orphan who became a Zen monk. Forced to choose between his pacifist beliefs and serving out his years in the army (required of all Korean youth), Samu Sunim deserted and fled to Japan. In 1967, with the aid of some friends, he migrated to New York City and began to teach meditation. In 1968 he moved to Montreal where he worked for the next few years improving his English. He also became a Canadian citizen and married. In 1972 he moved to Toronto where a Korean-Canadian community existed, but his initial plans to begin a center were frustrated by a lengthy illness. Only in 1975 did he resume his meditation schedule. By 1979 his support had grown to the point that a building could be purchased, and the Zen Buddhist Temple of Toronto was established and in 1980, incorporated.

In 1981 Alexander Lundquist was sent to Ann Arbor, Michigan, to found a temple. The following year Samu Sunim ordained him a monk, with the name "Sanbul Sunim." Later that year, the Zen Buddhist Temple-Ann Arbor was incorporated.

Both temples of the Zen Lotus Society conduct daily meditation sessions, instruct beginners in basic meditation, and hold regular weekend meditation retreats. Quarterly, Samu Sunim holds extended five-to seven-day retreats. Temple members are very active in social affairs and devote time to the peace movement. The society is developing a Buddhist Peace Cemetery. Members also participate in the Buddhists Concerned for Animals.

**Headquarters:** Zen Buddhist Temple-Toronto, 46 Gwynne Avenue, Toronto, Ontario, Canada M6K 2C3; Zen Buddhist Temple-Ann Arbor, 1214 Packard Road, Ann Arbor, Michigan 48104.

**Membership:** In 1984 the society reported three centers, one each in Canada, the United States, and Mexico. In the United States, there were 50 members with an additional 150 members in other centers.

**Periodical:** *Spring Wind-Buddhist Educational Forum,* 1214 Packard Road, Ann Arbor, Michigan 48104.

## Chinese Buddhists

For general information about Chinese Buddhists, please see pages 424-26 of Volume 2 of the *Encyclopedia of American Religions.*

### ★ 107 ★
### The Shrine of the Eternal Breath of Tao

The Shrine of the Eternal Breath of Tao was founded by Master Ni, Hua-Ching, who began his study of Taoism as a child in China. After the Chinese Revolution, he moved to Taiwan and continued his studies. Eventually he became a teacher of Taoism and its related martial and healing arts. During the 1970s he moved to the United States and began to teach in Los Angeles.

Master Ni teaches the universal law of subtle energy response. Everything in the universe is a manifestation of energy in either its grosser or its more subtle states. Understanding and developing the proper response to the energies of one's environment will bring harmony to one's life. The practice of Taoist meditation, martial arts (kung fu and t'ai chi ch'uan), and medical practices (acupuncture and herbs) assist in attaining a balanced relationship to life. The universal law of response is basic to all spiritual practices.

**Headquarters:** College of Tao and Traditional Chinese Healing, 117 Stonehaven Way, Los Angeles, California 90049.

**Membership:** Not reported. In 1982 the shrine had two centers, one in Los Angeles and one in Malibu, California. There were an estimated 100 members.

**Sources:**

Ni, Hua-Ching. *Tao, the Subtle Universal Law and the Integral Way of Life.* Malibu, Calif.: Shrine of the Eternal Breath of Tao, 1982.

## Western Buddhists

For general information about Western Buddhists, please see pages 434-35 of Volume 2 of the *Encyclopedia of American Religions.*

### ★ 108 ★
### The American Buddhist Movement

The American Buddhist Movement was founded in 1980 as an independent Buddhist order to promote Buddhism in America and ordain Buddhist monks. Rather than following any particular school of Buddhism, the movement respects all traditions as equal and encourages the unity of Buddhist thought and practice. Theravada, Mahayana, and Vijrayana Buddhists participated in the movement's founding. In defining its peculiar role, the movement asserts that an American form of Buddhism is possible and that Westerners do not have to adopt Asian cultural forms to be Buddhists.

The movement has established a variety of structures to perpetuate its program. Classes are offered on a variety of Buddhist concerns, including introduction to the several distinctive national traditions. Periodically, an *American Buddhist Directory* is published. Plans have been announced to build a permanent center in the New York City area to house a meditation hall, library, and lecture room.

Membership in the movement is open to all Buddhists and activities have been designed to serve those primarily affiliated with the movement as well as those affiliated with other groups. Leadership is invested in a four-person board of directors. Kevin R. O'Neill has served as its president since its inception.

**Headquarters:** 301 West 45th Street, New York, New York 10036.

**Membership:** In 1984 the movement reported 200 members in three centers.

**Educational Facilities:** Buddhist College, 225 Lafayette Street, New York, New York 10012.

**Periodical:** *American Buddhist Newsletter,* 301 West 45th Street, New York, New York 10036.

**Sources:**

*The American Buddhist Directory.* New York: The American Buddhist Movement, 1982.

# Chapter 22

# New Unaffiliated Religious Bodies

For general information about New Unaffiliated Religious Bodies, please see
pages 445-46 of Volume 2 of the *Encyclopedia of American Religions.*

## Miscellaneous Churches

### ★109★
### Church of Pan

The Church of Pan was founded in 1970 by Kenneth Walker
and members of a nudist colony in rural Rhode Island. The
organization of the church was occasioned by the request
of two members to be married in the nude and the inability
of the group to locate a minister to perform the ceremony.
They decided to form a church and Walker became the
minister.

The Church of Pan espouses naturalist principles. Reverence
and devotion is directed toward the Creator, and actions
follow patterns discerned to be in concert with the Creator's
designs and purposes. While engaged in altruistic actions
which attempt to modify the harshness of nature, in line with
the destiny of creation, the church denounces human actions which have destroyed life-supporting systems and
polluted nature. Humans have the task of maintaining the
balance of life on the planet.

The church also opposes the distortions of human society
in its treatment of sexuality. Forgetting the naturalness of
sex, society tends to view it either as sinful or something
to be marketed.

The church is headquartered at a nudist colony managed
by Walker. Members are active in the promotion of en-
vironmental concerns. As might be expected from the nature
of its beginning, the church has experienced difficulties over
its status as a tax-exempt religious organization.

**Headquarters:** R.R. 3, Box 189, Foster, Rhode Island 02825.

**Membership:** In 1983 the church reported thirty families,
all members of the one congregation in Rhode Island.

### ★110★
### The Church of the Creator

The Church of the Creator was founded in 1973 by Ben
Klassen, its pontifex maximus. The occasion for the
establishment of the church was the publication of Klassen's

book, *Nature's Eternal Religion,* in which the basic perspective of the church was fully discussed. Klassen expanded his
ideas in *The White Man's Bible,* published in 1981.

The church summarizes its objectives as the survival, expansion, and advancement of the white race. It follows the laws
of nature, i.e., creativity, rather than Christianity. It rejects
the idea of God, the supernatural, and the afterlife. The
highest law of nature is the right of any species to survival,
expansion, and advancement of its own kind. The white race
is nature's finest achievement, and its future is the epitomy
of the law of nature. Jews, blacks, and other "colored" people are considered objects of hate.

**Headquarters:** Box 5908, Lighthouse Point, Florida 33064.

**Membership:** Not reported. Only one small congregation is
known.

**Sources:**

Klassen, Ben. *Nature's Eternal Religion.* Lighthouse Point, Fla.:
The Church of the Creator, 1973.

_____. *The White Man's Bible.* Lighthouse Point, Fla.: The
Church of the Creator, 1981.

### ★111★
### International Council of Community Churches

The International Council of Community Churches was formally organized in 1946, but possesses a history which begins
in the early nineteenth century when nonsectarian community churches began to appear as an alternative to the formation of separate denominationally-affiliated congregations.
Such community churches were especially welcomed in communities too small to support more than one viable congregation. Over the years, such congregations have frequently retained a fiercely independent stance. To their number
were added other independent congregations which had
separated from denominational structures and adopted a
nonsectarian stance.

In the wake of the ecumenical movement in the early twentieth century, the most visible symbol being the Federal
Council of Churches of Christ formed in 1908, many congregations merged across denominational lines, some form-

ing independent federated or union churches, dropping all denominational affiliation. During this period, some community churches began to see, in light of their years of existence apart from denominational boundaries, that they had a particular role vis-à-vis Christian unity.

A first attempt to build a network of community churches was known as The Community Church Workers of the United States. At a national conference of individuals serving community churches in Chicago in 1923, a committee formed to hold a second conference and outline plans for a national association. Organization occurred the next year and Rev. Orvis F. Jordan of the Park Ridge (Ill.) Community Church was named as secretary. He later became the first president of the group. The organization continued for over a decade, but died in the 1930s due to lack of support.

A second organization of community churches was also begun in 1923 among predominantly black congregations. Representatives of five congregations gathered in Chicago in the fall of 1923 to form The National Council of the Peoples Community Churches (incorporated in 1933 as the Biennial Council of the People's Church of Christ and Community Centers of the United States and Elsewhere). Rev. William D. Cook, pastor of Metropolitan Community Church in Chicago, served as the first president.

Unable to gain recognition from the Federal Council of Churches, the independent community churches began a second attempt at organization in the last days of World War II. Rev. Roy A. Burkhart, pastor of First Community Church of Columbus, Ohio, led in the formation of the Ohio Association for Community Churches in 1945. The next year representatives from nineteen states and Canada met and formed the National Council of Community Churches.

Almost immediately, the black and white groups began to work toward a merger. The merger, accomplished in 1950, created the International Council of Community Churches with a charter membership of 160 churches. By 1957 the several foreign congregations had ceased their affiliation with the council and the word "International" was dropped. In 1969 the name was changed to National Council of Community Churches. In 1983, however, foreign congregations in Canada and Nigeria affiliated and in 1984 the original name was again assumed.

There is no doctrinal statement shared by the council or its member churches, though most churches share a liberal ecumenical-minded Protestant perspective. The council describes itself as committed to Christian unity and working "toward a fellowship as comprehensive as the spirit and teachings of Christ and as inclusive as the love of God."

The council is a loosely organized fellowship of free and autonomous congregations. The national and regional officers facilitate communication between congregations and serve member congregations in various functions, such as representing them at the Consultation on Church Union and coordinating the securing of chaplains in the armed services.

**Headquarters:** c/o Rev. J. Ralph Shotwell, Executive Director, 900 Ridge Road, Suite LL 1, Homewood, Illinois 60430.

**Membership:** In 1984 the council reported 250 member congregations with 175,000 members and 350 ministers. In ad-

dition, the council serves more than 1,000 other churches (membership unknown). The council allows dual membership, and approximately five percent of the member churches have a second denominational affiliation.

**Educational Facilities:** As a matter of policy, the council has no educational institutions or mission projects of its own. It endorses and encourages member churches to support individual schools and missions that meet a council standard of being "postdenominational," and of promoting Christian unity while meeting human need.

**Periodicals:** *The Christian Community; The Pastor's Journal,* c/o Rev. J. Ralph Shotwell, Executive Director, 900 Ridge Road, Suite LL 1, Homewood, Illinois 60430.

**Sources:**

*National Council of Community Churches, Directory.* Homewood, Ill.: National Council of Community Churches, 1982.

Shotwell, J. Ralph. *Unity without Uniformity.* Homewood, Ill.: Community Church Press, 1984.

## ★ 112 ★
## Mahikari of America

Mahikari of America is an outpost of one of the so-called "New Religions" of Japan, the Sukyo Mahikari or the True Light Supra Religious Organization. Mahikari was founded by Okada Yoshikazu (1901-1974), a member of a prominent Samurai family. During World War II he was severely injured and developed tuberculosis. When as a result of the bombing of Tokyo he lost everything, he turned to religion and joined the Sekai Kyussei Kyo (Church of World Messianity) [see Vol. 2, p. 479]. From it he found the healing he sought. Then in 1959 he had a revelation from Su no kami-sama (the Lord God) in which he was entrusted with a cleansing-healing mission. The following year he founded Mahikari, originally called the Lucky and Healthy Sunshine Children. He later changed the name to the Church of True-Light Civilization.

Mahikari closely resembles the Sekai Kyussei Kyo. The main practice of Mahikari, radiating the True-Light, termed *okiyome* (purification) or *Mahikari no waza* (the method of Mahikari) is taught in a three-day class (*kenshu*). During kenshu participants are given a pendant, the *omitama*. A person wearing the omitama can transmit the True-Light through their hands. The True-Light heals, opens the recipient to God, removes spirits attached to the individual, and purifies the body by removing toxic substances. Okada taught that eighty percent of all the suffering in the world was caused by disincarnate spirits attaching themselves to individuals.

Okada Yoshikazu is regarded as the physical embodiment of the god Yoni-masi-o-amatsu, and is known as Sukuin-ushisama (Saviour). He continued to receive revelations throughout his life. These revelations have been collected into two books, *Goseigenshu,* or Book of Revelations, and *Norigotoshu,* or Book of Prayers, which serve as scripture for the group.

After Okada's death in 1974, the movement split into two factions, Sekiguchi Sakae was formally installed as the new leader of the church. Shortly after his installation, however, Okada's adopted daughter claimed that she was the rightful heir. Following a lawsuit, the Supreme Court of Japan in 1978 ruled in favor of Sekiguchi and awarded him the headquarters' property. Okada's daughter Sachiko, called Keijusama by her followers, established a new headquarters in Kanagawa Prefecture and reorganized those loyal to her as the Sukyo Mahikari. Mahikari of America is affiliated with Sukyo Mahikari.

Mahikari of America was organized in 1973, and the first *dojo* (center) was established in Los Angeles.

**Headquarters:** 6470 Foothill Boulevard, Tujunga, California 91042.

**Membership:** In 1982 there were fifteen centers in the United States, plus one each in Puerto Rico and Montreal. An estimated several thousand people are affiliated with Mahikari.

**Sources:**

Davis, Winston. *Dojo.* Stanford, Calif.: Stanford University Press, 1980.

Tebecis, A.T. Mahikari. *Thank God for the Answers at Last.* Tokyo: L.H. Yoko Shuppan, 1982.

*Yokoshi Norigoto Shu.* Los Angeles: Kekai Mahikari Bunmei Kyodan of America, 1977.

★113★
### The Temple of Bacchus

The Temple of Bacchus was formed in 1978 by Bishop H. Carlisle Estes, the temple's pastor. Bacchus, also known as Dionysus, was the ancient Greek god of food and drink. Estes claimed in 1975 that Bacchus revealed to him the temple's teachings, which have been published in a pamphlet, *The Book of Bacchus.* The temple believes that there is one God, known by many names, and that Bacchus is His disci-ple. Bacchus decreed that Estes should form a church to worship God and ordered that it be a place of joy and celebration. Bacchus taught that everything God created is good and humans should enjoy the pleasures of the body—food, wines, music, creative activity, and the arts. However, all should be enjoyed in moderation. Excess in any area leads to illness and pestilence and the disfiguring of bodily form.

According to the revelation, Bacchus has decreed daily worship with feasting and dancing. Six days of bacchanals are followed by a day of fasting and rest. Priests, bishops, and cardinals of the church assist in the preparation of the daily feast with a primary responsibility for preventing the rituals from becoming repetitive and stereotyped.

Almost from its founding, the temple has been a subject of controversy. Critics charged Bishop Estes and his assistant, Cardinal Vincent Morino, with operating a restaurant under the guise of a temple in order to circumvent local zoning laws which had previously denied them permission to open a restaurant in the building occupied by the temple. They further charged that the nightly bacchanals, in which those in attendance are asked to contribute a stated donation and in return receive a full meal, are in fact not religious events at all. The controversy has led to several law suits which are, as of the time of this writing, still pending and which will determine the future of the temple.

The temple is one of several religious bodies chartered by the Universal Life Church of Modesto, California (see Vol. 2, p. 459).

**Headquarters:** RD 2, Box 51, Wells, Maine 04090.

**Membership:** In 1979 the church reported 125 members of the single congregation in Maine, with new congregations beginning in Honolulu and in Wiltshire, England.

**Sources:**

Estes, H. Carlisle. *The Book of Bacchus.* Wells, Maine: Temple of Bacchus, 1978.

# Appendix: Religious Group Name/Status Changes

The Appendix was prepared for the Supplement to *The Encyclopedia of American Religions* to treat religious groups that have undergone a change in name or status since the first edition.

Appearing alphabetically by religious group name, all entries in the Appendix include a sequential entry number (the sequence continues from the main section), name of religious group, and a brief annotation. All entries in the Appendix are indexed in the Religious Group Index.

The annotations for Appendix entries are introduced by one of three standard phrases, depending on the status of the religious group. Appearing in boldface at the beginning of the annotation, the standard phrases used are as follows:

1) **Defunct.** Used for religious groups known to have gone out of existence since publication of the first edition of *The Encyclopedia of American Religions*. Only groups whose demise has been directly verified are listed. Volume and page number of the first edition are noted for historical information on the group.

2) **Merged.** Used for religious groups which have merged into already existing bodies or into completely new churches. Volume and page number of the first edition are noted for historical information on the former church body. For new churches that have come into existence as a result of merger and are included in the Supplement, the main entry number is noted.

3) **New Name.** Used for religious groups whose names have changed since publication of the first edition of *The Encyclopedia of American Religions*. In most cases, the change had little effect upon the doctrine or teachings of the group. For a few, such as the Institute of Ability, the name change represented a radical change in direction for the group. The original name, along with its volume and page number from the first edition, is given in the new name entry.

★114★
**A Candle**

**Defunct:** For historical information, see Vol. 1, p. 475.

★115★
**American Eastern Orthodox Church (Martin)**

**Defunct:** For historical information, see Vol. 1, p. 79.

★116★
**American Holy Orthodox Catholic Eastern Church (Sherwood)**

**Defunct:** For historical information, see Vol. 1, p. 76.

★117★
**American Muslim Mission**

**New Name:** The World Community of Islam in the West (see Vol. 2, p. 341) changed its name to American Muslim Mission.

★118★
**American Rationalist Federation**

**New Name:** The Rationalist Association (see Vol. 1, p. 157) changed its name to American Rationalist Federation.

★119★
**American Zen College**

**New Name:** The Kwan Yin Zen Temple, Inc. (see Vol. 2, p. 424) changed its name to American Zen College.

★120★
**Americans First, Inc.**

**Defunct:** For historical information, see Vol. 1, p. 158.

★121★
**Ansaru Allah Community**

**New Name:** The Nubian Islamic Hebrew Mission (see Vol. 2, p. 343) changed its name to Ansaru Allah Community.

★122★
**Ansaru Free Assembly**

**New Name:** The Viking Brotherhood (see Vol. 2, p. 296) changed its name to Ansaru Free Assembly.

★123★
**Apostolic Catholic Church of the Americas**

**New Name:** The American Orthodox Catholic Church (Zeiger) (see Vol. 1, p. 38) changed its name to Apostolic Catholic Church of the Americas.

★124★
**Aryo-Christian Church of St. George of Cappadocia**

**Defunct:** For historical information, see Vol. 2, p. 155.

★125★
**Association for Christian Development**

**New Name:** The Associated Churches of God (see Vol. 1, p. 474) changed its name to Association for Christian Development.

★126★
**Association for the Understanding of Man**

**Defunct:** For historical information, see Vol. 2, p. 132.

★127★
**Atlantion Wicca**

**Defunct:** For historical information, see Vol. 2, p. 278.

★128★
**Bavarian Illuminati**

**Defunct:** For historical information, see Vol. 2, p. 262.

★129★
**Bennu Phoenix Temple of the Hermetic Order of the Golden Dawn**

**Defunct:** For historical information, see Vol. 2, p. 261.

★130★
**Bodha Society of America, Inc.**

**Defunct:** For historical information, see Vol. 2, p. 174.

★131★
**Buddhist World Philosophical Group**

**Defunct:** For historical information, see Vol. 2, p. 435.

★132★
**The Builders**

**New Name:** The Brotherhood of the Sun (see Vol. 2, p. 45) changed its name to The Builders.

★133★
**Christ Catholic Church**

**New Name:** The Christ Catholic Church (Diocese of Boston) (see Vol. 1, p. 38) changed its name to Christ Catholic Church.

★134★
**Christian Bible Students Association**

**Defunct:** For historical information, see Vol. 1, p. 492.

★135★
**Church of Jesus Christ (Cutlerite)**

**Merged:** The Church of Jesus Christ (Cutlerite) (see Vol. 2, p. 21) merged into the True Church of Jesus Christ (Cutlerite).

**★136★**
**Church of Satanic Brotherhood**

**Defunct:** For historical information, see Vol. 2, p. 303.

**★137★**
**Church of the Awakening**

**Defunct:** For historical information, see Vol. 2, p. 197.

**★138★**
**Church of the Four Leaf Clover**

**Defunct:** For historical information, see Vol. 2, p. 105.

**★139★**
**Church Universal and Triumphant**

**New Name:** The Summit Lighthouse (see Vol. 2, p. 160) changed its name to Church Universal and Triumphant.

**★140★**
**Circle of Inner Truth**

**Defunct:** For historical information, see Vol. 2, p. 131.

**★141★**
**Community of Micah (Fabrengen)**

**Defunct:** For historical information, see Vol. 2, p. 326.

**★142★**
**Cosmerism**

**Defunct:** For historical information, see Vol. 2, p. 133.

**★143★**
**Dancers of the Sacred Circle**

**Defunct:** For historical information, see Vol. 2, p. 288.

**★144★**
**Delphic Coven**

**Defunct:** For historical information, see Vol. 2, p. 275.

**★145★**
**Delphic Fellowship**

**Defunct:** For historical information, see Vol. 2, p. 293.

**★146★**
**Dianic Wicca**

**Defunct:** For historical information, see Vol. 2, p. 276.

**★147★**
**Earthstar Temple**

**New Name:** The New England Coven of Welsh Traditional Witches (see Vol. 2, p. 272) changed its name to Earthstar Temple.

**★148★**
**Evangelical Christian Church (Wesleyan)**

**New Name:** The Holiness Christian Church of the United States of America (see Vol. 1, p. 221) changed its name to Evangelical Christian Church (Wesleyan).

**★149★**
**Evangelical Orthodox (Catholic) Church in America (Non-Papal Catholic)**

**Merged:** The Evangelical Orthodox (Catholic) Church in America (Non-Papal Catholic) (see Vol. 1, p. 41) merged into the Orthodox Catholic Church in America.

**★150★**
**Evangelical Orthodox Church**

**New Name:** The New Covenant Apostolic Order (see Vol. 2, p. 447) changed its name to Evangelical Orthodox Church.

**★151★**
**Family of Love**

**New Name:** The Children of God (see Vol. 2, p. 452) changed its name to Family of Love.

**★152★**
**Fellowship of Christian Men**

**Defunct:** For historical information, see Vol. 2, p. 470.

**★153★**
**First Century Church**

**Defunct:** For historical information, see Vol. 2, p. 238.

**★154★**
**Foundation Faith of God**

**New Name:** Foundation Faith of the Millenium (see Vol. 2, p. 229) changed its name to Foundation Faith of God.

**★155★**
**Free Protestant Episcopal Church**

**Merged:** The Free Protestant Episcopal Church (see Vol. 1, p. 54) merged into the Apostolic Catholic Church of the Americas (see Supp., entry 16).

**★156★**
**The Free Thinkers of America**

**Defunct:** For historical information, see Vol. 1, p. 156.

**★157★**
**Goddian Organization**

**Defunct:** For historical information, see Vol. 1, p. 153.

★158★
**Hilltop House Church**

**Defunct:** For historical information, see Vol. 2, p. 461.

★159★
**Hollywood Coven**

**Defunct:** For historical information, see Vol. 2, p. 273.

★160★
**Holy Order of Briget**

**Defunct:** For historical information, see Vol. 2, p. 284.

★161★
**International Missionary Society, Seventh Day Adventist Church Reform Movement, American Union**

**New Name:** The SDA Reform Movement (see Vol. 1, p. 466) changed its name to International Missionary Society, Seventh Day Adventist Church Reform Movement, American Union.

★162★
**International Pentecostal Holiness Church**

**New Name:** The Pentecostal Holiness Church (see Vol. 1, p. 261) changed its name to International Pentecostal Holiness Church.

★163★
**International Sivananda Yoga Vedanta Centers**

**New Name:** The True World Order (see Vol. 2, p. 365) changed its name to International Sivananda Yoga Vedanta Centers.

★164★
**Johannine Daist Communion**

**New Name:** The Free Primitive Church of Divine Communion (Dawn Horse Fellowship) (see Vol. 2, p. 368) changed its name to Johannine Daist Communion.

★165★
**Katharsis**

**Defunct:** For historical information, see Vol. 2, p. 48.

★166★
**Liberal Catholic Church, Province of the United States (San Diego)**

**New Name:** The Liberal Catholic Church (Miranda, Calif.) (see Vol. 2, p. 152) changed its name to Liberal Catholic Church, Province of the United States (San Diego).

★167★
**Life Action Foundation**

**New Name:** The House of Love and Prayer (see Vol. 2, p. 326) changed its name to Life Action Foundation.

★168★
**Ministry of Universal Wisdom**

**Defunct:** For historical information, see Vol. 2, p. 205.

★169★
**Minnesota Baptist Association**

**New Name:** The Minnesota Baptist Convention (see Vol. 1, p. 379) changed its name to Minnesota Baptist Association.

★170★
**Missionaries of the New Truth**

**Defunct:** For historical information, see Vol. 2, p. 463.

★171★
**Monastery of the Holy Protection of the Blessed Virgin Mary**

**New Name:** Sri Ma Anandamayi Monastery (see Vol. 2, p. 384) changed its name to Monastery of the Holy Protection of the Blessed Virgin Mary.

★172★
**Morse Fellowship**

**Defunct:** For historical information, see Vol. 2, p. 121.

★173★
**Nemeton**

**Defunct:** For historical information, see Vol. 2, p. 292.

★174★
**Neo-Dianic Faith**

**Defunt:** For historical information, see Vol. 2, p. 291.

★175★
**New Age Church of Christ**

**New Name:** The Bridge to Freedom (see Vol. 2, p. 159) changed its name to New Age Church of Christ.

★176★
**New York Sacred Tantrics**

**Defunct:** For historical information, see Vol. 2, p. 381.

★177★
**North American Episcopal Church**

**Merged:** The North American Episcopal Church (see Vol. 1, p. 54) merged into the American Episcopal Church.

★178★
**Old Orthodox Catholic Patriarchate of America**

**New Name:** The Christ Orthodox Catholic Exarchate of Americas and Eastern Hemisphere (see Vol. 1, p. 37) changed its name to Old Orthodox Catholic Patriarchate of America.

★179★
**Old Roman Catholic Church in North America**

**New Name:** The Old Roman Catholic Church (English Rite) (see Vol. 1, p. 43) changed its name to Old Roman Catholic Church in North America.

★180★
**Old Roman Catholic Church in the U.S.**

**Defunct:** For historical information, see Vol. 1, p. 42.

★181★
**Open Goddess**

**Defunct:** For historical information, see Vol. 2, p. 282.

★182★
**Order of Osirus**

**Defunct:** For historical information, see Vol. 2, p. 278.

★183★
**Ordo Templi Orientis (Roanoke, Virginia)**

**Defunct:** For historical information, see Vol. 2, p. 260.

★184★
**Ordo Templi Satanas**

**Defunct:** For historical information, see Vol. 2, p. 304.

★185★
**Orthodox Old Roman Catholic Church, II (Skelton)**

**Merged:** The Orthodox Old Roman Catholic Church, II (Skelton) (see Vol. 1, p. 41) merged into the Byzantine Catholic Church (see Supp., entry 18).

★186★
**Our Lady of Endor Coven, the Ophite Cultus Satanus**

**Defunct:** For historical information, see Vol. 2, p. 301.

★187★
**Pagan Way**

**Defunct:** For historical information, see Vol. 2, p. 289.

★188★
**Pan-African Orthodox Christian Church**

**New Name:** The Black Christian Nationalist Church (see Vol. 2, p. 334) changed its name to Pan-African Orthodox Christian Church.

★189★
**People's Temple Christian (Disciples) Church**

**Defunct:** For historical information, see Vol. 2, p. 224.

★190★
**Polish Catholic Church**

**Defunct:** For historical information, see Vol. 1, p. 36.

★191★
**Presbyterian Church in the United States**

**Merged:** The Presbyterian Church in the United States (see Vol. 1, p. 135) merged into the Presbyterian Church (U.S.A.) (see Supp., entry 21).

★192★
**Primitive Church of Jesus Christ (Bickertonite)**

**Merged:** The Primitive Church of Jesus Christ (Bickertonite) (see Vol. 2, p. 19) merged into the Church of Jesus Christ (Bickertonite).

★193★
**Process Church of the Final Judgment**

**Defunct:** For historical information, see Vol. 2, p. 230.

★194★
**Prophetic Herald Ministry**

**Defunct:** For historical information, see Vol. 1, p. 450.

★195★
**Rajneesh Foundation International**

**New Name:** The Rajneesh Meditation Center (see Vol. 2, p. 385) changed its name to Rajneesh Foundation International.

★196★
**Reformed Soto Zen Church**

**New Name:** The Zen Mission Society (see Vol. 2, p. 418) changed its name to Reformed Soto Zen Church.

★197★
**Renaissance Church of Beauty**

**New Name:** The Brotherhood of the Spirit (see Vol. 2, p. 45) changed its name to Renaissance Church of Beauty.

★198★
**Runic Society**

**Defunct:** For historical information, see Vol. 2, p. 297.

★199★
**Saiva Siddhanta Church**

**New Name:** The Subramaniya Yoga Order (see Vol. 2, p. 369) changed its name to Saiva Siddhanta Church.

**★200★**
**Sanatana Dharma Foundation**

**New Name:** The Institute of Ability (see Vol. 2, p. 223) changed its name to Sanatana Dharma Foundation.

**★201★**
**School of Esoteric Christianity**

**Defunct:** For historical information, see Vol. 2, p. 63.

**★202★**
**Serbian Orthodox Church in Diaspora**

**New Name:** The Serbian Orthodox Diocese for the United States and Canada (see Vol. 1, p. 69) changed its name to Serbian Orthodox Church in Diaspora.

**★203★**
**Seventh Day Baptist General Conference U.S.A. & Canada, Ltd.**

**New Name:** The Seventh-Day Baptist General Conference (see Vol. 1, p. 401) changed its name to Seventh Day Baptist General Conference U.S.A. & Canada, Ltd.

**★204★**
**Sisters of the Amber**

**Defunct:** For historical information, see Vol. 2, p. 123.

**★205★**
**Sonorama Society**

**Defunct:** For historical information, see Vol. 2, p. 379.

**★206★**
**Star of Truth Foundation**

**Defunct:** For historical information, see Vol. 1, p. 500.

**★207★**
**Thee Satanic Church**

**Defunct:** For historical information, see Vol. 2, p. 305.

**★208★**
**Thee Satanic Orthodox Church of Nethilum Rite**

**Defunct:** For historical information, see Vol. 2, p. 304.

**★209★**
**United Presbyterian Church in the United States of America**

**Merged:** The United Presbyterian Church in the United States of America (see Vol. 1, p. 124) merged into the Presbyterian Church (U.S.A.) (see Supp., entry 21).

**★210★**
**Vajradhatu**

**New Name:** Karma Dzong (Kargyupa Sect) (see Vol. 2, p. 432) changed its name to Vajradhatu.

**★211★**
**The Way International**

**New Name:** The Way Biblical Research Center (see Vol. 2, p. 449) changed its name to The Way International.

**★212★**
**WFLK Fountain of the World**

**Defunct:** For historical information, see Vol. 2, p. 39.

**★213★**
**The World Community**

**New Name:** Prema Dharmasala (see Vol. 2, p. 362) changed its name to The World Community.

**★214★**
**Yoga Research Foundation**

**New Name:** The International School of Yoga and Vedanta (see Vol. 2, p. 366) changed its name to Yoga Research Foundation.

**★215★**
**Yogiraj Sect (Swanandashram)**

**Defunct:** For historical information, see Vol. 2, p. 375.

# Religious Group Index

This index interfiles references to *The Encyclopedia of American Religions,* Volumes 1 and 2, first edition, with references to the first edition *Supplement.*

References in the index are identified as follows:

Italicized numbers refer to Volume 1 or Volume 2 of the first edition.
Page numbers follow the colon.

The italicized designation *Supp* refers to the *Supplement* to the first edition.
Entry numbers follow the colon.
Boldface numbers indicate a main entry.

*1* or *2* refers to Volume 1 or Volume 2 of the first edition; page numbers follow. *Supp* refers to the *Supplement* of the first edition; entry numbers follow. Boldface numbers indicate main entry.

*1* or *2* refers to Volume 1 or Volume 2 of the first edition; page numbers follow. *Supp* refers to the *Supplement* of the first edition; entry numbers follow. Boldface numbers indicate main entry.

Religious Group Index

*1* or *2* refers to Volume 1 or Volume 2 of the first edition; page numbers follow. *Supp* refers to the *Supplement* of the first edition; entry numbers follow. Boldface numbers indicate main entry.

Religious Group Index

*1* or *2* refers to Volume 1 or Volume 2 of the first edition; page numbers follow. *Supp* refers to the *Supplement* of the first edition; entry numbers follow. Boldface numbers indicate main entry.

1 or 2 refers to Volume 1 or Volume 2 of the first edition; page numbers follow. Supp refers to the Supplement of the first edition; entry numbers follow. Boldface numbers indicate main entry.

Religious Group Index

**Religious Group Index**

*1* or *2* refers to Volume 1 or Volume 2 of the first edition; page numbers follow. *Supp* refers to the *Supplement* of the first edition; entry numbers follow. Boldface numbers indicate main entry.

**Religious Group Index**

1 or 2 refers to Volume 1 or Volume 2 of the first edition; page numbers follow. Supp refers to the Supplement of the first edition; entry numbers follow. Boldface numbers indicate main entry.

Religious Group Index

*1* or *2* refers to Volume 1 or Volume 2 of the
first edition; page numbers follow. *Supp* refers
to the *Supplement* of the first edition; entry
numbers follow. Boldface numbers indicate
main entry.

*1* or *2* refers to Volume 1 or Volume 2 of the first edition; page numbers follow. *Supp* refers to the *Supplement* of the first edition; entry numbers follow. Boldface numbers indicate main entry.

*1* or *2* refers to Volume 1 or Volume 2 of the first edition; page numbers follow. *Supp* refers to the *Supplement* of the first edition; entry numbers follow. Boldface numbers indicate main entry.

**Religious Group Index**

*1* or *2* refers to Volume 1 or Volume 2 of the
first edition; page numbers follow. *Supp* refers
to the *Supplement* of the first edition; entry
numbers follow. Boldface numbers indicate
main entry.

1 or 2 refers to Volume 1 or Volume 2 of the first edition; page numbers follow. Supp refers to the Supplement of the first edition; entry numbers follow. Boldface numbers indicate main entry.

Religious Group Index

*1* or *2* refers to Volume 1 or Volume 2 of the first edition; page numbers follow. *Supp* refers to the *Supplement* of the first edition; entry numbers follow. Boldface numbers indicate main entry.

1 or 2 refers to Volume 1 or Volume 2 of the first edition; page numbers follow. Supp refers to the Supplement of the first edition; entry numbers follow. Boldface numbers indicate main entry.

Religious Group Index

*1* or *2* refers to Volume 1 or Volume 2 of the first edition; page numbers follow. *Supp* refers to the *Supplement* of the first edition; entry numbers follow. Boldface numbers indicate main entry.

*1* or *2* refers to Volume 1 or Volume 2 of the first edition; page numbers follow. *Supp* refers to the *Supplement* of the first edition; entry numbers follow. Boldface numbers indicate main entry.

*1* or *2* refers to Volume 1 or Volume 2 of the first edition; page numbers follow. *Supp* refers to the *Supplement* of the first edition; entry numbers follow. Boldface numbers indicate main entry.

*1* or *2* refers to Volume 1 or Volume 2 of the first edition; page numbers follow. *Supp* refers to the *Supplement* of the first edition; entry numbers follow. Boldface numbers indicate main entry.

Religious Group Index

*1* or *2* refers to Volume 1 or Volume 2 of the first edition; page numbers follow. *Supp* refers to the *Supplement* of the first edition; entry numbers follow. Boldface numbers indicate main entry.

Religious Group Index

# Personal Name Index

This index interfiles references to *The Encyclopedia of American Religions,* Volumes 1 and 2, first edition, with references to the first edition *Supplement.*

References in the index are identified as follows:

Italicized numbers refer to Volume 1 or Volume 2 of the first edition.
Page numbers follow the colon.

The italicized designation *Supp* refers to the *Supplement* to the first edition.
Entry numbers follow the colon.

Abbey, W.H.  *2:*482
Abbinga, Hermann F.  *1:*52
Abd 'Allah, Iman Isa, Ibn Abu Bakr Muhammed  *2:*343
Abdel-Messiah, Marcos  *1:*86
Abd-Ishu, Antonius  *1:*44
Abd-Ru-Shin. *See* Bernhardt, Oskar Ernst
Abdu'l-Baha  *2:*352; *Supp:*88
Abdul-Jabbar, Kareem  *2:*342
Abdullah al-Yafi-i, Sheikh  *Supp:*83
Abel  *Supp:*47
Abell, Theodore Curtis  *1:*155
Abernathy, Donald  *1:*29
Abhayananda, Swami  *2:*384
Abraham, David  *2:*450-51
Acker, Richard C.  *Supp:*14
Adair, Gregory R.P.  *1:*79
Adam, E.B.  *1:*478
Adam, Jack C.  *1:*53
Adams, A.P.  *1:*482, 497
Adams, Barry  *2:*48
Adams, Fred  *2:*287
Adams, John Quincey  *1:*309
Adams, Joseph H.  *Supp:*33
Adams, Ruth  *2:*244
Adamski, George  *2:*199, 201-2, 203
Addison, Clarence C.  *1:*303
Adler, Felix  *1:*156
Afton, Anita  *2:*124, 126
Agapoa, Tony  *2:*103
Agyeman, Jaramogi Abebe. *See* Cleage, Albert B.
Ahandakapila, Swami  *Supp:*97
Ahmad, Mirza Ghulam  *2:*340
Ahmed, Basher  *1:*44
Ahmed, Muhammed, Al Mahdi  *2:*343
Ahnfelt, Oscar  *1:*166
Aiken, John W.  *2:*197
Aiken, Louisa  *2:*197
Aitkin, Robert  *2:*419
Aivanhov, Omran Michael  *Supp:*72

Ajari. *See* Pemchekov-Warwick, Dr. N.G.
Akana, Akaiko  *2:*482
Akana, Francis K.  *2:*482
Akhnaton  *2:*189
Akizaki, Takeo  *2:*439
Akizaki, Yoshio  *2:*439
Al-Adawiya, Rabi'a  *2:*344
Alamo, Susan  *2:*446, 448
Alamo, Tony  *2:*446, 448
Alan, Jim  *2:*283
'Ala-ud-Din, Halveti Sheikh Ali  *Supp:*82
Albright, Jacob  *1:*177
Alcyone. *See* Krishnamurti, Jeddu
Alexander, Agnes Baldwin  *2:*352
Alexander, Archbishop  *1:*7
Alexander, Dr.  *2:*268
Alexander VI, Pope  *1:*17
Alexandros, Bishop  *1:*64
Alexis, Patriarch of Moscow  *1:*59-60
Al-Ghazali  *2:*344-45
Al-Habib, Muhammed, Ibn  *2:*346
Al-Hasan of Basra  *2:*343
Ali  *2:*336-37
Ali, Duse Mohammed  *2:*339
Ali, Noble Drew. *See* Drew, Timothy
Al-Jerrahi, Muzaffer Ozak, Sheikh  *Supp:*82
Alldaffer, Fannie  *1:*233
Alldaffer, Tracy  *1:*233
Allen, Asa Alonzo  *1:*283, 285
Allen, Ethan  *1:*150
Allen, J.H.  *1:*448
Allen, James  *2:*66
Allen, Richard  *1:*189-90
Allen, Stuart  *1:*435-36
Allingham, Cedric  *2:*199
Allred, Owen  *Supp:*59
Allred, Rulon C.  *2:*16, 17, 18; *Supp:*59, 61

Almeida, Florentino  *1:*309
Alpert, Richard  *2:*49, 194, 368, 382
Al Shadhili, Shaikh of Fez, Morocco  *2:*346
Alspaugh, Clair H.  *Supp:*35
Altisi, Jackie  *2:*204
Alvarez, Julius  *1:*44
Alvarez of Ceylon, A.F.X.  *1:*32
Al-Wahshi, Babaji  *2:*349-50
Alwood, Muriel C.  *1:*308
Ambrose, St.  *1:*15
Amenhotep IV  *2:*182, 209, 295
Amman, Jacob  *1:*335-36
Amritananda, Swami  *Supp:*97
Anandamayi, Sri Sri, Mataji  *2:*384
Anandamurti (ji), Shrii Shrii  *2:*381; *Supp:*94, 100
Anderson, Carl  *2:*199
Anderson, Lester B.  *2:*43
Anderson, Mrs.  *2:*187
Anderson, Wing  *2:*116
Andreae, Valentin  *2:*48
Andrew, J.J.  *1:*409-10
Andrews, E.A.  *2:*475
Andrews, James F.  *2:*475
Andrey, Bishop  *1:*66-67
Angelucci, Orfeo M.  *2:*199
Anson, Matthew  *1:*42
Anson, Peter  *1:*33
Appu, Radha  *2:*436
Arboo, Madame  *2:*270
Arechaga, Frederic de  *2:*298
Arius  *1:*2, 482
Arjan  *2:*387
Arminius, Jacob  *1:*113, 175
Armitage, Thomas  *1:*358
Armstrong, Garner Ted  *1:*471, 473, 475
Armstrong, Herbert W.  *1:*448, 471-72, 473, 475
Armstrong, Hunt  *1:*307
Arnold, David  *2:*33

Arnold, Eberhard  2:33
Arnold, Gottfried  1:342
Arnold, Kenneth  2:198
Arnold, Newton  2:151
Arnot, Andrew  1:125
Arvidson, Gary  1:475
Asbury, Francis  1:138, 175, 177, 179, 189, 190, 192
Ashiata, Shiemash  2:350
Ashitzu, Jitsuzen  2:401
Asoka  2:395, 396
Assagioli, Roberto  2:148
Astley, Norman  2:187
Astrid. See Moore, Jeanene
Athanasius, Patriarch of Alexandria  1:86
Athenagoras I, Patriarch  1:64
Atkin, William H.  2:152
Atkinson, W.W.  2:60
Atmananda  Supp:92
Attakai, Mary  2:196
Aubrey, George  1:278
Audrey, J.W.  Supp:30
Augustine, St.  1:11, 50, 456
Aurobindo, Ghose, Sri  2:373-74
Aurobindo, Sri  2:237
Austin, Mary  2:279
Austin, Tom  1:306
Avadhuta, Acharya Vimalananda  2:381
Averky, Archbishop  1:67
Awrey, Daniel  1:247
Ayau, Edward  2:482
Ayer, A.J.  1:152
Ayllon, Vasquez de  1:21

Baal Shem Tov, Israel  2:318, 323, 329
Baba. See Paramahansa, Swami Muktananda
Baba Ram Dass. See Alpert, Richard
Baba, Satya Sai  2:373
Babajan, Hazrat  2:347
Babaji, Guru  2:367
Bacchus  Supp:113
Backus, Isaac  1:372
Bacon, Francis  2:179
Bader, Augustine  1:458
Bagwell, J.D.  1:476
Baha'u'llih  2:352
Bailes, Frederick  2:56
Bailey, Alice La Trobe Bateman  2:48, 144, 145, 146, 147, 148, 149, 200, 245; Supp:67, 68
Bailey, Dorothy  2:169
Bailey, Foster  2:145, 147

Bailey, Mary  2:147
Baird, Thomas L.  1:186
Baker, Aleta  2:258
Baker, Charles F.  1:437
Baker, Dean  1:443
Baker, Frank  2:65
Baker, George. See Divine, Father Major J.
Baker, Martha  2:65
Baker, Mary. See Eddy, Mary Baker
Baker, Oscar M.  1:436
Baker, Richard  2:417
Balboa, Vasco Nunez de  1:21
Ballard, Donald  2:156, 158, 159
Ballard, Edna Wheeler (Lotus)  2:155, 156, 158, 159, 162
Ballard, Guy  2:155, 156, 158, 159, 160, 161, 162
Ballard, Marlin B.  2:480
Ballou, Adin  2:27
Ballou, Hosea  1:149
Banks, A.A.  1:394
Baptiste, Walt  2:391
Baradeus, Jacob  1:84
Barbeau, Archbishop Andre  Supp:8
Barber, M.E.  1:440, 441
Barbour, Nelson H.  1:481, 482
Barcynski, Leonard R.  Supp:70, 74
Barcynski, Vivian  Supp:70, 74
Barker, Frank  1:136
Barlow, John Y.  Supp:59
Barnabe, Julian  1:275
Barnes, Harry Elmer  1:155
Barnett, M.J.  2:54
Barrett, Francis  2:251, 252, 253, 254
Barrett, Harrison D.  2:96
Barrett, Thomas Ball  1:272
Barrington-Evans, W.A.  1:43
Barrow, R.G.  1:75
Barrows, Charles M.  2:54
Barth, Hattie M.  1:260
Barth, Karl  2:466
Barth, Kenneth L.  1:428
Barth, Paul T.  1:260
Bartholomew, St.  1:1, 2, 82
Bartkow, Paul  1:283
Bartlemen, Frank  1:24
Bartok, Eve  2:351
Barton, Michael X.  2:201
Bashir, Anthony  1:70, 77
Basil the Great, St.  1:86
Basilios, Abuna  1:87
Basilius Abdullah III  2:155
Bateman, Samuel  2:15
Bates, Joseph  1:459, 465
Bates, Lonnie  1:293
Bauer, Bishop Roy G.  Supp:7
Baughman, J.L.  2:64

Bausch, William J.  1:7, 20
Bautista, Margarito  Supp:59
Baxter, Richard  2:85, 93
Bayle, Pierre  1:152
Beachy, Moses  1:338
Bean, Scipio  1:190
Beckbill, W.W.  1:188, 189
Becker, Frank E.  2:435
Becker, Peter  1:342
Beckett, Thomas A.  1:4
Beckles, J.T.  1:79
Beckwith, Edwin Burt  2:151
Bedini, Gaetano  1:24
"Bee, the." See Bizich, Tracy B.
Begg, Mirza Wahiduddin  Supp:81
"Beggar, the"  2:386
Beidler, Paul  2:424; Supp:36, 104
Beissel, Conrad  1:400
Beitz, W.F.  1:103
Bell, E.N.  1:271, 288
Bellingham, Richard  2:279
Ben Ami  2:334
Ben Carter. See Ben Ami
Ben Israel, Naphtali  2:334
Benade, William  2:91
Benedetto, Francis di  Supp:3
Benedict, David  1:356
Benedict, Samuel Dorlin  1:39
Benik, Anthony  2:112
Benjamine, Elbert  2:187
Bennett, J.G.  2:35
Bennett, Paul  1:208
Bent, David W.  2:211
Berg, David  2:453
Berger, Morroe  2:339
Berkeley, George  2:53
Bernard, Pierre Arnold. See Coon, Peter
Bernard, St.  1:16
Bernardone, John. See Francis of Assisi
Berner, H. Charles  2:223
Bernhardt, Oskar Ernst  2:120
Berry, W.J.  1:388, 389
Bertiaux, Michael  2:265
Besant, Annie  2:139-40, 141, 142, 143, 144, 145, 150, 151, 165, 166, 376; Supp:68
Bethards, Betty  2:227
Bethurum, Truman  2:199
Bey, Hamid  2:149, 213, 214
Bhagat Singh Thind  2:387
Bhagawat, Sri Arunachala Bhakta  2:380
Bhajan, Yogi  2:388
Bhattacharya, Vijaya  2:436
Bias, Clifford  2:99, 100
Bickerton, William  2:19
Biedler, Paul  Supp:35, 36
Bill, Annie C.  2:78, 329
Billet, Grant Timothy  1:44, 45

---

Bingham, Mrs. Frank   *2*:55, 62
Bishop, Beatrice Gaulton   *2*:99
Bishop, Gladden   *2*:4
Bishop, John L.   *1*:494
Bizich, Tracy B.   *1*:498
Blackstone, William E.   *1*:412, 416
Blakeley, Jesse N.   *1*:211
Blanchard, Charles A.   *1*:430
Blau, Amram   *2*:323
Blaurock, George   *1*:322
Blavatsky, Helena Petrovna   *2*:86, 135-36, 139, 140, 141, 143, 144, 150, 157, 165, 167, 171, 199, 200; *Supp*:66
Blessing, William Lester   *1*:497-98
Blighton, Paul W.   *2*:190, 191
Blighton, Ruth   *2*:191
Blob, Charlotte   *2*:202
Blumhardt, Christoph   *2*:34
Boardman, William   *1*:202, 203
Boccaccio, Gaetano   *1*:487
Bodhisattvaguru, Father Satchak-rananda   *Supp*:96
Bodine, William L.   *1*:477
Boehm, Martin   *1*:177
Boehme, Jacob   *2*:179
Bohler, Peter   *1*:168
Boland, J.M.   *1*:204
Bolle, Simon   *Supp*:37
Bolle, Soren   *Supp*:37
Boltwood, Charles Denis   *1*:54; *Supp*:17
Bond, W. Allen   *1*:476
Bonewits, Isaac   *2*:253, 293
Bonhoeffer, Dietrich   *2*:466
Boniface, St.   *1*:11
Bonner, E.H.   *2*:470
Bonneville, Dr. George de   *1*:148
Booth, A.E.   *1*:422
Booth, Ballington   *1*:215
Booth, Harry L.   *2*:304
Booth, L.V.   *1*:394
Booth, Maud   *1*:215
Booth, William   *1*:214, 215
Boruta, Victor   *2*:264
Boryszewski, Francis Ignatius   *1*:36
Boswell, Lee   *2*:106
Bosworth, F.F.   *1*:283
Botkin, Gleb   *2*:286-87
Bottorff, O.B.   *1*:427
Boughan, Dan B.   *2*:113
Bow, Mary Martha   *2*:168
Bowden, Eileen   *2*:81
Bowe, J.   *1*:297
Bowling, Anna   *Supp*:22
Bowling, Hugh   *1*:263
Bownd, Nicholas   *1*:399
Bowne, Borden Parker   *1*:204
Bowne, Hugh   *1*:197, 198
Boyd, James   *1*:421, 422
Boyd, R.H.   *1*:393-94

Boyle, Cunningham   *1*:499
Boyle, Justin   *1*:34
Boynton, Paul   *Supp*:10
Boyse, John   *1*:131
Braden, Charles   *2*:140
Bradlaugh, Charles   *1*:152
Bradley, A.D.   *1*:293
Bradley, Lasserre, Jr.   *1*:388
Brady, Enid   *2*:212
Brandeis, Louis D.   *2*:314
Brandreth, H.R.T.   *1*:33
Branham, William   *1*:283
Brannon, Hiram T.   *1*:354
Brasher, John L.   *1*:203
Braswell, Herman Flake   *1*:499-500
Bray, David, Sr.   *2*:218
Brayton, Jean   *2*:259
Brayton, Richard M.   *2*:259
Breasted, James H.   *2*:293
Breese-Whiting, Kathryn   *2*:71
Brenneman, Daniel   *1*:332
Bresee, Phineas F.   *1*:219
Brett, Pliny   *1*:179, 230
Brewer, G.C.   *1*:406
Briggs, Charles A.   *1*:126
Briggs, Jason   *2*:10
Briggs, John Bigelow   *1*:477
Bright, Charlotte   *2*:101
Bright, John   *1*:313
Bright Star. *See* Young, June
Briller, James, Sr.   *1*:216
Brinkman, George   *1*:275
Brinser, Matthias   *1*:346
Brintone, Anne   *2*:279
Brisbane, Albert   *2*:26-27
Britten, Emma Harding   *2*:187
Broadbent, J. Leslie   *Supp*:61
Brock, Dr. and Mrs.   *2*:390
Brockman, Rev. Christopher L.   *Supp*:23
Bronson, R.T.   *2*:13
Brook, Peggy   *2*:79
Brooke, Anthony   *2*:122, 125
Brooke, Sir James   *2*:122
Brooks, Arthur Wolfort   *1*:51
Brooks, Fannie James   *2*:55
Brooks, James H.   *1*:412, 416, 424
Brooks, John P.   *1*:204, 218
Brooks, Nona L.   *2*:62
Broshears, Ray   *2*:457
Brostek, Mildred   *1*:265
Brother Francis. *See* Raymond, Ralph F.
Brother John   *2*:41
Brother Philip. *See* Williamson, George Hunt
Brothers, Richard   *1*:447, 494, 495
Brothers, William Henry Francis   *1*:32, 36, 39, 40-41, 76
Brown, E.D.   *1*:192
Brown, Gordon   *2*:79

Brown, Kingdon L.   *2*:111-12
Brown, P.W.   *1*:306
Brown, Ray O.   *1*:417
Brown, W. Montgomery   *1*:75
Brown, Walter X.   *1*:40; *Supp*:7
Browne, Robert   *1*:115
Brubaker, Jennie   *2*:290
Bruce, Robert, King of Scotland   *2*:9
Bruffett, Fred   *1*:208
Bruffett, Hallie   *1*:208
Bruggeman, David   *1*:415
Brunier, Nina Fern   *2*:246
Bryan, William   *1*:447
Bryant, Steve N.   *1*:269
Bryant, W.F.   *1*:247, 255
Bryant, W.R.   *Supp*:30
Bubar, David N.   *2*:238
Bubba Free John   *2*:368-69
Buber, Martin   *2*:310, 327, 328
Buchholtz, Frederic A.   *2*:274
Buchman, Frank   *2*:476
Buckland, Joan   *2*:284
Buckland, Raymond   *2*:279-80, 284
Buckland, Rosemary   *2*:279-80
Buckles, Edwin A.   *1*:266
Buczynski, Ed Hermes   *2*:275
Buddah. *See* Gautama, Siddhartha
Budge, E.A. Wallis   *2*:293
Bul-Ali   *2*:339
Buller, Voy M.   *1*:257
Bullinger, Ethelbert   *2*:449
Bullinger, Ethelbert William   *1*:417, 427, 434, 435, 436, 437, 439
Bultema, Harry   *1*:435, 437
Bultmann, Rudolf   *2*:466
Bunderlin, Johann   *1*:327
Bundy, George   *1*:432
Bunger, Fred S.   *2*:129
Bunjiro, Kawate   *2*:441
Bunker, John   *2*:99
Burgoyne, T.H.   *2*:187
Burke, Robert W.C.   *2*:64
Burkhart, Rev. Roy A.   *Supp*:111
Burkmar, Lucius   *2*:51
Burks, Arthur   *2*:111
Burns, Douglas Murray   *2*:402
Burns, James Edward   *Supp*:14
Burns, Robert Alfred   *1*:43, 46; *Supp*:4
Burns, Robert E.   *Supp*:8
Burruss, King Hezekia   *1*:226
Burton, Malcolm K.   *1*:142
Bushnell, Horace   *1*:117
Bussell, D.J.   *2*:213
Butler, Hiram Erastus   *2*:42

---

*1* or *2* refers to Volume 1 or Volume 2 of the first edition; page numbers follow. *Supp* refers to the *Supplement* of the first edition; entry numbers follow.

Personal Name Index

*1* or *2* refers to Volume 1 or Volume 2 of the
first edition; page numbers follow. *Supp* refers
to the *Supplement* of the first edition; entry
numbers follow.

1 or 2 refers to Volume 1 or Volume 2 of the
first edition; page numbers follow. Supp refers
to the Supplement of the first edition; entry
numbers follow.

129

Dov Baer, Rabbi, the Mittler Rebbe  2:321

Dow, Harry A.   2:153

Dow, Lorenzo   1:197

Dowd, F.B.   2:180

Dower, William H.   *Supp*:66

Dowers, Mary Martha. *See* Bow, Mary Martha

Dowie, John Alexander   1:247, 284; 2:472, 473

Dowling, Levi H.   2:94

Downing, Barry H.   2:200

Draft, Johnnie   *Supp*:29

Draves, W.A.   2:13

Dresser, Annetta   2:52, 54

Dresser, Horatio   2:54

Dresser, Julius   2:52, 54

Drew, Timothy   2:339, 341

Drummond, Henry   1:252, 253; 2:66

Duby, William Ralph   2:129, 130, 131

Duce, Ivy O.   2:347

Dugger, A.N.   1:479-80

Dugger, Charles Andy   1:480

Dugger, Effie   1:480

Dugger, Naomi   1:480

Dujom, Rinpoche   2:432

Duluth, Sieur Daniel Greysolon  1:21

Dunkley, Archibald   *Supp*:77

Dunnington, Lewis   2:56

DuPlessis, David J.   1:250-51

Durbin, Harold C.   2:110

Durham, Ron   1:406

Durham, W.H.   1:273, 280

Durkee, Steve   2:49

Duval, Pierre   1:124

Dvivedi, Manilal N.   2:359

Dwight, Timothy   1:118; 2:339

Dycus, W.M.   1:134

Dyson, Fred   2:447


Eachta Eacha Na   2:16

Earle, A.B.   1:202

Easton, Enos   1:469

Easwaran, Eknath   2:370

Eaton, E.L.   1:483

Eberhardt, Christoph   1:102

Eddy, Asa Gilbert   2:75

Eddy, Mary Baker   2:52, 53, 54, 74-78, 79, 328

Edminster, Clyde   1:451

Edson, Hiram   1:465

Edward VI, King of England  1:4, 49

Edwards, Jonathan   1:118, 375

Effendi, Shoghi   2:352-53; *Supp*:87, 88

Efuntola, King   2:269

Egli, Henry   1:337

Eichenstein, Lisher Y.   2:325

Eielsen, Elling   1:104

Eikerenkoetter, Rev. Frederick, II, 2:67; *Supp*:63

Einstein, Albert   *Supp*:88

Eklund, John Theodore   2:151, 152

Elizabeth I, Queen of England  1:4, 49, 114

Elliott, Herbert J.   2:480

Ellis, Henry Milton   2:72

Ellison, Jim   *Supp*:48

Elton, Eve   2:66

Emerson, Ralph Waldo   1:149; 2:26, 359; *Supp*:62

Emery, George   2:217

Emry, Sheldon   1:450-51

Enderle, Herman   2:290

Enfantin, Barthe'lemy Prosper  2:25

Engel, Jacob   1:346

Engel, Leopold   2:128

Englert, Paul   1:154

Enochs, Emmet Neil   1:55

Enos, Leonard   2:436

Entfelder, Christian   1:327

Ephesus   1:7

Erasmus, Desiderius   1:18, 19

Erdmann, Paul   2:46

Ericson, Denis   1:73

Errico, Rocco   2:72

Erwitt, Boris   2:435

Esbjorn, Lars Paul   1:94

Eschmann, John   1:382

Eshelman, M.M.   1:448

Estes, Bishop H. Carlisle   *Supp*:113

Estrada, Jose Manuel, Ven. Sat Arhat (Missionary)   *Supp*:71

Eusebius of Caesarea   1:9, 82

Eustace, Herbert W.   2:79

Eutyches, Archimandrite   1:82

Evans, J. Ellwood   *Supp*:45

Evans, Warren Felt   2:52, 53, 54

Evokim, Archbishop   1:77

Ewart, Frank J.   1:287, 288

Ewing, Finis   1:133


Faitlovitch, Jacques   2:330

Fambough, William   1:180

Fanning, Tolbert   1:405

Faquaragon, Alexandro B.   1:311

Fard, W.D.   2:341

Farrakhan, Abdul Haleem   *Supp*:79

Farrell, Fr. Michael   *Supp*:2

Farrow, Lucy   1:296

Farwell, William   2:67

Father Divine   2:224-25

Fauth, Gordon   1:480

Fedchenkov, Benjamin   1:61

Fehervary, Thomas   1:39; *Supp*:8

Feild, Reshad   *Supp*:84

Feldman, Mark   2:264

Ferguson, Joseph T.   2:65

Ferguson, Mabel G.   1:308

Ferguson, Robert A.   2:104

Ferguson, T.P.   1:224

Ferguson, William   2:210

Ferriere, Serge Raynaud de la, Sat Guru (Master)   *Supp*:71

Fesi, John Dominic   *Supp*:7

Fetting, Otto   2:13

Feuerbach, Ludwig   1:152

Fichte, Johann   2:53

Fife, Sam   1:500

Filer, Clifford   1:235

Fillmore, Charles   2:55, 57, 59, 73

Finch, Ralph G.   1:212

Finleyson, John   1:447

Finney, Charles G.   1:202, 224; 2:2

Firmilian, Archiman Drite   1:68

Firmilian, Bishop   1:69

Fisher, David   2:292

Fisher, George   1:208

Fisk, Alfred G.   2:467

Fist, Fletcher   2:45

Fitch, Charles   1:461

Fitch, Ed   2:289, 290

Fitch, Lillian G.   1:286

Fitch, William   1:286

Fitzgerald, B.J.   2:103

Flanders, Lloyd   2:18

Flanders, Moroni   2:18

Fleischmann, Konrad Anton  1:381-82

Flenner, Millard J.   1:449

Fletcher, Emery   2:21

Fletcher, Jack   2:131

Fletcher, John   1:247, 261

Fletcher, Pat   2:131

Fletcher, R.J.   2:21

Flexer, Dorothy Graff   2:100, 109

Flexer, Russell J.   2:109

Flexor, Dorothy   2:100

Flowers, Amanda   2:99

Flowers, J. Roswell   1:271

Fludd, Robert   2:178

"Fly, the." *See* Kaiser, Elworth Thomas

Flynn, W.W.   1:46

Ford, Arnold Josiah   2:331, 333

Ford, Arthur   2:98, 226

Ford, Henry   1:156

Ford, Jack   1:235

Ford, Lewis   1:305

Ford, Patricia du Mort   *Supp*:6

Forrest, Julia O.   2:101

Fort, Charles   2:200

Fosdick, Harry Emerson  *1*:126
Foster, Charles  *2*:2
Foster, Randolph S.  *1*:202, 203
Foster, Robert  *2*:5
Foster, Mrs. Thomas  *2*:401
Fourier, Charles  *2*:26
Fox, Arthur H.  *2*:462
Fox, Diane  *2*:462
Fox, Emmet  *2*:55, 64, 66
Fox, George  *1*:329, 347, 348, 349
Fox, Kate  *2*:94, 96
Fox, Margaretta  *2*:96
Fox, Selena  *2*:283
Fox, Stephen S.  *2*:474
Francesca, Aleuti.  *See* Francis, Marianne
Francescon, Louis  *1*:280
Francis, Marianne  *2*:208, 209
Francis of Assisi, St.  *1*:6, 13
Francis Xavier, St.  *2*:411
Franck, Sebastian  *1*:327
Francke, August Hermann  *1*:159-60, 400
Frangquist, David  *2*:293
Franke, Elmer E.  *1*:467
Frankfort, Henri  *2*:293
Franklin, Benjamin  *1*:405
Frantson, Frederick  *1*:167
Frater Achad. *See* Jones, Charles Stanfield
Frater Ichedemel. *See* White, Nelson H.
Frater 132. *See* Smith, Winifred T.
Frater 210. *See* Parsons, John W. (Jack)
Frazer, Dudley  *1*:278, 279
Frazier, Henry D.  *2*:235
Frazier, R.O.  *1*:317
Frederick I  *1*:457
Frederick II  *1*:457
Frederick Wilhelm III, King of Prussia  *1*:139
Fredricksen, Norman C.  *2*:107
Freeman, Carole  *2*:123
Freking, F.W.  *Supp*:3
French, H. Robb  *1*:236, 241
Freytag, F.L. Alexander  *1*:492
Friedlander, Solomon  *2*:325
Friedman, Mordecai Shlomo  *2*:325
Friedman, Moses  *2*:325
Fries, Howard  *1*:46
Fris, H.V.  *Supp*:4
Frisby, Neal  *1*:283, 284
Froehlich, Samuel Heinrich  *2*:471
Frogostein, Harold E.  *Supp*:66
Fromke, DeVern  *1*:443
Frost, Gavin  *2*:283
Frothingham, Octavius Brooks  *1*:151
Frumentius, Bishop  *1*:86
Fry, Daniel  *2*:206-7

Fujita, Reisai  *2*:437
Fujuhana, Kyodo  *2*:411
Fuller, Richard  *1*:367
Fuller, W.E.  *1*:261, 298
Fullerton, Alexander  *2*:142, 143
Fults, Pam  *2*:296
Fung, George D.  *2*:427
Fung, Paul F.  *2*:427
Funk, Christian  *1*:329

Ga, Macario V.  *Supp*:13
Gaard, Conrad  *1*:449
Gaddafi, Muammar  *2*:454
Gaebelein, Arno E.  *1*:426
Gaines, James A.  *Supp*:17
Galerius  *1*:8, 9
Galphin, John  *1*:392
Gamble, Charles  *1*:277
Gampopa  *2*:432
Gandhi, Mohandas K.  *2*:362, 385
Gandhi, Virchand A.  *2*:392
Ganneau, Mr.  *2*:253
Garcia Peraga, Juanita  *1*:286
Gardner, Gerald  *2*:266, 279
Gardnerm, Jack E.  *2*:235
Garlichs, Herman  *1*:139
Garman, W.O.H.  *1*:429
Garr, A.G.  *1*:265
Garrett, Leroy  *1*:406
Garrettson, Freeborn  *1*:190
Garrique, Florence  *2*:147
Garvey, Marcus  *2*:331, 339, 340;  *Supp*:77
Gasan, Jito  *2*:415
Gaskin, Stephen  *2*:47
Gasquoine, Earl P.  *Supp*:7
Gasteiner, Lovie Webb  *2*:175
Gates, Walter L.  *2*:13
Gattell, Benoni B.  *2*:118
Gauntlett, B.E.R.  *2*:150
Gautama, Siddhartha  *2*:393, 403, 405, 407, 410, 428, 436;  *Supp*:104
Gay, Ben F.  *2*:461
Gay, Marvin  *1*:477
Gayatri Devi, Srimata  *2*:361
Gayman, Daniel  *Supp*:47, 58
Gaynor, Annie Nicol  *Supp*:24
Gebelin, Count de  *2*:253
Geddes, Francis  *2*:467
Geirroldsson, Svein  *2*:296
Gelberman, Joseph H.  *2*:328
Gelesnoff, Vladimir M.  *1*:439
Gellatly, Alexander  *1*:125
Gentzel, Charles Boyd (Mark)  *2*:202
George, David  *1*:392
George, James Hardin  *1*:53
Georgins I. *See* Newman, Hugh George de Willmott
Gerling, Helene  *2*:102

Gerling, J. Bertram  *2*:102
Germain, St.  *2*:156, 157, 162, 164, 165
Germer, Karl Johannes  *2*:256, 260
Gestefeld, Ursula  *2*:54
Geyer, Heinrich  *1*:254
Gibbons, James Cardinal  *1*:25
Gibson, Joan  *2*:73
Gibson, John Paul  *2*:127
Gilbert, Nathaniel  *1*:189
Gilbert, Violet  *2*:209
Ginsburg, Steven  *2*:458
Girandola, Fr. Anthony J.  *Supp*:2
Giri, Nirmalananda  *2*:384
Glanvill, Joseph  *2*:85, 93
Glas, John  *1*:402
Gleason, Matt  *2*:244
Glendenning, Bishop of Scotland  *2*:9
Glendenning, Maurice Lerrie  *2*:8-9
Glendenonwyn  *2*:9
Glover, George Washington  *2*:75
Glover, Goodwife  *2*:86
Goddard, Dwight  *2*:401
Goerz, David  *1*:338
Goetz, Warren H.  *2*:212
Gold, E.J. *See* Al-Wahshi, Babaji
Goldman, Billy  *2*:15
Goldsmith, Emma  *2*:81
Goldsmith, Joel  *2*:80-81
Goldwater, Barry  *2*:469
Gonyo, Elrick  *Supp*:1
Gooding, Paul  *1*:345
Goodman, Steele  *2*:107
Goodrich, P.W.  *Supp*:11
Goodrich, Roy D.  *1*:492
Gordon, Adoniram J.  *1*:203, 416, 424
Gordon, Charles Robert  *2*:245
Gorman, George F.  *2*:198
Gortner, Marjoe  *1*:245
Goss, H.A.  *1*:288
Gottula, Gerard W.  *2*:238
Govan, John George  *1*:444
Govinda, Lama Anagarika  *2*:433
Grad, Bernard  *2*:84
Graham, Eli  *1*:376
Grant, Frederick  *1*:419, 422, 423
Grant, Heber J.  *2*:15
Grant, Kenneth  *2*:260, 261
Grant, W.V.  *1*:283, 284
Granville, Lord  *1*:163
Grave, Richard  *2*:121-22
Gravely, M.  *1*:288
Graves, James R.  *1*:372

Personal Name Index

Graves, Robert  2:287
Graves, Samuel R.  2:279
Gray, Charles W.  1:225, 226
Gray, Garver C.  1:310
Grebel, Conrad  1:322
Greed, John J.  Supp:2
Greeley, Andrew  1:27
Greely, Horace  2:94
Green, Alyce  2:379
Green, Elmer  2:240, 379
Greenbaum, Leon  2:78
Greenblatt, Joan  2:380
Greenblatt, Matthew  2:380
Greenwald, Levi Isaac  2:325
Gregory, Bishop  1:69
Gregory, St., the Illuminator  1:82
Gregory I the Great, Pope  1:10-11
Gregory VII, Pope  1:11-12
Gregory XVII, Pope. See De la
  Trinite, Father Jean
Grew, Henry  1:463
Grier, Albert C.  2:64
Griffith, Benjamin  1:366
Griffith, Glenn  1:236, 237, 240,
  242
Griggs, Russ  2:453
Grimes, Simon  2:433
Grochowski, Leon  1:36
Groeneveld, H.D.G.  2:91
Gross, Darwin  2:233
Grover, Iver C.  1:282
Groves, Anna  1:444
Grubber, James  1:252
Gruber, Eberhard Ludwig  2:35
Gruber, J.A.  2:35
Grumbein, Henry  1:347
Guibbory, Moses  2:327
Guillen, Miguel  1:306
Gulotti, Miraglia  1:37
Gunaratana, Mahathera Henepola
  2:403
Gunn, Beatrice  2:264
Gupta, Yogi  2:375
Guray, Nicolas  2:109
Gurdjieff, George Ivanovitch
  2:348-51
Gurley, Zenos  2:10
Gurney, John  1:201, 351, 353
Guterman, Aryeh  2:325
Guthrie, Colin J.  1:38
Guthrie, Wayne A.  2:126
Guynes, H. Don  2:467

Haan, Gysbert  1:120
Haddad, S.J.  2:113
Hagar, Mordecai  2:324

Hagen, Walter  2:241
Hak Ja Han  2:226
Hakeem Abdul Rasheed  Supp:63
Hakuin  2:415
Halberstamm, Benzion  2:324
Halberstamm, Solomon  2:324
Halberstamm, Yekutiel Jehudah
  2:324-25
Halberstamm, Zevi  2:324
Haldane, James  1:402
Haldane, Robert  1:402
Haldeman, I.M.  1:412, 417
Halevy, Joseph  2:330
Halhed, Nathaniel Brassey  1:447
Hall, Duane  Supp:58
Hall, Franklin  1:287
Hall, Gerald  Supp:58
Hall, H.R.  1:315
Hall, Joseph E.  2:173
Hall, Manly Palmer  2:186, 191
Hall, Verna M.  1:450
Halsey, Tarna  2:124, 201
Halsey, Wallace C.  2:201
Halyburton, Thomas  1:168
Hamatheite, M. Zidoneo  1:46
Hamblen, J.H.  1:188, 189
Hamel, Guy F. Claude  1:41, 45-46;
  Supp:18
Hamid  Supp:84
Hammett, William  1:179
Hammond, David  2:384
Hampton, Charles  2:151, 152,
  153, 154
Hanby, S.R.  1:288
Hancock, Pauline  2:14
Hand, Beth R.  2:111
Haney, Milton L.  1:203
Hanish, Otoman Zar-Adusht  2:444
Hann, Amos  Supp:28
Hansadutta, Swami  Supp:99
Hanson, Ernest  2:244
Harby, Isaac  2:316
Hardegg, Mr.  2:37
Harden, Thomas  1:305
Harding, A.L. Mark  1:43
Hargis, Billy James  2:469
Hargrove, E.T.  2:142
Hariot, Thomas  1:152
Harkness, Dr. Georgia  1:46
Harlowe, Marie  2:435
Harper, H.C.  1:407
Harris, C.W.  1:300
Harris, Martin  2:4
Harrison, Carl B.  1:443
Harrison, Donald D.  2:293, 294
Hartley, Thomas  2:89, 285
Hartley, William  2:143
Harvani, Hazrat Khwara Usman
  Supp:81
Harvey, Donald  Supp:87
Harvey, Robert C.  Supp:10

Harwood, J.H.  1:430
Hauska, Martinek  2:24
Haven, Gilbert  1:203
Hawaweany, Raphael  1:70
Hawkins, Israyl Bill  Supp:55
Hawkins, Jacob  Supp:55, 56
Hawley, Mr.  2:3
Hays, Raymond  1:305
Haywood, G.T.  1:288, 291, 296
Head, Mr.  1:495
Head, Mrs.  1:495
Healy, Patrick  Supp:1
Heath, Mary Louise  2:451
Heath, Oliver  2:451
Heatwole, Gabriel D.  1:332
Hedrick, Granville  2:12
Heefner, Steve  2:449
Hegg, Verner  2:167
Heideman, Arthur Leopold  1:106,
  107, 108
Heideman, Paul A.  1:108
Heidenreich, Alfred  2:167
Heil, W.F.  1:197
Heiman, Thomas  2:202
Heindel, Max  2:181
Heinlein, Robert  2:304
Heller, Rev. Patrick A.  Supp:22
Hellman, Sylvia  2:366
Helwys, Thomas  1:360
Hembee, Maud  1:235
Hendy, John  1:444
Hendy, William  1:444
Henge  2:288, 292
Henninges, H.C.  1:486
Henry VIII, King of England
  1:4, 11, 49
Hensley, Becky  2:474
Hensley, George Went  1:304
Hensley, Kirby J.  2:459, 460
Hepker, George H.  2:219
Herford, Ulric Vernon  1:44;
  Supp:17
Herman, Mordecai  2:331
Hernandez, J.A.  1:307
Hernandez y Esperon, Angel Maria
  1:308
Herr, Francis  1:331
Herr, John  1:331
Herrigel, Wilhelm  Supp:88
Herven, Dawn  2:451
Herven, John  2:451
Herzl, Theodore  2:314
Herzog, Eduard  1:31, 32, 35
Heschel, Abraham Joshua  2:325
Heughan, Elsie  1:211
Heyer, J.C.F.  1:102
Heynemann, Barbara  2:35
Hibbert, Joseph  Supp:77
Hickerson, John  2:480
Hickey, L.D.  2:18
Hicks, Donald  Supp:28

---

*1 or 2* refers to Volume 1 or Volume 2 of the
first edition; page numbers follow. *Supp* refers
to the *Supplement* of the first edition; entry
numbers follow.

Hicks, Elias  *1*:351
Hieronimus, Robert  *2*:240
Higbee, C.L.  *2*:5
Higgens, Minnie  *2*:187
Higgins, Jerry  *2*:98
Higgins, Melvin  *2*:362
Higginson, Thomas Wentworth  *1*:151
Higuchi, Kiyoko  *2*:479
Hilarion, Master  *Supp*:66. *See also* Blavatsky, Helena Petrovna
Hillebrand, Wilhelm  *2*:401
Hillyer, Nelson D.  *1*:43
Hilton, Henry  *1*:253
Himes, Joshua  *1*:459, 460
Hindmarsh, Robert  *2*:89
Hinds, Robert  *Supp*:77
Hinkins, John-Roger  *2*:233
Hinkle, George M.  *2*:4
Hinton, Daniel C.  *1*:34, 36
Hippolytus  *1*:15
Hippolytus of Alexandria  *1*:455
Hirai, Kinza Riuge  *2*:401
Hirai, Ryowa  *2*:404
Hirai, Ryuki  *2*:416
Hirai, Tatsusho  *2*:404
Hirsh, R.H.  *1*:489
Hisamatsu, Shin-ichi  *2*:423
Hitchcock, William Mellon  *2*:194
Hitler, Adolf  *Supp*:68
Hobson, Elizabeth  *2*:93
Hoch, Daniel  *1*:340
Hochweber, Wilhelm  *2*:167
Hocking, W.E.  *1*:127
Hockley, Fred  *2*:254
Hodge, Charles  *1*:375
Hodgson, William B.  *2*:339
Hodson, Richard  *2*:139
Hodur, Francis  *1*:35, 36
Hoefle, John J.  *1*:488, 489
Hoeksema, Herman  *1*:121
Hoeller, Stephan  *2*:155
Hoffman, Bernie Lazar  *2*:448
Hoffman, Enid  *2*:219
Hoffman, George W.  *1*:195
Hoffmann, Christopher  *2*:36-37
Hofmann, Albert  *2*:193
Hofmann, Melchior  *1*:320, 458
Hoiles, C. Douglas  *Supp*:26
Holdeman, John  *1*:334
Holloway, Gilbert N.  *2*:235
Holloway, June  *2*:235
Holmes, Ernest  *2*:55, 56, 60, 73
Holmes, Fenwicke  *2*:60, 68
Holmes, Stewart  *2*:423
Holmgren, A.A.  *1*:272
Holsinger, Henry R.  *1*:343, 345
Holstine, Henry  *1*:281
Holt, William  *1*:354
Holz, Richard  *1*:215
Homer, Alfred  *2*:112

Homer, Gladys A.  *2*:112
Honen  *2*:397, 410, 438
Honey, C.A.  *2*:201-2
Hong, Frederick  *2*:427
Hooker, Thomas  *1*:118
Hooper, Ivy  *2*:99
Hoosier, Harry  *1*:189
Hoover, Christian  *1*:346
Hopkins, Emma Curtis  *2*:54, 55, 62, 63, 65
Hopkins, Israel Eliezer  *2*:325
Hopkins, Samuel  *1*:126
Horioka, Chimyo  *2*:423
Horner, Jack  *2*:223, 224
Horner, Ralph G.  *1*:213
Horning, Moses  *1*:332, 333
Hornshuh, Fred  *1*:274
Horowitz, David  *2*:327
Horwitz, Rabbi Jacob Isaac  *2*:320
Hoskins, I.F.  *1*:489
Hoskins, R.K.  *1*:156
Hoton, Mr.  *2*:4
Houdini, Harry  *2*:96, 213
Hough, Joseph Damien  *1*:42-43; *Supp*:7
Houser, Alvin E.  *1*:409
Houteff, Victor T.  *1*:467
Howard, D.H.  *2*:460
Howard, Luther S.  *1*:276
Howard, Peter  *2*:477
Howe, Julia Ward  *1*:147
Howell, James  *1*:191
Howell, Leonard  *Supp*:77
Howgill, Francis  *1*:348
Hoyt, David  *2*:453
Hoyt, Robert  *1*:27
HPB. *See* Blavatsky, Helena Petrovna
Hua, Hsuan  *2*:428
Huba, Ihor  *1*:72
Hubbard, L. Ron  *2*:221, 257, 258
Hubbard, Ron, Jr.  *2*:223
Hubmaier, Balthasar  *1*:321
Hudler, Rev. James  *Supp*:22
Huffman, H.B.  *1*:236
Hugh, John  *2*:169
Hugh, Paola  *2*:169
Hughes, Frank Ellsworth  *Supp*:69
Hughes, Thomas I.C.  *1*:468
Hui-k'o  *2*:413
Hui-neng  *2*:413
Humbard, Rex  *1*:431; *2*:477
Humble, Floyd  *2*:100, 101
Humphreys, Fr. John J.  *Supp*:2
Hung-jen  *2*:413
Hunsberger, Ephraim  *1*:340
Hunt, Ernest  *2*:401
Hunt, Roland  *2*:169
Hunter, Edwin Wallace  *1*:39
Hunter, Neva Dell  *2*:219
Huntley, Clyde M.  *1*:499

Huntley, Florence  *2*:116
Hurtienne, E.A.  *2*:234
Hus, John  *1*:161, 457; *2*:24
Huss, Alfred E.  *1*:124
Hut, John  *1*:321, 322, 458
Hutchison, Anne  *Supp*:44
Hutchison, W.O.  *1*:281
Hutter, Jacob  *1*:320; *2*:31
Huxley, Aldous  *Supp*:62
Huxley, Julian  *1*:152
Huxley, Thomas Henry  *Supp*:25
Hyde, George Augustine  *1*:76
Hymenaeus Alpha. *See* McMurty, Grady

Iakovos, Archbishop  *1*:64, 65, 66, 73
Ianofan, Bishop  *1*:73
Ichazo, Oscar  *2*:239
Ieyasu  *2*:411
Iijima, Kanjitsu  *2*:408
Ikeda, Daisaku  *2*:409
Illiana. *See* Afton, Anita
Imamura, Kanmo  *2*:412
Imamura, Yemyo  *2*:400, 412
Inge, William R.  *2*:149
Ingersoll, Robert G.  *1*:156; *Supp*:25
Innocent III  *1*:12, 13
Innocent VII  *1*:17
Inskip, John S.  *1*:203
Ioshanna, *See* Norman, Ruth
Ireland, Richard  *2*:108
Irenaeus  *2*:85
Ireney, Archbishop  *1*:46
Ironside, Harold S.  *1*:413, 430, 438
Irvine, William  *1*:444, 445
Irving, Edward  *1*:252, 458
Irwin, Benjamin Hardin  *1*:247, 261
Isaacson, Gerry  *2*:113
Isaacson, Robert  *2*:113
Islands, Andreu  *1*:58
Isobe, Hosen  *2*:416
Israel, Patriarch David  *Supp*:60
Israel of Stolin, Rabbi  *2*:320
Itkin, Michael-Francis  *1*:44, 45; *2*:458
Ito, Shinjo  *2*:406

Jablonski, Murshid Moineddin  *2*:346
Jablonsky, Daniel Ernest  *1*:162
Jackson, Antoinette  *2*:477
Jackson, J.H.  *1*:394
Jackson, Jesse  *Supp*:79
Jackson, Mary  *1*:301

*1* or *2* refers to Volume 1 or Volume 2 of the first edition; page numbers follow. *Supp* refers to the *Supplement* of the first edition; entry numbers follow.

Personal Name Index

King, Eugene K.   *Supp*:86
King, Francis   2:255, 258, 279
King, George   2:207
King, Godfre-Ray. *See* Ballard, Guy
King, J.H.   1:261, 262
King, Martin Luther   2:468
King, Reginald B. (Rex)   *Supp*:86
King, Robert   2:150
King, Ruth L.   *Supp*:86
King, Samuel   1:133
King, Theodore Q.   *Supp*:86
King, Thomas   *Supp*:86
King, W.L.   1:238
Kingham, Emma   2:107
Kingham, John   2:107
Kinghorn, Michael   2:293
Kingold, Charles   *Supp*:74
Kingston, Charles W.   2:15
Kingston, John Ortel   2:15
Kingston, Merlin   2:18
Kirkland, R. Lee   1:427
Kirkland Seeress   2:4
Kiyoto, Kameo   2:442
Klassen, Ben, Pontifex Maximus
    *Supp*:110
Kleps, Arthur   2:194, 195
Klimovicz, Joseph   1:37
Knapp, Martin Wells   1:210
Kneitel, Judy   2:280
Kneitel, Tom   2:280
Knight, Albion W.   *Supp*:15
Knight, Gareth   2:263
Knight, W.S.M.   *Supp*:17
Knoch, Adolph Ernst   1:417, 439
Knorr, Nathan H.   1:486
Knowles, William   1:198
Knox, John   1:113, 114
Ko Bang   *Supp*:105
Kobo Daishi   2:404
Koch, Gerka   1:450
Koehler, Stephan   1:102
K'on-dkon-mch'og Rgyal-po   2:433
Kongo, Gedatsu   2:405, 406
Konko, Setsutane   2:442
Konko Daijin. *See* Bunjiro, Kawate
Koorie, Hanna   1:84
Kopp, E. Paul   1:283
Kopp, Leroy M.   1:282
Korteniemi, Solomon   1:105
Kosen, Imakita   2:415
Koshi, Shuntetsu   2:422
Koshiway, Jonathan   2:196
Koskela, John   1:108
Koski, Marie   2:102
Koun, Yamada, Roshi   2:419
Kovacezich, Iriney, Bishop of Spring-
    boro   1:69
Kozlowska, Maria Franciska. *See*
    Sister Felicia
Kozlowski, Anthony   1:35
Krewson, John W.   1:489

Kripalvanandji, Swami Shri   2:369
Krishna   2:355, 357, 372, 374
Krishna, Gopi   2:383
Krishna Venta. *See* Pencovic,
    Francis H.
Krishnamurti, Jeddu   2:140-41, 376;
    *Supp*:68
Kristof, Civet   1:74
Kriyananda, Swami [Temple of Kriya
    Yoga]. *See* Higgens, Melvin
Kriyananda, Swami [Ananda Medi-
    tation Retreat]. *See* Walters, J.
    Donald
Kroll, Maria   *Supp*:7
Ku Kai. *See* Kobo Daishi
Kuang, Stephen   1:441
Kuhlman, Kathryn   1:283, 286
Kumarji, Muni Sushil   2:391
Kumoto, Paul K.   2:69
Kunga, Lama, Thartse Rinpoche
    2:433
Kupihea, Margare   2:218
Kuriyama, Joshin   2:406
Kusch, Andrew   1:72
Kushi, Michio   2:431
Kuvalayanandaji, Swami   2:383
Kwan Tai   2:426
Kyrillos VI, Pope   1:86
Kyritis, Theodore   1:65-66

LaDue, Mrs. Francis A.   *Supp*:66
Lady Cybele   2:274
Lady Dierdre   2:280
Lady Rowen. *See* Buckland,
    Rosemary
Lady Sara   2:295-96
Lady Sheba   2:274, 277, 278
Lady Theos. *See* Kneitel, Judy
Laestadius, Levi   1:104
Lafayette, Marquis de   1:22
Laird, Margaret   2:80
Lake, John D.   1:283, 284
Lalibela, King   1:86
Lambert, W. Noel   1:31
Lamboune, Arthur E.   1:436
Lamech, Brother   1:400
Lammers, Arthur   2:217
Lamsa, George M.   2:72
Landas Berghes, Prince de   1:31,
    32, 33, 39, 40
Landbeck, Christoph Friedrich
    2:128
Lane, Isaac   1:194
Lane, Robert W.   *Supp*:4
Lang, Ruth H.   1:500
Langford, Jack   1:446
Langlois, Kongo   2:419
Lanting, Ronald E.   2:304
Lao-Tzu   2:425, 430
Lapp, William Arnold   2:228
Larkin, Clarence   1:412, 417

Larson, Christian D.   2:61
Larson, Thore   1:104
LaSalle, Robert de   1:21
Las Casas, Bartholomew de   1:21
Lashley, James F.A.   1:75-76
Laveau, Marie   2:268
LaVey, Anton Szandor   2:300,
    302-3, 304
Lavy, Solomon   *Supp*:42
Law, William   2:5
Law, Wilson   2:5
Lawrence, Joshua   1:384
Lawrence, Reginald   2:109
Lawrence, Tommie   1:295
Lawson, Alfred William   2:464
Lawson, R.C.   1:292
Layne, Meade   2:117
Lea, H.C.   1:31
Leadbeater, Charles W.   1:34;
    2:140, 141, 150, 151, 152;
    *Supp*:68
Leary, E.K.   1:233
Leary, Timothy   2:194, 195
LeBaron, Alma Dayer   2:16, 17
LeBaron, Alma, Jr.   2:16
LeBaron, Benjamin F.   2:16
LeBaron, Ervil   2:16, 17; *Supp*:59
LeBaron, Floren   2:16, 17
LeBaron, Joel   2:16, 17, 18
LeBaron, Owen   2:16
LeBaron, Ross Wesley   2:16, 17
Ledbetter, Hoy   1:406
Lee, Mother Ann   2:36
Lee, Carl Q.   2:472
Lee, Gloria   2:200-201, 202, 204
Lee, Jessie   1:389
Lee, Witness   1:441, 443
Leeser, Isaac   2:315, 316
Le Galyon, Carolyn Barbour   2:73
Leibrecht, Walter   2:466
Leiden, Jan of   1:326
Leifeste, Harriette   2:113
Leighton, Edward M.   2:113
Leiner, Samuel Solomon   2:325
Leiner, Yeruchem   2:325
Lennox, Ruth Scoles   2:161
Lenz, Dr. Frederick   *Supp*:92
Leo, John   1:27
Leo X, Pope   1:17
Leo XIII, Pope   1:25
Leon, Moses de   2:252
Leonard, Gladys Osborne   2:94
Leonard, T.K.   1:273
Leskinen, Andrew   1:108
Lessing, Kitty   2:273
Lever, Marshall   2:131, 132

*1* or *2* refers to Volume 1 or Volume 2 of the first edition; page numbers follow. *Supp* refers to the *Supplement* of the first edition; entry numbers follow.

Personal Name Index

Lever, Quinta  *2*:132
LeVesque, Doris C.  *2*:206
Levi, Eliphas  *2*:251, 252, 253, 254
Levington, William  *2*:91, 94-96
Levy, Clifton Harby  *2*:329
Lewellyn, Joe S.  *1*:257
Lewis, H. Spencer  *2*:182, 183
Lewis, Janet Stine  *2*:106
Lewis, Joseph  *1*:156
Lewis, Murshid Ahmed Christi Samuel L.  *2*:50, 346
Lewis, Ralph M.  *2*:183
Lewis, Sol  *2*:111
Lewis, William A.  *2*:334
Lichtenberger, Arthur  *1*:46
Lichtenstein, Morris  *2*:329
Lichtenstein, Tehilla  *2*:329
Liebman, Joshua  *2*:56
Lienart, Cardinal  *1*:26, 47
"Light of the World, the." *See* Fife, Sam
Lilly, William  *2*:178
Linden, Jan van der  *Supp*:67
Lindsey, Gordon  *1*:283, 284
Lindsey, Holden  *2*:202
Lindsey, Theophilus  *1*:149
Lindstrom, Paul  *1*:431
Lines, Gregory  *2*:153
Lines, Samuel Gregory  *1*:34, 36
Linn, Matthew  *1*:125
Lipa, Mark I.  *1*:66
Lipscomb, David  *1*:405
Lisle, George  *1*:392
Litch, Josiah  *1*:459
Little, R.J.  *1*:421
Little, Robert Wentworth  *2*:179, 180
Litzman, Warren  *1*:310, 311
Livingston, John Henry  *1*:119
Lloyd, Frederick Ebenezer  *1*:33, 36, 75, 76
Lloyd, Robert J.  *1*:410
Lloyd, Sherman Russell  *2*:10
Lochbaum, Ada  *1*:289
Lochbaum, Charles  *1*:289
Lodru, Lama  *2*:433
Long, J.A.  *2*:143
Long, Max Freedom  *2*:219
Long, S.E.  *1*:436
Lono, Sam  *2*:218
Lorber, Jakob  *2*:128
Lorrance, Arleen  *2*:236
Louis X, Minister. *See* Farrakhan, Abdul Haleem
Love Israel. *See* Erdmann, Paul
Lowande, Alexander A.  *2*:480

Lowe, W.J.  *1*:422, 423
Lozowick, Lee  *Supp*:91
Lueken, Veronica  *Supp*:5
Luk, A.D.K.  *2*:165
Luke and Mark  *2*:133
Lully, Marc  *2*:265
Lund, Harold Woodholl  *2*:80
Lundeberg, K.O.  *1*:104
Lundquist, Alexander  *Supp*:106
Luntz, Alfred  *2*:117
Luther, C. David  *Supp*:19
Luther, Martin  *1*:19, 89-90, 110, 112, 319, 320, 358, 482; *Supp*:20
Lynch, Joseph B.  *1*:216
Lyons, Charles E.  *2*:106

McAdow, Samuel  *1*:133
McAlister, R.E.  *1*:287, 288
McCabe, Joseph  *1*:157
McCarthy, Charles C.  *Supp*:1
McClenny, L.P.  *1*:430
McClintock, Lorene  *2*:81
McCollough, Walter  *1*:302
McConnell, Lela G.  *1*:232
McCroskey, Dee L.  *1*:439
MacDonald, George  *1*:252
MacDonald, James  *1*:252
MacDonald, Margaret  *1*:252
MacDonald, William  *1*:203
Mace, Alfred  *1*:419
McFarland, Morgan  *2*:276
McGivern, Farley  *2*:476
McGready, James  *1*:132-33
McGuire, George Alexander  *1*:75, 76
Machen, J. Gresham  *1*:127
McIlvenna, Ted  *2*:455
McIntire, Carl  *1*:127, 128, 129, 130, 377, 427
Mack, Alexander  *1*:341, 343
MacKall, Warren  *1*:314; *Supp*:34
MacKenin, Charles  *1*:259
Mackenzie, Kenneth R.H.  *2*:180, 254
Mackillop-Fritts, Ivan  *Supp*:6
McKinley, Wilson  *2*:450
Mackintosh, Charles H., C.H.M.  *1*:416
McKinzie, James O.  *1*:266
McLain, C.E.  *1*:436
McMasters, John  *2*:223
McMurty, Grady  *2*:260
McPhail, M.L.  *1*:486, 487
McPherson, Aimee Semple  *1*:265, 273-74, 280, 283
McPherson, H.S.  *1*:273
McPherson, Rolf K.  *1*:274
McWilliams, Ruth  *2*:227
Madhusudandasji, Dhyanyogi Mahant, Maharaji  *Supp*:90
Madole, James H.  *2*:296

Maezumi, Hakuyu Taizan, Roshi  *2*:418
Mahan, Asa  *1*:202
Mahaprabhu, Chai Tanya  *2*:372
Mahara, Buaji  *2*:389
Maharaj, Brahmananda Saraswati, Jagda-Guru Bhagwan of Jyotir-Math  *2*:379
Maharaj, Narayanananda, Swami  *Supp*:95
Maharji Ji  *2*:370-71
Maharji, Shri Hans Ji  *2*:370
Maharji, Upasni  *2*:347
Maharshi, Sri Ramana  *2*:368, 380
Mahavira, Vardhamana  *2*:39
Mahinda, Prince  *2*:396
Maimonides, Moses  *2*:311
Maine, V. Jean  *2*:265
Maitreya  *2*:433, 434
Makemie, Francis  *1*:116
Makery, Bishop of Uman  *1*:62
Maki, Victor  *1*:108
Mal Bhag  *Supp*:101
Malcolm X  *2*:341; *Supp*:79
Mallatt, Jean  *1*:500
Malone, Emma  *1*:352
Malone, Walter  *1*:352
Mancinelli, Leo Gregory  *1*:41
Mandefro, Liake  *1*:87
Mangan, Howard  *2*:100
Mangum, John D.  *2*:467
Mann, Mildred  *2*:63
Manning, Al G.  *2*:285
Manoogian, Sion  *1*:1
Manoogian, Torkom  *1*:84
Mantell, Thomas  *2*:198
Manter, R.A.  *1*:226
Manuel, Franco  *1*:312
Mar Georgius [The Autocephalous Syro-Chaldean Church of North America]. *See* Newman, Hugh George de Willmott
Mar Georgius [Holy Orthodox Church in America]. *See* Plummer, George Winslow
Mar Jacobus. *See* Herford, Ulric Vernon
Mar John Emmanuel. *See* Brooks, Arthur Wolfort
Mar Laurentius. *See* James, Earl Anglin
Mar Thomas Theophilus. *See* Beckles, J.T.
Mar Uzziah. *See* Schlossberg, Bertram S.
Mar Yokhannan. *See* Stanley, John M.
Marangella, Joel  *Supp*:85, 86, 87
Marchenna, Richard Arthur  *1*:42, 43; *2*:457; *Supp*:2, 4, 7
Marcx, Frances  *2*:131

*1* or *2* refers to Volume 1 or Volume 2 of the first edition; page numbers follow. *Supp* refers to the *Supplement* of the first edition; entry numbers follow.

**136**

Marday, Bishop  *1*:68
Mari, St.  *1*:81
Marine, Frederick B.  *1*:311
Mark, St.  *1*:86
Marks, William  *2*:10, 11
Marley, Bob  *Supp*:77
Marlowe, Christopher  *1*:152
Marpalotsa  *2*:432
Marquette, Jacques  *1*:19, 21
Marrs, B.F.  *1*:471
Marrs, Roy  *1*:471
Marshall, Edward G.  *Supp*:14
Marshall, Hanlon Francis  *1*:34
Martell, Leo Louis  *2*:253, 276-77
Martenson, John  *1*:167
Martha Theresa, Most Rev. *See* Mohring, Martha Jo
Martin, Abraham  *1*:332
Martin, Ernest L.  *1*:474
Martin, Jonas  *1*:332
Martin, R.L.  *1*:226
Martin, Rabia A.  *2*:347
Martin, Samuel H.  *2*:18
Martin, Thomas  *1*:80
Marx, Karl  *1*:152
Mary Stuart, Queen of England  *1*:49
Maryona  *2*:120
Mason, C.H.  *1*:224, 296, 298
Massey, Julius  *Supp*:3
Mast, Don  *2*:42
Master Ni, Hua-Ching  *Supp*:107
Master Sun W.K.  *Supp*:71
Mather, Cotton  *1*:117, 118, 160; *2*:85, 93
Mather, Increase  *2*:85, 93
Mathers, MacGregor  *2*:251, 254, 256, 261
Mathijs, Jan  *1*:326; *2*:25
Matlock, L.C.  *1*:209
Matrisciana, Pat  *2*:447
Matsuda, Masaharu  *2*:69
Matsuo, Jotei  *2*:400
Matsuoka, Soyu  *2*:419
Matthew, Arnold Harris  *1*:30-32, 33, 42, 43; *2*:150, 151
Matthew, James  *2*:153
Matthew, Wentworth Arthur  *2*:331, 333
Matthews, Edward M.  *2*:152, 153, 154; *Supp*:11
Matthews, James A.  *2*:466
Matthews, Joseph Wesley  *2*:466
Mattingley, Woods  *2*:216
Maximinus  *1*:8
Mayol, Santiago  *1*:308
Mazda, Anuru  *2*:443
Meacham, Joseph  *2*:36
Mead, G.R.S.  *2*:140
Mead, Frank S.  *1*:418
Medaris, J.B.  *Supp*:12

Medley, M.S.  *2*:462
Meeker, Lloyd Arthur  *2*:217
Meher Baba  *2*:347, 348
Meir, Verahmiel Yehuda  *2*:324
Meishu-sama. *See* Okada, Mokichi
Meissner, Linda  *2*:446, 450, 453
Melanchthon, Philip  *1*:92
Mellor, Eloise  *2*:172
Menander  *2*:395
Mendes, Henry Pereira  *2*:317
Mendiondo, Samuel  *1*:309
Merrill, Stephen  *1*:203
Merritt, Mickleberry  *1*:180
Merritt, Timothy  *1*:202
Merwan Sheriar Irani. *See* Meher Baba
Messmer, Franz Anton  *2*:51, 85, 86, 93
Metelica, Mike  *2*:45
Methodius, St.  *1*:73, 161
Metz, Christian  *2*:35
Metzger, Karl  *2*:256, 260
Meyer, Ann Porter  *2*:231
Meyer, Jacob O.  *1*:478-79
Meyer, Kent  *1*:158
Meyer, Masheikh Wali Ali  *2*:346
Meyer, Peter Victor  *2*:231
Meyerhofer, Gottfried  *2*:128
Michael, Hedwig  *2*:38
Michaelius, Jonas  *1*:119
Middleton, E. Russell  *1*:191
Mikael, Gabre Kristos  *1*:87
Mikesell, Winifred Ruth  *2*:106
Miki, Nakayama  *2*:440-41
Miki, Tokuchika  *2*:478
Miki, Tokuharu  *2*:478
Milarepa  *2*:432
Militz, Annie Rix  *2*:55, 65
Milivojevitch, Dionisije  *1*:68-69, 72
Miller, E.W.  *2*:246
Miller, G. Ogden  *Supp*:13
Miller, Harry  *2*:38 .
Miller, John  *2*:42
Miller, Mark I, Bishop. *See* Skelton, Oliver W.
Miller, William  *1*:424, 459-61, 462, 463, 493
Milligan, T.  *2*:273
Mills, Edward  *2*:64
Mills, Mary L.  *1*:279
Mills, Michael Keyfor  *1*:496
Mintern, Michael J.  *2*:472
Minzey, Willie  *2*:299
Mishra, Rammurti Sriram  *2*:380, 384
Misra, Shankar  *2*:389
Mitchell, A.C.  *1*:216
Mitchell, John  *1*:429
Mitchell, Mr. and Mrs. John  *2*:423

Miura, Isshu, Roshi  *2*:420
Miyake, Shina  *2*:439
Miyamoto, Ejun  *2*:400
Miyao, Katsuyoshi  *2*:439
Moeller, Charles  *2*:238
Mohammed  *2*:230, 335, 336
Mohring, Martha Jo  *Supp*:69
Mohring, Merle D., Sr.  *Supp*:69
Molay, Jacques de  *2*:252
Moldovan, Andrei  *1*:67
Moncado, Hilario Comino  *1*:48
Monroe, Eugene Crosby  *2*:39
Montague, Mr.  *2*:4
Montanus  *1*:455
Montgomery, G.H.  *1*:307
Montgomery, James  *1*:165
Montgomery, William  *1*:448
Moody, Dwight L.  *1*:203, 412, 416, 424, 430
Moon, Sun Myong  *2*:226
Moore, Jeanene  *2*:202
Moore, Thomas E.  *1*:214
Moore, Trevor  *1*:78
Moorehead, William G.  *1*:424
Moorhouse, Harry  *1*:424
Morais, Sabbato  *2*:317
Moreh Tsedek  *2*:334
Moreno, John M.  *1*:79
Morgan, G. Campbell  *1*:412
Morino, Cardinal Vincent  *Supp*:113
Moroni, Angel  *2*:16
Morrell, Richard M.  *2*:463
Morrill, Richard B., His Beatitude Metropolitan  *Supp*:18
Morris, Daniel  *1*:477
Morris, E.C.  *1*:393
Morris, E.J.  *1*:298
Morris, J.H.  *1*:298
Morris, Judah  *2*:313
Morris, Marion  *2*:475
Morris, Samuel  *2*:480
Morris, Thomas  *1*:198
Morrison, William J.C.  *1*:354
Morse, Elwood  *2*:121
Morse, Louise  *2*:121
Morusca, Policarp  *1*:67
Mory, C.A.  *1*:421
Moses  *2*:309, 311; *Supp*:60
Moses, Alfred Geiger  *2*:329
Moses, Tom  *1*:269
Moses David. *See* Berg, David
Moshier, Bud  *2*:60
Moshier, Carmen  *2*:60
Moss, Harold  *2*:294
Moss, Loring I.  *Supp*:38

*1* or *2* refers to Volume 1 or Volume 2 of first edition; page numbers follow. *Supp* re to the *Supplement* of the first edition; numbers follow.

Mother Boats  2:299
Mother Divine. *See* Ritchings,
    Edna Rose
Mother Trust  2:105-6
Mott, Lucretia  1:147
Motycha, A.  1:165
Moyle, Olin  2:327
Mozumdar, Akhoy Kumar  2:461
Mudge, James  1:204
Mueller, George  1:382
Muhammad, Elijah  2:341;
    *Supp*:78, 79, 80
Muhammad, Emmanuel Abdullah
    *Supp*:78
Muhammad, Wallace Deem  2:342;
    *Supp*:78
Muhammad, Wallace Fard
    *Supp*:78
Muhammed, Iman Isa Abd'Allah
    Ibn Abu Bakr  2:343
Muhammed, Mirza Ali, the Bab
    2:351-52
Muhlenberg, Henry Melchior
    1:94
Mulford, Prentice  2:54
Mulholland, John F.  2:425
Muller, Ralph J.S.  2:40
Mullins, Eustace  1:156
Mumford, John. *See* Ahandakapila,
    Swami
Mumford, Stephen  1:400
Muncaster, David A.  2:463
Mundo, Laura  2:201
Müntzer, Thomas  1:320-21, 322,
    455, 458
Muriel Isis. *See* Tepper, Muriel R.
Murphy, Richard  2:452
Murphy, Ural R.  2:228
Murray, John  1:129, 148, 149
Murray, Margaret  2:266, 286, 302
Murro, Jonathan  2:171
Muschell, Helen  2:244
Musiel, Ruth  2:113
Musser, Guy  2:15
Musser, Joseph White  2:15, 16;
    *Supp*:59
Myers, Harvey  2:390
Myers, John  1:443
Myers, Mary L.  2:164, 175
Myers, Michael  2:283
Myers, Oscar H.  1:266
Myman, Martin  2:245
Myneta, Mary  2:161
Myoko, Naganuma  2:409

Nachman of Bratslav  2:323

*1* or *2* refers to Volume 1 or Volume 2 of the
first edition; page numbers follow. *Supp* refers
to the *Supplement* of the first edition; entry
numbers follow.

Nagaraj, Babaji  2:377
Nagasaki, Toyokichi  2:416
Nagorka, Diane S.  2:102
Nagorka, Henry J.  2:102
Nakagawa, Soen, Roshi  2:419,
    420-23
Nakazono, Jilau  2:443
Nanak  2:386, 387, 388, 390
Nanda, Jyotir Maya  2:366
Napier, Marie Mae  2:173
Narayaniah  2:140
Nast, William  1:203
Natall, Ramon  2:117
Neal, Eli N.  1:288; *Supp*:30
Nee, Watchman  1:440-41, 443
Nee Shu Tsu. *See* Nee, Watchman
Nelson, Buck  2:199
Nelson, Herman F.  *Supp*:13
Nelson, Norman  2:292
Neruda, Milton James  2:295
Nesnick, Mary  2:281
Nestorius  1:2, 80
Neth, Joseph Edwards  *Supp*:11
Nevada Slim. *See* Turner, Dallas
Nevin, John Williamson  1:117
Newbrough, John Ballou  2:94, 115
Newcomb, Vesta  2:38
Newell, Chris  2:279
Newell, Simon  2:279
Newhouse, Flower A.  2:170
Newman, Hugh George de Willmott
    1:44, 46; 2:155; *Supp*:17
Newman, John Henry  1:51
Newton, Benjamin W.  1:418
Newton, Frank  2:436
Nichiren  2:396, 397, 398, 407
Nichols, L.T.  1:234
Nichols, William Albert  1:51, 77
Nicodemus, Master  2:101
Neibuhr, H. Richard  1:117
Niebuhr, Reinhold  1:117
Nikon, Patriarch of Moscow  1:62
Ni'matullah, Nur-ad-din M.
    *Supp*:83
Nishijimi, Kakuryo  2:400
Nitschman, David  1:162, 163, 164
Nityananda, Bhagwan Sri  2:367,
    368
Nityananda, Tantracharya  *Supp*:94
Niwano, Nikkyo  2:409
Nizami, Hassan  2:347
Noble, Abel  1:400
Nobunaga, Oda  2:410
Noebel, David  2:470
Noli, Fan S.  1:37, 66
Noonan, Allen  2:49
Norman, Ernest L.  2:209
Norman, Jennie. *See* Brubaker,
    Jennie
Norman, Ruth  2:209
Norris, J. Frank  1:373-74

Novack, Michael  2:289
Novack, Penny  2:289
Novak, Michael  1:27
Noyes, John Humphrey  2:29
Nuncios  1:18
Nurbakhsh, Dr. Javad  *Supp*:83
Nurse, Goodwife  2:271
Nyima, Choskyi, Panchen Rinpoche
    2:434
Nyland, W.A.  2:349

Oberholtzer, John H.  1:339-40
O'Brien, Carl  1:475
Odhner, Philip  2:92
Odyian  2:432
Officer, Samuel E.  1:291
Ofiesh, Aftimios  1:37, 51, 77, 78
Ogamisama. *See* Sayo, Kitamura
Ogasawara, Sen-sei Koji  2:442
O'Hair, J.C.  1:417, 435, 436, 437,
    438
O'Hair, Madalyn Murray  1:158;
    *Supp*:24
O'Halloran, Richard  1:31
Ohsawa, George  2:430
Oiler, Ted  1:281
Okabe, Gakuo  2:411
Okada, Itsuki  2:479
Okada, Mokichi  2:479
Okada, N. Daisama  2:479
O'Kelly, James  1:138, 179, 402
Okimegamisama  2:440
Olazabal, Francisco  1:306, 307,
    308
Olcott, Henry Steele  2:135, 139,
    140, 141, 403
Old Billy  2:330
Oliver, Lum  1:134
Olmitz, Iowa  1:247
Olney, Oliver  2:4
Olsen, Ivan E.  1:433
Olson, Culbert L.  1:157
Oncins Hevia, Jose G.  1:65
One Mighty and Strong  2:16
O'Neal, H. Edwin  2:228
O'Neal, Lois  2:228
O'Neill, Kevin R.  *Supp*:108
O'Neill, Thomas  2:96
Oom the Omnipotent. *See* Coon,
    Peter
Opie, W.E.  1:433
Origen  1:148, 455, 456
Orr, C.E.  1:209
Orser, George W.  1:397
Orth, Mina Blanc  1:451
Osborn, T.L.  1:283
Osborn, William  1:203
Ostrander, Sheila  2:86
Otsuka, Kanichi  2:442
Otterbein, Philip  1:177
Ouspensky, P.D.  2:348

*1* or *2* refers to Volume 1 or Volume 2 of the
first edition; page numbers follow. *Supp* refers
to the *Supplement* of the first edition; entry
numbers follow.

Personal Name Index

*1* or *2* refers to Volume 1 or Volume 2 of the first edition; page numbers follow. *Supp* refers to the *Supplement* of the first edition; entry numbers follow.

140

Runcorn, Ora  *1*:471
Runyon, Poke  *2*:287
Russell, Alexander  *2*:415
Russell, Bertrand  *1*:152; *Supp*:25
Russell, C.F.  *2*:258
Russell, Charles Taze  *1*:278,
    481-85, 486, 487, 488, 489, 490,
    492, 497
Russo, M.  *2*:114
Ruth, C.W.  *1*:221
Rutherford, J.R.  *1*:484-85, 487,
    489, 491, 492
Ryan, Francis J.  *Supp*:8
Ryan, Leo J.  *2*:225
Ryzy-Ryski, Vladyslav  *1*:78

Saarenpaa, Mikko  *1*:106
Sabin, Oliver C., Jr.  *2*:78
Sabir, Makhdum Ala'u'd'-Din-Ali
    Ahmad  *Supp*:81
Sad-eyed Seer of Lublin. *See*
    Horwitz, Rabbi Jacob Isaac
Sadiq, Mufti Muhammad  *2*:340
Sadler, John  *1*:447
Sahab, Shiv Dayal Singh, Param
    Guru Shri  *2*:389
Sahn, Master Seung, Sunim
    *Supp*:105

Sailsbury, W.L.  *2*:114
Saint-Charles, Bishop  *2*:265
St. Clair Nurse, Archbishop Glad-
    stone  *1*:75
Saint-Martin, Louis Claude de
    *2*:251, 264

Saint-Omer, Geoffrey de  *2*:251
Saint-Simon, Claude Henry  *2*:25
St. Therese of Lisieux  *Supp*:5
Sakal, Sekiguchi  *Supp*:112
Sakyamuni. *See* Gautama, Siddharta
Saliba, Philip  *1*:70
Salonen, Neil A.  *2*:227
Samarian, William  *1*:244
Samon, Sergius  *1*:74
Sams, Clarence Francis  *1*:389
Samu Sunim  *Supp*:106
Samuel, Athanasius Y.  *1*:86
Samuel, William  *2*:80
Samuel the Prophet  *2*:84-85
Sanbul Sunim. *See* Lundquist,
    Alexander

Sandai-sama. *See* Okada, Itsuki
Sande, Frances  *2*:167, 168
Sandeman, Robert  *1*:402
Sander, J.A.  *1*:181
Sanders, Alex  *2*:280
Sanders, Maxine  *2*:280
Sandine, Himler B.  *1*:141
Santamaria, John  *1*:280
Santamaria, Rocco  *1*:280
Saraswati, Ma Yogashakti  *Supp*:13

Saraswati, Niranjananda, Swami
    *Supp*:97
Saraswati, Satyananda, Swami
    *Supp*:97
Saraswati, Viswananda  *2*:364
Saraydarian, H.  *2*:148
Sariputra  *2*:395
Sarkar, Prabhat Ranjan. *See*
    Anandamurti(ji), Shrii Shrii
Sarkar Sahab, Param Guru. *See*
    Sinha, Sri Kamta Prasad
Sarkissian, Karekin  *1*:84
Sasaki Joshu, Roshi  *2*:423
Sasaki, Ruth Fuller Everett
    *2*:416, 420
Sasaki, Shigetsu. *See* Sasaki,
    Sbkei-an, Roshi
Sasaki Sokei-an, Roshi  *2*:416, 420
Sasmus, Kev Singh  *2*:390
Satchidananda, Swami  *2*:364
Sattler, Michael  *1*:320, 321-22
Saul, King of Israel  *2*:85, 92
Sava, Bishop of Canada  *1*:69
Sava, St.  *1*:68
Savoy, Gene  *Supp*:73
Sawyer, Don  *2*:278
Sawyer, Elizabeth  *2*:278
Sawyna, Wasyl  *1*:53
Sayo, Kitamura  *2*:439-40
Sazanami, Shizuka  *2*:412
Schackford, Charles  *1*:150
Schaffer, James  *1*:228
Schechter, Solomon  *2*:317
Schellenberg, Abraham  *1*:341
Schelling, Friedrich  *2*:53
Scheppe, John C.  *1*:288
Schiffner, Alexander  *1*:450
Schlatter, Michael  *1*:139
Schlossberg, Bertram S.  *Supp*:17
Schmid, Otto  *1*:444
Schmitt, Charles P.  *1*:311
Schmitt, Dorothy E.  *1*:311
Schmucker, Samuel S.  *1*:94, 95
Schmul, H.E.  *1*:236, 240
Schneersohn, Joseph Isaac  *2*:319,
    321
Schneersohn, Menachem Mendel
    (1789-1866)  *2*:321
Schneersohn, Menachem Mendel
    (1902)  *2*:322
Schneersohn, Samuel  *2*:321
Schneersohn, Sholom Dov Baer
    *2*:321
Schneider, Abe  *1*:223
Schneider, William H.  *Supp*:14
Scholte, Hendrik  *1*:120
Schraub, Philip  *2*:173
Schroeder, Ethel  *2*:79
Schroeder, Lynn  *2*:86
Schucman, Dr. Helen  *Supp*:64
Schuler, Bob  *1*:445

Schwarz, F.W.  *1*:254
Schwarz, Jack  *2*:240
Schweikert, J.E.  *1*:44
Schweitzer, Albert  *2*:385
Schwenckfelder, Caspar  *1*:320,
    327, 347
Scofield, C.I.  *1*:413, 416-17
Scott, F.C.  *1*:300
Scott, George  *1*:166
Scott, Joseph L.  *1*:256
Scott, Orange  *1*:209
Scroggie, William Graham  *1*:412
Seabury, Samuel  *1*:50
Seale, Ervin  *2*:64, 328
Seebach, Ehrenfried  *1*:102
Seinertson, Geneva  *2*:216
Seinertson, Wayne  *2*:216
Seki, Eikaku  *2*:405
Sekida, Katsuki  *2*:419
Selassie, Haile ("Power of the Holy
    Trinity")  *1*:87; *Supp*:77
Sellers, Ernest William  *1*:308
Sellers, L.O.  *1*:264
Semple, Robert  *1*:273
Seng-ts'an  *2*:413
Senntao, Mysikiitta Fa Empress
    *2*:243
Sensenig, Aaron  *1*:334
Senzaki, Nyogen  *2*:419, 421
Seo, Kyung Bo  *2*:422; *Supp*:104
Sepulveda, Carlos  *1*:308
Sergi, Archbishop of Australia
    *1*:72
Sergius, Patriarch  *1*:60, 61, 77
Serra, Junipero  *1*:19
Servetus, Michael  *1*:112, 148
Seth-Klippoth, Rev.  *2*:304
Seton, Mother Elizabeth  *1*:24
Severus, Lucius Septimus  *1*:8
Sexton, Elizabeth A.  *1*:260
Seymour, W.J.  *1*:248, 270, 296
Shaheen, Michael  *1*:70
Shakarganj, Baba Farid  *Supp*:81
Shaku, Sokatsu  *2*:415
Shaku, Soyen  *2*:401, 415, 435
Shakyamuni. *See* Gautama,
    Siddhartha
Shapira, Elimelekh, of Dinov  *2*:325
Sharpe, Pauline  *2*:202
Shaw, William  *1*:495
Sheba, Queen of  *Supp*:77
Sheehan, Edmund Walter  *2*:152-53
Sheen, Fulton J.  *2*:56
Shelburne, G.B., Jr.  *1*:407
Shell, Robert E.L.  *2*:260
Shelley, Gerald George  *1*:42, 43;
    *Supp*:2

*1* or *2* refers to Volume 1 or Volume 2 of the
first edition; page numbers follow. *Supp* refers
to the *Supplement* of the first edition; entry
numbers follow.

Shelley, Lee  *1*:223
Shelley, Percy Bysshe  *1*:152
Shelton, Robert  *1*:278
Shelton, S. McDowell  *1*:292-93
Shen, C.T.  *2*:429
Shenouda III, Pope  *1*:86
Shepherd, Robert T.  *Supp*:11
Sherlock, Bonnie  *2*:275
Sherwin, George J.  *1*:451
Sherwood, Cyril John Clement  *1*:75, 76
Shields, T.T.  *1*:377
Shigemura, Daisy  *2*:81
Shi'itte, Yadadi  *2*:117
Shimano, Eido Tai  *2*:419, 422
Shimaza, Mrs. Taneko  *2*:69
Shimizu, Shinjun  *2*:411
Shimun XXIII, Eshai  *1*:81
Shin, Gosung  *Supp*:104
Shin, Il Kwon  *2*:424
Shinn, Asa  *1*:178
Shinran  *2*:397, 410
Shirayama, Ryoichi  *2*:412
Shivananda, Swami  *Supp*:95
Shoemaker, Michael  *2*:368
Short, David William  *1*:300
Shott, David  *Supp*:3
Shypylka, Theodore  *1*:71
Sibley, Ebenezer  *2*:253
Sibthorpe, W.M.  *1*:423
Sidebottom, Ike T.  *1*:438
Sigismund, John  *1*:148
Simon XVII, Abraham  *1*:44
Simonian, Elisha  *1*:84
Simons, Menno  *1*:325, 326, 327-28, 334, 335; *2*:31
Simpson, Albert Benjamin  *1*:203, 222, 273, 283
Sinclair, John C.  *1*:275
Sinclair, Lily  *2*:303
Singh, Avtar  *Supp*:101
Singh, Bishwanath. *See* Nityananda, Tantracharya
Singh, Boota  *Supp*:101
Singh, Bakht  *1*:441
Singh, Chavan  *2*:38
Singh, Gobind  *2*:387
Singh, Gurbachan  *Supp*:101
Singh, Jaimal, Baba  *2*:389, *Supp*:101
Singh, Kahn  *Supp*:101
Singh, Kirpal  *2*:389, 390, 391
Singh, Sant Ajaib  *2*:391
Singh, Sant Darshan  *2*:391
Singh, Sawan  *2*:389, 390
Singh, Suda  *2*:232

Singh, Thakar  *2*:391
Sinha, Sri Kamta Prasad  *2*:389
Sinkler, Lorraine  *2*:81
Sirat, Mr. and Mrs. Lee  *2*:435
Sis, Cilicia  *1*:82
Sisk, H.C.  *1*:211
Sister Felicia  *1*:36
Sivananda, Swami  *2*:364, 365, 366; *Supp*:96, 97
Skagg, Dewey E.  *1*:471
Skelton, Oliver W.  *Supp*:18
Skikiewicz, John  *1*:34
Skikiewicz, Roman W.  *Supp*:7
Skillman, Robert N.  *2*:244, 245
Skinner, Calvin S.  *2*:331
Skinner, Floyd  *1*:241
Skrypnyk, Mstyslaw  *1*:71
Skutch, Judith  *Supp*:64
Slack, George  *1*:297
Slade, Henry  *2*:96
Slater, Harold  *2*:275
Sloane, Herbert Arthur  *2*:302
Smale, Joseph  *1*:248
Smith, Aaron  *2*:18
Smith, B.  *1*:226
Smith, Clarence  *2*:114
Smith, David J.  *Supp*:50
Smith, E.D.  *1*:226
Smith, Elias  *1*:402
Smith, Emma  *2*:14
Smith, Enid  *2*:207
Smith, Frank Madison  *2*:11
Smith, Freda  *2*:456
Smith, Grover S.  *1*:312
Smith, Henry Preserved  *1*:126
Smith, Hiram  *2*:4, 5
Smith, Huston  *2*:197
Smith, Israel Alexander  *2*:11
Smith, Johann Oscar  *2*:480
Smith, Joseph, Jr.  *1*:446, 458, 497; *2*:1-5, 8, 9, 10, 11, 12, 13, 16, 17, 19, 20, 39; *Supp*:47, 58, 60
Smith, Joseph, III  *2*:11
Smith, Julian L.  *1*:38
Smith, Justa  *2*:84
Smith, Lucien  *1*:188
Smith, Marcie P.  *2*:70
Smith, Michael  *2*:289
Smith, Payne  *1*:52
Smith, R. Pearsall  *1*:203
Smith, W. Wallace  *2*:11
Smith, William  *2*:10
Smith, Winifred T.  *2*:257
Smitley, Richard E.  *1*:129
Smyth, John  *1*:359-60, 365, 395
Snethen, Nicholas  *1*:178
Snow, L.D.  *1*:478; *Supp*:53
Snow, Samuel S.  *1*:461
Snow, Wallace  *Supp*:29
Snyder, Gary  *2*:420
Soares, Basilius  *1*:44

Soares, Rose  *1*:275
Socinius  *2*:148
Socrates  *2*:83
Soen Sa Nim  *Supp*:105
Sohrab, Ahmad  *Supp*:88
Sojourner, William  *1*:395
Sokolowski, Joseph G.  *Supp*:7
Solomon, King  *Supp*:77
Solomon, Paul  *2*:133
Sonoda, Shuyei  *2*:400
Sophronios, Bishop  *1*:77
Soror Veritas. *See* White, Anne
Sorrow, Watson  *1*:263
Sosa, Arthuro Rangel  *1*:308, 309
Souris, Joachim  *1*:65, 78, 79
Southcott, Joanna  *1*:493, 494, 495
Sowders, William  *1*:278, 279
Sowell, M.S.  *1*:226
Spalding, Baird  *2*:120
Spangler, David  *2*:125
Spark, Jered  *1*:149
Sparks, Jack  *2*:448
Sparks, T. Austin  *1*:443
Spataro, Francis C.  *Supp*:87
Speed, James Hughes  *2*:202
Spence, James  *2*:121
Spencer, Herbert  *1*:147
Spencer, Mrs. Ivan Q.  *1*:277
Spencer, Rev. Ivan Q.  *1*:277
Spencer, Peter  *1*:193
Spener, Philipp Jacob  *1*:159, 408
Spern, Angelo C.  *2*:464
Spilsbury, John  *1*:360
Spiru, Athenagoras  *1*:64
Sprague, Lillian  *1*:220
Sprengel, Anna  *2*:254-55
Spruit, Herman Adrian  *2*:153, 154; *Supp*:6, 69, 70, 96
Spurling, R.G.  *1*:247, 254
Spurling, Richard, Jr.  *1*:254, 255
Stadsklev, C.O.  *1*:451
Stam, Cornelius  *1*:437-38
Standridge, W.E.  *1*:428
Stanewick, Phyllis  *2*:288
Stanewick, Richard  *2*:288
Stanford, Ray  *2*:132
Stanford, Rex  *2*:132
Stanley, Christopher C.J.  *1*:41, 44; *Supp*:18
Stanley, John M.  *1*:55; *Supp*:17
Stanton, George  *Supp*:74
Starazewski, Felix  *1*:37
Starkey, Cyrus A.  *1*:42, 44
Stasek, George  *2*:155
Stauffer, Jacob  *1*:333
Stebbins, Genevieve  *2*:187
Steele, Arthur  *1*:129
Steele, Daniel  *1*:203
Stehlik, Edward Michael  *Supp*:3
Steinberg, Paul  *Supp*:64
Steiner, Rudolf  *2*:165, 166, 167, 181

---

*1* or *2* refers to Volume 1 or Volume 2 of the first edition; page numbers follow. *Supp* refers to the *Supplement* of the first edition; entry numbers follow.

Tomlinson, Homer  *1*:257, 258, 306
Tomlinson, Milton A.  *1*:257, 258
Tomo Geshe Rinpoche. *See* Kalzang, Geshe Ngawang
Tonella, Peter A.  *1*:43
Torbet, Robert  *1*:359
Torkillus, Reorus  *1*:94
Torrey, R.A.  *1*:203, 430
Toruian, Levon  *1*:83
Tosh, Peter  *Supp*:77
Toups, Mary Oneida  *2*:270
Tovey, Pete  *1*:310
Trager, Elizabeth  *1*:265
Traina, A.B.  *1*:478, 479
Trask, John  *1*:399
Treacy, John  *Supp*:3
Treleaven, John W.  *Supp*:14
Trescott, John W.  *Supp*:50
Trifa, Valerian D.  *1*:67
Trine, Ralph Waldo  *2*:54
Trotman, A.S.  *1*:75
Trott, G.A.  *1*:407
Trotter, William  *1*:416
Troward, Thomas  *2*:55, 61
Troxell, Hope  *2*:167, 170
Truesdell, Alden  *2*:63
Truesdell, Neil  *2*:63
Trungpa, Chogyam, Rinpoche  *2*:432
Truppa, Gedun  *2*:434
Trust, Josephine De Croix. *See* Mother Trust
Tsong-kha-pa  *2*:399
Tsuji, Kenyru  *2*:411
Tsunesaburo, Makiguchi  *2*:408
Tulga, Chester  *1*:378, 379
Tulku, Tarthang, Rinpoche  *2*:431
Tulku, Trungpa  *2*:432
Turiyananda, Swami  *Supp*:95
Turner, Alexander Tyler  *1*:77
Turner, Dallas  *2*:247
Turner, George  *1*:494, 495
Turner, Lucy Evelyn  *1*:280
Turner, Dr. Roy John  *1*:280
Turner, Mrs. Roy John  *1*:280
Twersky, Aaron  *2*:323
Twersky, Alexander  *2*:324
Twersky, David  *2*:324
Twersky, Isaac  *2*:324
Twersky, Israel Jacob  *2*:324
Twersky, Jacob Joseph  *2*:324
Twersky, Menahem Nahum Ben Zevi  *2*:323
Twersky, Mordecai  *2*:323
Twitchell, Paul  *2*:232
Tyarks, William F.  *1*:75, 76

Tyberg, Judith M.  *2*:237, 374
Tywman, Harrison J.  *Supp*:33
Tyndale, William  *1*:113

Uklein, Simeon  *1*:63
Ulrich, Anthony  *1*:162
Umbach, Penny  *2*:100
Underhill, Evelyn  *2*:149
Underwood, May  *1*:444
Undsorfer, Samuel  *2*:325
Updegraff, David B.  *1*:353
Upham, T.C.  *1*:202
Uranda. *See* Meeker, Lloyd Arthur

Vajirathammasophon, Ven Phrak-hru  *Supp*:102
Valentine, Michael  *2*:463
Van Baalen, J.K.  *1*:121
Van Camp, Harlaw  *1*:477
Van der Linden, Jan. *See* Linden, Jan van der
Van Grasshof, Carl Louis. *See* Heindel, Max
Van Hoof, Mary Ann  *Supp*:3
Van Polen, Evangeline  *2*:162
Van Polen, Garman  *2*:162
Van Raalte, D. Albertus  *1*:120
Van Rijckenborgh, J.  *2*:183
Van Steenoven, Cornelius  *1*:5, 29
Van Tassel, George  *2*:205
Van Thiel, J.J.  *1*:31
Vanden Berg, Gerald  *1*:122
Vander Mey, J.  *1*:121
Vanderwood, Ralph  *1*:188
Vanore, Andrew Lawrence  *Supp*:7
Vargas, E.B.  *1*:188
Varick, James  *1*:192
Varlet, Dominique Marie  *1*:5, 29
Varnell, A.F.  *1*:295
Vassallo, Calvin C.  *2*:429
Vasudevadas  *2*:362, 363
Vedder, Henry C.  *1*:359
Venta, Krishna. *See* Pencovic, Francis H.
Ver-Koilen, Dale  *2*:419
Veronica, Phyllis  *2*:204
Vest, Dean  *2*:17-18
Viall, John S.  *1*:370
Vick, Beauchamp  *1*:374
Vilatte, Joseph Rene  *1*:30, 33, 35, 36, 37, 40, 44, 47, 75
Vimalananda, Dadaji  *Supp*:100
Vincent, Isabella  *1*:246
Vinita, Thera Bope  *2*:403
Vipartes, Sigismund  *1*:40, 44
Virgil, Raymond P.  *1*:289
Vishtapa, Hystaspes  *2*:443
Vitikka, Anti  *1*:105
Vivekananda, Swami  *2*:359, 360, 361, 401
Vladimir, Bishop  *1*:73

Vladimir I. *See* Propheta, Walter M.
Voglesong, Jack  *2*:238
Vogt, Virgil  *2*:42
Voliva, Wilbur Glenn  *2*:472
Voltaire, Francois Marie Arouet  *1*:150
Von Carlstadt, Andreas  *1*:91
Von Koerber, Hans Nordewin  *2*:128
Von Puttkamer, Alexander  *1*:382
Von Scholte, Joann  *1*:29
Vrienis, Pangraties  *1*:65
Vries, Roland de  *2*:390

Wadle, L. Paul  *1*:34, 76; *Supp*:69
Wagner, Belle M.  *2*:187
Wagner, Henry  *2*:187
Wai, Chuen  *2*:427
Wains. *See* Speed, James Hughes
Waite, A.E.  *2*:252, 255
Wakefield, H.C.  *1*:134
Wakefield, Wesley H.  *1*:215
Wakefield, William J.  *1*:215
Waldner, Michael Schmied-Michel  *2*:31, 32
Waldo, Peter  *1*:482
Waldrop, Donald L.  *2*:215
Walker, George  *1*:444
Walker, Helen V.  *2*:64
Walker, Kenneth  *Supp*:109
Walker, Thane  *2*:349
Wall, Aaron  *1*:339
Wall, N.J.  *1*:420
Wallace, Baird  *2*:212
Wallace, Orville  *1*:279
Walsh, John T.  *1*:462, 463
Walter, Darius  *2*:32
Walters, J. Donald  *2*:363
Walthall, Jethro  *1*:246-47
Walther, Carl Fredinand Wilhelm  *1*:94, 98
Wangyal, Geshe  *2*:431
Wannarat, Phra, Supreme Patriarch  *Supp*:102
Ward, Henry Dana  *1*:459
Ward, Robert  *1*:375
Wardall, Ray M.  *2*:151, 152
Wardley, James  *2*:36
Warfield, Benjamin  *1*:117
Warhentin, Bernard  *1*:338
Warner, Daniel S.  *1*:204, 207-8 209
Warner, James K.  *Supp*:49
Warren, Sterling  *2*:204
Washington, William  *1*:225
Wasson, David  *1*:151
Waters, Charles E., Sr.  *1*:303
Waters, John H.  *1*:380, 381
Waterstraat, Wilhelm  *1*:41
Watkins, Gary  *2*:223
Watson, Winfield  *2*:18

*1* or *2* refers to Volume 1 or Volume 2 of the first edition; page numbers follow. *Supp* refers to the ***Supplement*** of the first edition; entry numbers follow.

Personal Name Index

# Publications Index

This index interfiles references to *The Encyclopedia of American Religions,* Volumes 1 and 2, first edition, with references to the first edition *Supplement.*

References in the index are identified as follows:

Italicized numbers refer to Volume 1 or Volume 2 of the first edition.
Page numbers follow the colon.

The italicized designation *Supp* refers to the *Supplement* to the first edition.
Entry numbers follow the colon.

1 or 2 refers to Volume 1 or Volume 2 of the
first edition; page numbers follow. *Supp* refers
to the *Supplement* of the first edition; entry
numbers follow.

148

*1* or *2* refers to Volume 1 or Volume 2 of the first edition; page numbers follow. *Supp* refers to the *Supplement* of the first edition; entry numbers follow.

**Publications Index**

*1* or *2* refers to Volume 1 or Volume 2 of the first edition; page numbers follow. *Supp* refers to the *Supplement* of the first edition; entry numbers follow.

1 or 2 refers to Volume 1 or Volume 2 of the first edition; page numbers follow. Supp refers to the Supplement of the first edition; entry numbers follow.

Publications Index

Nasha Batkiwschyna  *1*:72
N.A.T. Newsletter  *2*:125
Nation  *Supp*:25
National Baptist Voice  *1*:393
National Spiritualist Reporter, The  *2*:99
Natorei Karta  *2*:323
Nature's Eternal Religion  *Supp*:110
Nauvoo Expositer  *2*:5
Nazarene Messenger  *1*:220
Nazarene News  *1*:238
Needed Truth  *1*:420
Negro World  *2*:339
Nelly Heathen  *2*:299
Nemeton  *2*:292
Nemeton Newsletter  *2*:292
Neo-Dharma Notes  *2*:402
New Age Forum, The  *2*:112
New Age Thought  *2*:231
New America  *2*:297
New Angelus for the New Age, The  *2*:173
New Aurora  *1*:370
New Birth  *2*:452
New Birth Christian Community Quarterly Journal  *2*:128
New Broom, The  *2*:276
New Church Education  *2*:91
New Church Life  *2*:91
New Creation, The  *1*:487
New Day, The  *2*:481
New Era  *2*:8
New Life  *2*:452
New Life Fellowship  *Supp*:57
New Manna  *2*:452
New Nation News  *2*:454
New Religions of Japan  *2*:399
New Text of Spiritual Philosophy and Religion, A  *2*:103
News and Needs  *1*:399
News Bulletin  *1*:137
News from Martinus Institute  *2*:118
News of the Churches  *1*:442
Newsletter  *Supp*:85
Newsletter (Arising Sun IFO's)  *2*:212
Newsletter (Association for the Understanding of Man)  *2*:133
Newsletter (Christian Community)  *2*:167
Newsletter (Cosmic Star Temple)  *2*:210
Newsletter (New England Institute of Metaphysical Studies)  *2*:264

Newsletter (Oliver C. Sabin, Jr.)  *2*:78
Newsletter (Prosperos)  *2*:349
Newsletter (Quimby Center)  *2*:220
Newsletter (Seich-No-Ie)  *2*:69
Newsletter (Superet Light Center)  *2*:106
Newswatch Magazine  *Supp*:50
New York Christian Advocate  *1*:460
Nihongi  *2*:438, 442
Norigotoshu  *Supp*:112
North Star Baptist, The  *1*:380
Northern Independent, The  *1*:212
Northwest Friend  *1*:354
Not So Secret Doctrine  *2*:349
Notes from Our Church Organ  *1*:495
Notes from Woodsong  *2*:80
Notes on the New Testament  *1*:170
Numerical Bible, The  *1*:419

Oahspe  *2*:94, 115
Occident and Jewish Advocate  *2*:315-16
Ocean of Theosophy  *2*:141
Odinist, The  *2*:298
Ogamisama's World Wide Newsletter  *2*:440
Ohio Bible Fellowship Visitor, The  *1*:429
Old Brethren's Reasons, The  *Supp*:41
Old Faith Contender  *1*:387
Old Paths Advocate  *1*:407
One Church  *1*:41
Ontological Thought  *2*:218
Opas  *1*:108
Oracle  *2*:451-52
Oracles of Mohonri  *Supp*:60
Order of the Sons of Zadok, The  *Supp*:60
Order of the Universe  *2*:431
Orion  *2*:228
Ortho  *1*:77
Orthodox Catholic Herald  *1*:74
Orthodox Observer, The  *1*:64
Orthodoxy  *1*:77
Other Sheep  *1*:221
Our Church  *1*:62
Our Herald  *1*:290
Our Hope  *1*:426
Our Lady of the Roses, Mary Help of Mothers  *Supp*:5
Our Missionary  *1*:38
Our News and Views  *2*:132
Our Saviour Has Arrived  *Supp*:80
Outside the Camp  *1*:439

Pace  *2*:477

Pagan, The  *2*:289
Pagan/Occult/New Age Directory  *2*:274
Pastoral Counseling  *1*:38
Pastor's Journal, The  *Supp*:111
Path, The  *2*:141
Path of Truth, The  *2*:74
Pearls of Wisdom, The  *2*:161
Pentecostal Evangel, The  *1*:272
Pentecostal Free Will Baptist Messenger, The  *1*:268
Pentecostal Herald (Pentecostal Church of God of America)  *1*:275
Pentecostal Herald (United Pentecostal Church)  *1*:294
Pentecostal Holiness Advocate, The  *1*:262
Pentecostal Messenger, The  *1*:276
Pentecostal Power  *1*:282
Pentecostal Witness  *1*:260
People's Mouthpiece, The  *1*:292
Pietisten  *1*:166
Pilgrim, The  *Supp*:41
Pilgrim News  *1*:239
Pillar of Fire  *1*:231
Pillars of Light  *2*:163
Pisgah Journal, The  *1*:316
Pistis Sophia  *Supp*:60
Plain Truth, The  *1*:471, 473
Plainer Words  *1*:436
Plan of the Ages, The (1881)  *1*:483
Polskikatolik  *1*:36
Portal  *2*:72
Power for Abundant Living  *2*:449
Prayers and Poems from Mother's Heart  *Supp*:93
Precursor  *2*:90
Presbyterian Journal, The  *1*:136
Presbyterian Life  *1*:140
Presbyterian Survey  *1*:136; *Supp*:21
Present Testimony, The  *1*:441
Present Truth  *1*:488
Present Truth of the Apocalypsis, The  *1*:489
Primary Point  *Supp*:105
Primitive Baptist, The  *1*:387
Primitive Baptist Directory  *1*:388
Primitive Baptist Library Quarterly  *1*:388
Primitive Messenger, The  *1*:389
Primitive Methodist Journal, The  *1*:198
Principles and Practices of the Rosicrucians  *2*:181
Proceedings  *2*:206
Process  *2*:229
Process, The  *2*:230
Progress Journal  *1*:464

*1* or *2* refers to Volume 1 or Volume 2 of the first edition; page numbers follow. *Supp* refers to the *Supplement* of the first edition; entry numbers follow.

152

*1* or *2* refers to Volume 1 or Volume 2 of the first edition; page numbers follow. *Supp* refers to the *Supplement* of the first edition; entry numbers follow.

---

*1* or *2* refers to Volume 1 or Volume 2 of the
first edition; page numbers follow. *Supp* refers
to the *Supplement* of the first edition; entry
numbers follow.

# Subject Index

This index interfiles references to *The Encyclopedia of American Religions,* Volumes 1 and 2, first edition, with references to the first edition *Supplement.*

References in the index are identified as follows:

Italicized numbers refer to Volume 1 or Volume 2 of the first edition.
Page numbers follow the colon.

The italicized designation *Supp* refers to the *Supplement* to the first edition.
Entry numbers follow the colon.

*1* or *2* refers to Volume 1 or Volume 2 of the first edition; page numbers follow. *Supp* refers to the *Supplement* of the first edition; entry numbers follow.

**158**

*1* or *2* refers to Volume 1 or Volume 2 of the
first edition; page numbers follow. *Supp* refers
to the *Supplement* of the first edition; entry
numbers follow.

*1* or *2* refers to Volume 1 or Volume 2 of the first edition; page numbers follow. *Supp* refers to the *Supplement* of the first edition; entry numbers follow.

160

*1* or *2* refers to **Volume 1** or **Volume 2** of the first edition; page numbers follow. *Supp* refers to the *Supplement* of the first edition; entry numbers follow.

Subject Index

---

*1* or *2* refers to Volume 1 or Volume 2 of the first edition; page numbers follow. *Supp* refers to the *Supplement* of the first edition; entry numbers follow.

**Subject Index**

1 or 2 refers to Volume 1 or Volume 2 of the first edition; page numbers follow. Supp refers to the Supplement of the first edition; entry numbers follow.

Subject Index

1 or 2 refers to Volume 1 or Volume 2 of the first edition; page numbers follow. Supp refers to the Supplement of the first edition; entry numbers follow.

*1* or *2* refers to Volume 1 or Volume 2 of the
first edition; page numbers follow. *Supp* refers
to the *Supplement* of the first edition; entry
numbers follow.

Subject Index

*1* or *2* refers to Volume 1 or Volume 2 of the first edition; page numbers follow. *Supp* refers to the *Supplement* of the first edition; entry numbers follow.

*1* or *2* refers to Volume 1 or Volume 2 of the first edition; page numbers follow. *Supp* refers to the *Supplement* of the first edition; entry numbers follow.

Subject Index

*1* or *2* refers to Volume 1 or Volume 2 of the first edition; page numbers follow. *Supp* refers to the *Supplement* of the first edition; entry numbers follow.

**Subject Index**

*1* or *2* refers to Volume 1 or Volume 2 of the first edition; page numbers follow. *Supp* refers to the *Supplement* of the first edition; entry numbers follow.

172

*1* or *2* refers to Volume 1 or Volume 2 of the
first edition; page numbers follow. *Supp* refers
to the *Supplement* of the first edition; entry
numbers follow.

Subject Index

1 or 2 refers to Volume 1 or Volume 2 of the first edition; page numbers follow. Supp refers to the Supplement of the first edition; entry numbers follow.

Subject Index

Zendo   2:417, 419, 420, 421, 422, 424

Zion   Supp:58

Zion, Ill.   2:472-73

Zion Publishing House   2:472

Zionism   2:310, 314, 317, 322

Zoroastrianism   2:245, 352, 443

Zuni, N. Mex.   1:38

Zurich, Switzerland   1:112; 2:224